Production and Operations Manual and Guide

Production and Operations Manual and Guide

Lewis R. Zeyher, CMC

Prentice-Hall, Inc., Englewood Cliffs, N.J.

Prentice-Hall International, Inc., *London*
Prentice-Hall of Australia, Pty. Ltd., *Sydney*
Prentice-Hall of Canada, Ltd., *Toronto*
Prentice-Hall of India Private Ltd., *New Delhi*
Prentice-Hall of Japan, Inc., *Tokyo*

Library of Congress Cataloging in Publication Data

Zeyher, Lewis R
  Production and operations manual and guide.

  Includes bibliographical references and index.
  1. Production management. I. Title.
TS155.Z42   658.5   75-5537
ISBN 0-13-725275-7

Printed in the United States of America

ABOUT THE AUTHOR

Lewis R. Zeyher has been President of Zeyher Associates, Management Consultants, Jenkintown, Pennsylvania, for twenty years. His total experience covers more than thirty-five years in a hundred different plants involving a wide variety of positions from factory manager to vice-president of manufacturing.

Mr. Zeyher has conducted industrial management seminars for business leaders in this country and abroad, and he has been active as a lecturer and teacher on management subjects. He is a Fellow of the Society for Advancement of Management, a Division of the American Management Association, and he holds the Society's Advancement of Management Award for his two books, *Cost Reduction in the Plant* and *Production Manager's Desk Book,* both published by Prentice-Hall. He is also a Founding Member of the Institute of Management Consultants.

He received his B.S. degree in Mechanical Engineering from Lafayette College, and has completed graduate studies at Pennsylvania, Columbia and Rutgers Universities.

Other books by the author:

Cost Reduction in the Plant
Production Manager's Desk Book
Production Manager's Handbook of Formulas and Tables

Getting the Most from This Book

This book was written to consolidate, under one cover, proven solutions to profit-depressing problems of the typical manufacturing plant and operations company (warehousing, distribution centers and trucking activities). New operating ideas, improved methods successfully introduced in many companies, and the more effective use of modern management controls are presented in detail. This is not an exposition on theoretical and untried approaches for better management—but a source of practical answers, based on years of shirt-sleeve experience gained in many and varied types of businesses. These methods and ideas have been successfully applied under all kinds of conditions, obstacles and skepticisms, and in spite of some employee resistance and executive passivity. They work—to boost efficiencies, productivity and profits. And they'll work for you, whatever your company size or product line.

In the past several decades business problems have multiplied at an accelerated pace. In order to cope effectively with this condition, managers at all levels should make every effort to improve their modern management knowledge and expertise. The paramount thrust of this book is to provide aids, practices, systems, programs, plans, forms, standards, controls, objectives, new approaches, and, most of all, to motivate and stimulate the reader to improve his overall management performance.

Typical of the practical features this manual offers are:

FIFTEEN WAYS THIS BOOK WILL BE HELPFUL

(1) If you are not satisfied with the performance of your manufacturing engineering department, examine Chapter 1. This chapter focuses on "designing for manufacturability." Product development engineers sometimes design a new product highly acceptable to marketing executives but impossible to manufacture at a cost the customer will accept, or so designed that it does not *fully* utilize the company's

equipment and available skills. A review of the section on "Analysis for Manufacturability" will provide a guide for you to use in checking your own operations. In addition, a 26-item checklist is provided.

(2) If you are unhappy about your record in meeting customer delivery promises, Chapter 2 provides cues for a complete overhauling and audit of your present system with suggestions for improvement.

(3) With the Federal Government's emphasis on safety and accident prevention, review Chapter 3 which provides 41 suggestions for safe practices covering lift-truck, hand-truck and carrier loading and unloading operations. In addition, a 30-item checklist is presented for improving your material's handling methods.

(4) Should you desire to involve employees in cost reduction, develop an employee suggestion plan (see Chapter 4 for explanation and method). By utilizing MTM for analysis, one employee made a saving of 27% by improving the work place layout; another employee eliminated an "aside part" operation and made a 100% saving in direct labor costs. By using work simplification principles, the sequence of operations of a crew of five was rearranged and with the expenditure of $500, the crew was reduced to three through a production employee's suggestion. In another plant a production clerk's suggestion won an award of $5,000 for her methods change resulting in substantial material savings.

(5) If you think it time to make an audit of your work standards and/or incentive pay plan, study Chapter 5. You may find loose standards and unaccounted-for methods changes that require new standards. Poorly maintained standards can be very costly as well as causing employee unrest.

(6) With new factory and warehouse space construction costs soaring, companies should review their inventory turnover rates. Before planning to add warehouse space or to build additional floor space in your factory, it would be well to make an effort to increase your turnover index. Great savings are usually possible here. Some actual examples revealed that a textile mill had $2,000,000 excess inventory with an estimated annual loss of $400,000 at 20% cost of carrying inventory. The interest alone at 7% was costing $140,000 annually. An electronics firm also was losing $42,000 a year because of a $210,000 excessive inventory. See Chapter 6.

(7) In this age of energy shortages, establish your utilities costs, then check Chapter 7 for the proper tools to use for measuring these plant costs. Then take definitive actions. A cost reduction checklist for both machine and energy is also provided.

(8) One important potential area for cost savings is minimizing machine downtime. In one company, with over 100 automatic screw machines on a two-shift operation, a study revealed that 35% of the scheduled machine time was consumed by downtime. By introducing a preventive maintenance system, this was eventually reduced to 15%. A $900,000 annual saving in unabsorbed burden was estimated to have been saved. See Chapter 7.

(9) Should you be looking for a new plant or warehouse site location, see Chapter 9. Also, for proper analysis you will need to know cost elements of construction—site selection, construction cost factors, facility design factors, building materials and building code restrictions. These are all discussed.

(10) Executives and managers at all levels have a continuous job of training others, but how much do they know about the *principles of learning?* A great deal about this subject is discussed in Chapter 11.

(11) Methods of computing performance objectives are discussed in Chapter 12. One example covers an outline of a method used in computing the Personnel Department's Performance Index and another example presented covers a Key Employee Bonus Plan, based on company profits and the measured performance of participants in the plan.

(12) An example of a formal cost reduction program effectively employed by major corporations is outlined in Chapter 13. In an initial 12-month period in one company, 150 different projects reduced costs $2,000,000. This represented a 5% savings on an annual expense budget of $40,000,000.

(13) If you would like to know how to control operations in your company distribution centers, read Chapter 15. The introduction of work standards in warehouses, examples of actual dray delivery standards of a large petroleum products company, truck travel time standards, and use of powered trucks and related warehouse functions all are covered.

(14) If you are undecided about operating your own trucks or using common carriers, see the suggested breakdown of expenses for analysis outlined in Chapter 16. Also included are complete instructions for training drivers, outlined by the American Petroleum Institute and used here with their permission.

(15) Operating executives like to receive their reports regarding events and actions in the area of their responsibilities promptly and accurately. See an actual example of the advantages of a complete computerization of operating control reports of a major company. Also presented are techniques for solving business problems by Quantitative Analysis. Refer to Chapter 18.

Here are some additional ways in which this manual can point the way to greater efficiencies and higher profits in manufacturing operations:

...Outlines company situations requiring the need for engineering planning for manufacture; tells how manufacturing engineering is the hub in the wheel of smooth technical operations; discusses designing for manufacturability, analysis for manufacturability, designing for automation, project engineering; and provides a checklist for improved performance. (See Chapter 1.)

...Sets forth practical production control planning for manufacture, through examination of your organization structure, staff and direction; covers implementing the plan, controlling and auditing your system. (See Chapter 2.)

...Points the way to better plant layout, production flow and material handling; covers factors that influence layout, guiding fundamentals, flow planning principles, proper selection of equipment; includes list of safe practices in lift-truck, hand-truck and carrier loading and unloading operations. (See Chapter 3.)

...Tells how better to use methods engineering techniques and Work Simplification principles; discusses involvement of employees in cost reduction programs and the best way to introduce an employee suggestion plan. (See Chapter 4.)

...Depicts methods of controlling production with engineered work standards; lists advantages of using work standards as a control, keeping standards up to date, auditing your system, maintaining supervisory and production employee interest in standards; provides a checklist for improving employee productivity through their use. (See Chapter 5.)

...Informs you on methods to use to improve your inventory turnover rate, sample calculations, cost of carrying inventory; tells how to reduce excessive inventories; provides suggested list of remedial actions. (See Chapter 6.)

...Advises you on plant engineering and preventive maintenance methods and the responsibilities of the plant engineer; names tools for measuring plant efficiences; provides checklist for cost reduction ideas for both machine and energy; shows how to determine downtime costs; lists the great advantages of preventive maintenance systems. (See Chapter 7.)

...Recommends quality control and inspection practices; examines the costs; reviews the economical aspects of decisions on the amount and type of inspection to maintain; shows how to determine the best organizational structure for your particular plant; specifies quality responsibilities, quality engineering, inspection procedures; tells how to make an effective analysis of quality control costs. (See Chapter 8.)

...Acquaints you with methods of determining the geographic location and control of warehouses, of calculating the most economical shipping terminal site between two sources; discusses cost elements of construction, warehouse planning processes, order picking, assembly disciplines, and how to measure warehouse performance and controlling costs. (See Chapter 9.)

...Reviews the advantages of a well-staffed and competent industrial engineering function. Covers such items as scope of the function, type of organization, maintaining proper relationships between line and staff functions, and includes a checklist for improving performance. (See Chapter 18.)

...States the importance to the manager of fully developing employees and discusses the key forces influencing training; explains the *principles of learning* in some depth; suggests teaching aids; comments on learning curves, overlearning, spacing of practice periods, differences between rote and logical learning, associative learning, multimedia instruction techniques; gives examples of downward, upward and across communications. (See Chapter 11.)

...Tells how you can establish performance objectives for line and staff personnel. Explains purpose of performance appraisals and the advantages to both top and middle management and to their subordinates. Provides examples of why some evaluation plans fail, importance of their proper maintenance, and suggests several plans for your consideration. A list of factors to consider when conducting an employee performance review is also presented. (See Chapter 12.)

...Specifies how to program for cost reduction attacks, including determining dimensions of plan, establishing goals and timetables, and outlines a complete plan used successfully by major corporations. Other topics included are the fixing of responsibility, setting goals and securing budgetary allowance. A cost reduction checklist also is presented. (See Chapter 13.)

...Relates in detail how to make capital investment decisions by quantitative analysis, the economics of such decisions, the explanation of the payback, return on investment, total-life average or full-life performance and average rate of return methods. (See Chapter 14.)

...Pinpoints methods to use in controlling operations at your distribution centers, including the introduction of work standards in warehousing with actual examples of dray delivery and truck travel-time standards. Other subjects covered are warehouse operations with manpower only, and with powered trucks, disbursement procedures, housekeeping, and general precautions. (See Chapter 15.)

...Recommends how to better manage your trucking operations—first deciding whether to operate your own trucks or to use common carriers, with a breakdown of expenses, suggested cost reduction possibilities, explanation of piggyback and containerization. A complete drivers' training program is included, excerpted, with permission, from American Petroleum Institute's "Drivers' Handbook." This covers vehicle inspection, general instructions, tires, 27 items of driving practices, special precautions for railroad grade crossings, truck breakdowns, and traffic accidents. (See Chapter 16.)

...Presents a program for reducing excessive paperwork, including forms design and control, preparing and analyzing paper flow charts, examining floor layout and conducting a space analysis, designing a distance-usage index, exhibit of 37-item questionnaire, example of an "activity schedule of positions" handling all forms and its analysis of an actual situation in industry, as well as a 46-item list of questions for paperwork improvement. (See Chapter 17.)

...Depicts a thorough review of an actual example, taken from industry, of a complete computerization of operating control reports for plant and operations managers. Describes the fundamental characteristics of solving business problems by this method: precision, reliability and accuracy, manageability, machine-readability, unambiguity, versatility and consistency. Indicates 22 items of advantages for plant management and a sampling of actual examples of cost savings realized through systems use. (See Chapter 18.)

Lewis R. Zeyher

To all employees who conscientiously aid and cooperate in effectively implementing management programs for improved operations.

ACKNOWLEDGMENTS

Grateful thanks are expressed to the persons who helped in the preparation of this book: to my wife for her patient and thorough editing of the manuscript, and to Guss C. Timm, John W. Hannon, Norman S. Tyler, Bruno A. Moski, W.H. Pilkenton, Richard Burdick and J.F. McKenna for their interest and help.

The following companies also kindly cooperated in assisting me: Atlantic Richfield Co., Maynard Research Council Incorporated, Tyco Industries, Inc., Bruno A. Moski Associates, Western Electric Co., Maytag Co., and American Petroleum Institute.

Table of Contents

Production and Operations
Manual and Guide

1

Advanced Engineering Planning for Manufacture

The operations of the manufacturing engineering department affect virtually all manufacturing line departments. An error, poor judgment, an omission of fact, or careless or gross incompetency can only create additional problems for you. The undesirable conditions also compound your operating losses. To achieve efficient and low cost plant operations you must have top performance in this key department.

Company situations requiring the need for engineering planning for manufacture include:

(a) The development of a new product.
(b) Changes in the demand and design of an existing product, including styling.
(c) Conversion of a process-type fabrication to a progressive production line when dictated by increased volume.
(d) New addition to plant or new plant.
(e) New capital equipment.
(f) Plant-wide modernization program.
(g) Cost reduction program involving changes in methods and tooling.
(h) Changes in specifications.

These factors may bring about the need for new manufacturing facilities. The problem of forecasting demand and setting up a program for production requires a thorough analysis of the data from the various manufacturing departments. The extent of these analyses depends on the complexity of the changes in the manufacturing processes.

[1]MANUFACTURING ENGINEERING: HUB IN THE WHEEL
OF SMOOTH TECHNICAL OPERATIONS

In this department the emphasis is on technical competence. A deficiency here will create a chain reaction, seriously affecting a number of other departments. Incompetency, negligence, poor judgment, omissions of important data, indolence, procrastinations and related abortive actions cannot be tolerated in this keystone of all technical operating areas. (See Exhibit 1-1.)

Should the manufacturing engineering manager fail to have an engineering background he should be well backed up by a capable man, skilled in this function. It often happens, however, that a strong technically oriented supervisor is weak in other facets of his responsibilities. A good leader, familiar with these shortcomings, will supplement them with his greater abilities. What are the responsibilities of the head of this department? For the medium-to-large, typical metal working plant they are briefly as follows: (taken from an actual job description)

(a) *Specific* (Paragraph headings only)
    (1) Approval Signatures
    (2) Scheduled Plant Committee Meetings
    (3) Sign for Invoices
    (4) Liaison Function—Sales, Manufacturing and Product Engineering
    (5) Assign Work
    (6) Exercise Surveillance
    (7) Production Departments (for aid and consultation)
    (8) Special Products
    (9) Review Design Analysis Drawings
    (10) Place Purchase Orders
    (11) Overtime Control
    (12) Union Grievances
    (13) Review Product Engineering Specifications, both preliminary and final

(b) *General:*
    (14) Conduct Staff Meetings
    (15) Training
    (16) Discipline
    (17) Job Descriptions Compliance
    (18) Organization and Planning
    (19) Communications
    (20) Salary Review
    (21) Screen and Approve New Employees
    (22) Attendance
    (23) Housekeeping
    (24) Telephone Contacts
    (25) Work Sampling
    (26) Cooperation with Other Departments
    (27) Other Related Duties

---

[1] Lewis R. Zeyher, *Production Manager's Desk Book* (Englewood Cliffs, N.J.: Prentice-Hall, Inc., copyright © 1969), p. 54, lines 4-23.

MANUFACTURING ENGINEER FUNCTIONS AND INTERDEPARTMENT RELATIONS

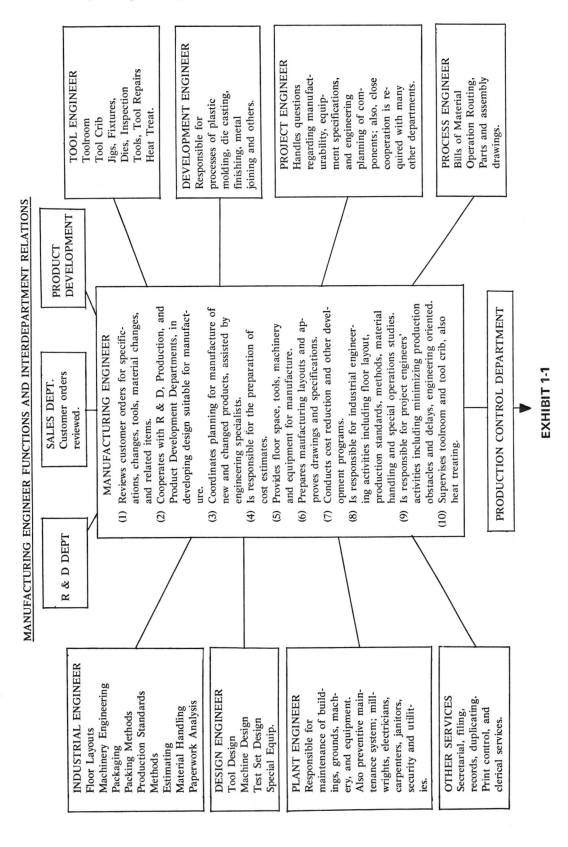

R & D DEPT

SALES DEPT. Customer orders reviewed.

PRODUCT DEVELOPMENT

TOOL ENGINEER
Toolroom
Tool Crib
Jigs, Fixtures,
Dies, Inspection
Tools, Tool Repairs
Heat Treat.

DEVELOPMENT ENGINEER
Responsible for processes of plastic molding, die casting, finishing, metal joining and others.

PROJECT ENGINEER
Handles questions regarding manufact-urability, equip-ment specifications, and engineering planning of com-ponents; also, close cooperation is re-quired with many other departments.

PROCESS ENGINEER
Bills of Material
Operation Routing,
Parts and assembly
drawings.

MANUFACTURING ENGINEER

(1) Reviews customer orders for specific-ations, changes, tools, material changes, and related items.

(2) Cooperates with R & D, Production, and Product Development Departments, in developing design suitable for manufact-ure.

(3) Coordinates planning for manufacture of new and changed products, assisted by engineering specialists.

(4) Is responsible for the preparation of cost estimates.

(5) Provides floor space, tools, machinery and equipment for manufacture.

(6) Prepares manufacturing layouts and ap-proves drawings and specifications.

(7) Conducts cost reduction and other devel-opment programs.

(8) Is responsible for industrial engineer-ing activities including floor layout, production standards, methods, material handling and special operations studies.

(9) Is responsible for project engineers' activities including minimizing production obstacles and delays, engineering oriented.

(10) Supervises toolroom and tool crib, also heat treating.

INDUSTRIAL ENGINEER
Floor Layouts
Machinery Engineering
Packaging
Packing Methods
Production Standards
Methods
Estimating
Material Handling
Paperwork Analysis

DESIGN ENGINEER
Tool Design
Machine Design
Test Set Design
Special Equip.

PLANT ENGINEER
Responsible for maintenance of build-ings, grounds, mach-ery, and equipment. Also preventive main-tenance system; mill-wrights, electricians, carpenters, janitors, security and utilit-ies.

OTHER SERVICES
Secretarial, filing, records, duplicating. Print control, and clerical services.

PRODUCTION CONTROL DEPARTMENT

EXHIBIT 1-1

DESIGNING FOR MANUFACTURABILITY

[2]No design is satisfactory until the particular problems of manufacture achieve a satisfactory economic balance between the demands of the user and the costs of manufacture. The design engineer must know the production processes and manufacturing methods in order to complete his design responsibility. Sometimes the responsibility for a manufacturable design is divided between two organizations, one which proposes a unit that can be manufactured by laboratory and skilled worker techniques, and the other which reworks that design to fit the needs of production. Both departments are concerned with design, and regardless of the division, there is one design problem to be considered—designing for manufacturability.

In order for the design engineer to design manufacturable products, he or his organization must have a *practicable* understanding of the capabilities of the currently used manufacturing machines and processes. Periodic review of the capabilities of the foundry processes, of the material removal processes, and of the assembly procedures is a *most* useful procedure for the design engineer. A complete review of the current capabilities consists of:

(a) Investment casting
(b) Shell molding
(c) Plastic encapsulation
(d) Ultrasonic machinery
(e) Printed wiring
(f) . . . . and a myriad of the presently acceptable manufacturing techniques.

The consideration of manufacturing processes is a course in itself. It is important, however, that the designer have an adequate background in currently used techniques, or that he have the advice and working cooperation of those who do have that knowledge. The designer should be able to recognize those methods that are the most economical of initial investment, labor and time. Any design that is made without proper consideration of such factors will probably require revision before production is started.

(a) Tooling Costs[3]

The designer may design a part for which there are often many ways that the part can be manufactured. It can be machined from a block of metal, it can be forged, or it can be cast or molded. Each method has a different cost for tooling to make even the first part. Consequently, the method specified often depends on the number to be produced. If the demand for the part will be small the major cost of manufacture is the initial tooling. Therefore, it is desirable to design and dimension the part for manufacture on general purpose material removal machines that require little tooling. Only when the volume justifies it, is it advantageous to consider processes with initial tooling costs.

Example:
Ho Scale Electric Trains and Freight Truck Cost Reduction.

---

[2] Used by permission of the Western Electric Company, New York, N.Y. *Planning for Manufacture,* 2nd Edition, copyright © 1965, p. 103, 104, 105.

[3] *Ibid.*

New method—one shot complete mold, eliminates five operations by changing material from *steel* and *zamac* to *plastic* and tooling from *stamping* to *die cast*—

	Old Method	New Method
Material	Steel, Zamac, Brass	Plastic (Delrin)
Process	Stamping (9 operations)	Die Cast (4 operations)
Cost/1,000		
Material	$11.08	$ 8.55
Labor	22.60	10.52
	$33.68	$19.07
Savings:	....	$14.61
Per Cent Savings:	$\dfrac{\$14.61}{33.68}$	43%

Sales Features

....improved product

(1 Pulls more cars (72 vs 18).

( )Better appearance.

(3)Cars roll easier and quieter (due to use of Delrin).

(4)Due to reduction in manufacturing cost—can sell cheaper.

Example: Precision Woodworking Shop

New method substitution of *African Mahogany* for *Walnut* by staining mahogany to make a Walnut finish.

Material costs (*at time of this writing*):

   Walnut   83c / sq. ft., 3/8" thick

   Mahogany 47c / sq. ft., 3/8" thick

Cost/box	Old Method	New Method
Material	$ 5.81	$3.29
Labor	6.19	6.19
Total	$12.00	$9.48

Savings.........$12.00 — $9.48 = $2.52/box

Per cent savings	$\dfrac{\$ 2.52}{\$12.00}$	21%

Total savings: 10,000 boxes sold annually X $2.52 = $25,200.00

Note: Characteristics of woods very similar—mahogany more easily available, grain and finish of mahogany (stained to walnut finish appearance) looks better, improves saleability of product.

Note: Both of these also represent Value Analysis examples due largely to sales features.

(b) Available Machines and Materials

In designing a product the following cost considerations should be observed:

(1) Utilize available machines as much as possible.

(2) Volume to be produced—this will affect type of tooling, among other factors.

(3) Make or buy—try to have direct control of the maximum of manufacturing processes.

(4) Select proper materials that are suitable for product quality, durability and economical maching costs. This may require some compromising between the conflicting demands.

(c) Factory Physical Limitations

Other important cost considerations are the layout and physical limitations which may affect cost: A few of these follow:

(a) The physical dimensions and weight of product that can be manually handled by people; and, will new handling equipment be necessary?

(b) Will product be too high for doors, too wide for present aisles or too awkward for transport by elevators?

(c) Will assembly areas require dust-free areas and clean air—will costly air conditioning be necessary?

(d) Will assembly operations require special clothing or expensive safety equipment?

(e) Will disagreeable odors and nearby noisy machinery dictate relocation of assembly area?

(f) Will undesirable vibrations caused by nearby heavy equipment, require changes or modifications in assembly benches, or to the offending equipment?

ANALYSIS FOR MANUFACTURABILITY[4]

This analysis should encompass the following:

(a) Is the design mechanically sound? Have the proper materials been selected? Are the cross sections adequate to insure design intent? Do formed parts have proper radii at the bends? Are castings properly designed with correct fillets? Are screws, rivets, and fastening devices of the proper size?

(b) Can the design be simplified? Is it unnecessarily complicated?

(c) Can the part or assembly be made on available machines with the customary tooling?

(d) Could minor changes be made to reduce the cost of manufacture?

(e) Have all parts been properly dimensioned and the proper tolerances specified to ensure correct assembly and interchangeability?

(f) Are the mechanical requirements practical and reasonable?

(g) On designs involving electrical requirements are the requirements practical and reasonable?

(h) Are the mechanical and electrical requirements adequate to ensure meeting the design intent?

In order to accomplish proper end result, very close liaison must be maintained between the manufacturing engineer and the R & D, product development and/or the customer's engineers. This can be done by obtaining checking prints or preliminary engineering sketches from the design engineer or conferring with him before the designs are formulated. Changes and modifications can be incorporated in the early design stages more easily than after final drawings and specifications have been issued.

---

[4] Used by permission of the Western Electric Company, New York, N.Y. *Planning for Manufacture,* 2nd edition, copyright © 1965, p. 108.

DESIGNING FOR AUTOMATION

Factors to consider include the following:

(a) Volume of product and cost of manufacture.
(b) A better utilization of machine tools.
(c) Adding feedback controls to mechanized tools already developed.
(d) The suitable grouping of machines.
(e) Mechanical and sequential handling and/or transport from one machine to another.

The advantages:

(a) Lower unit costs.
(b) More uniform and better quality product.
(c) Less material waste due to minimum rejection rate.
(d) Provides greater output of product for floor space needed.
(e) Improves employee working conditions.
(f) Use of preventive maintenance becomes mandatory.
(g) Less dirt, noise and confusion.
(h) More square feet of floor area per worker.
(i) More interesting work because it is less routine.
(j) Less manual handling thereby reducing accidents.
(k) Reduced construction costs due to less floor space required.
(l) Increases reliability in meeting customer delivery schedules.

PROJECT ENGINEERING

The following is an actual job description of a group leader of project engineers in a 1,000-employee, metal working plant:

(1) Function

He is responsible for the direct supervision of all project engineers, including the assignment of work, following up on progress and the completion of jobs; he exercises surveillance over work performance, quality and quantity of work, and accuracy and thoroughness as well as technical competence. He also acts as a guide, coach, and technical consultant to his subordinates and to other manufacturing department supervisors, and in so doing his activities will reach into all phases of manufacturing. He will also have contacts with other company departments, particularly where it concerns processing, tooling, machine repairs, new equipment, rework, quality, cost reduction, engineering changes, designs and related items.

(2) Duties and Responsibilities

In the following, and in the interest of brevity, only sub-headings will be indicated. It also should be understood that there may be many variations in job descriptions depending on product-mix, types and complexity of product, size of plant, equipment and organization.

(a) *Specific:*

    (1) Follow-up on jobs running

    (2) Specialties (miniatures)

    (3) Assign work

    (4) Exercise surveillance

    (5) Employee suggestions

    (6) Supervises design chief

    (7) New equipment

    (8) Product engineering & technical sales

    (9) Processing engineering

  (10) Technical service

  (11) Production problems

  (12) Used equipment

  (13) Tool room foreman

  (14) Attend meetings

  (15) Training subordinates

  (16) Maintaining discipline

  (17) Job description compliance.

  (18) Sampling work of project engineers: this includes taking a project, either just finished or in progress, and checking it thoroughly from its inception to last operation performed and examining it for the following:

    (a) Organization and planning of work

    (b) Judgment exercised

    (c) Engineering know-how and ingenuity

    (d) Processing (thoroughness, accuracy and completeness)

    (e) Design

    (f) Tooling and gaging

    (g) Paperwork

    (h) Quality of work

    (i) Cost factor

    (j) Dispatch (time to complete)

    (k) Follow-up

    (l) Appraisal of the operating performance of project

(*Note:* this item was developed due to its great importance.)

  (19) Quality control and inspection

  (20) Attendance

  (21) Paperwork and forms flow

  (22) Housekeeping

  (23) Communication

  (24) Planning

  (25) Telephone contacts

  (26) Cooperation with other departments.

CHECKLIST FOR IMPROVED PERFORMANCE[5]

(1) All positions should be covered by written job descriptions and kept current. Determine if the duties and responsibilities are being followed.

(2) Be constantly on the alert for continued technical incompetence. This creates confusion throughout the manufacturing departments, increases costs, lengthens the cycle time for order processing and may jeopardize customer relations. Do not permit this condition to exist.

(3) Do not accept slackness in the handling of discipline by your supervisors. Firmness in dealing with employees should always be expected.

(4) Assure yourself that all forms are executed promptly and that the necessary data and information called for in these forms are provided.

(5) Do not permit too many key employees to participate in the making of final engineering decisions. Their opinions should be encouraged but only one can be responsible for the results of these judgments. Make sure authorities have been properly delegated.

(6) In the transmittal of engineering data and information, leave nothing to chance. Non-technical employees should not be required to make a technical decision where a multiple choice is offered.

(7) Do not permit frequent engineering changes to be made, then changed, only to be followed by another reverting to the original decision. This naturally creates confusion and will produce a lack of confidence in the supervisor rendering them.

(8) Keep a check on the methods employed in the handling and distribution of new print releases and revisions. It generally is not fast enough, is incomplete and the obsolete prints are rarely collected and destroyed. You should have an effective print control procedure.

(9) Investigate filing practices. Too many employees receive copies of company communications who do not require them. This creates excessive filing.

(10) Examine existing floor layout plans of department. Are departments and desks effectively located? The elapse of time often brings changes in product-mix, employee turnover, and new customers; machinery is moved and procedures revised. These occurrences may dictate need for a new layout.

(11) Do you have enough check points on completeness, accuracy and legibility of forms being circularized? Periodically sample the flow of forms and look for evidence of these deficiencies.

(12) Consider a centralized filing system. Do not permit too many filing cabinets to occupy prime office space.

(13) Periodically check the routing and processing of work through the plant. Is the best and shortest route indicated? Are machine operations that have been eliminated still being shown on the process sheets?

---

5 Lewis R. Zeyher, *Production Manager's Desk Book,* (Englewood Cliffs, N.J.: Prentice-Hall, Inc., copyright © 1969), pp. 54-55.

(14) Can anything be done at one work station that will make the succeeding operation, at the next work station, easier? Does anyone ever investigate this?

(15) Occasionally check to determine if all approval signatures have proper significance. Does supervisor actually review, question, check, add, delete or contribute anything to form before affixing signature?

(16) Discourage the practice of supervisors and other key employees issuing important instructions verbally and without written confirmation. This refers particularly to instructions involving engineering data, procedures, methods and related information.

(17) Make sure your design engineers are realistic in their choice of tolerances.

(18) Assure yourself that the design section is cost conscious in their design work.

(19) Determine whether proper economical feeds and speeds have been established for all materials machined in your plant.

(20) Check on the planning of your project engineers—are they continuing to search for better and lower cost methods?

(21) Make sure your methods are standardized and have been properly described in writing.

(22) Determine if your design engineers are utilizing MTM charts when designing tools, fixtures and drill jigs.

(23) Are your engineers working closely with the quality control department in seeking ways to reduce scrap and rework? Insist that they do and follow up for compliance.

(24) Investigate your perishable tool and material control practices—are they tightly controlled?

(25) Does the supervisor of this department work closely with the quality analyst from the production control department? Assure yourself that he provides pre-production service to design engineering and manufacturing for new products.

(26) Do you have an effective control policy on the activities of your project engineers? Make sure their efforts are under supervisory control.

2

Production
Control Planning
for Manufacture

The manager of the production control department holds one of the most potent and vital of all key positions in the typical manufacturing plant. He is responsible for directing and coordinating the activities of the planning, receiving, scheduling, dispatching, materials handling, expediting, warehousing and shipping functions. The successful companies of the future will be expected to provide unusually good service, while producing a quality product with a minimum of cost. These objectives dictate the need for an effective organization, led by an aggressive supervisor within the framework of a flexible control system. In the performance of his responsibilities full support of all manufacturing departments is mandatory.

An effective system should enable you to determine, at any given time, the location and current status of each order and its future path indicated with the date of required completion. When unexpected changes are required in customer delivery dates, specifications, routing, or scheduling, the transactions will be efficiently executed with dispatch. Most importantly, the customer's promised shipping date will be met and a quality product will be received according to his specifications and in good condition.

To bring about these desirable results, a well-structured organization, competently staffed and effectively directed, is of the greatest importance. A discussion of these three requirements follows.

EXAMINING THE ORGANIZATION STRUCTURE, STAFF AND DIRECTION

(a) Organization Structure[1]

With so many people involved in the planning and action phases of this function, and with the need for careful coordination, the structure of the organization must be examined. Foremost in this examination these questions should be asked—what work is

---

[1] Lewis R. Zeyher, *Production Manager's Desk Book,* (Englewood Cliffs, N.J.: Prentice-Hall, Inc., copyright © 1969), pp. 1-3, 7.

to be done, who should do it, and what relationship will it have with other people and their functions?

In the very small company, the president and/or owner opens the mail, pulls out the customers' orders, reviews the credit status, and sorts out the orders where material is in finished stores from orders where the product must be manufactured. Then he takes the orders to be processed to his shop foreman and the other orders are given to the shipping clerk to take the product out of finished stores and ship to the customer. In this instance, communications are personal and direct, usually minimizing chances for error, lost orders, misunderstandings or need for involved expediting and/or dispatching routines. Paperwork is held to a few clerical transactions—no need for a lot of clerks, huge filing systems, volumes of forms flow, and the recurring dilemma, "What happened to the order for XYZ company that was placed two months ago?" In addition, the small company usually cannot afford to have too much money tied up in accounts receivable, and shipments are made promptly so billing can be immediately made. This is not true of the larger companies where you usually find a frantic rush during the last several days of each month so good billing can be shown for that period.

Growth and bigness generates complexity, some confusion, more overhead and definitely the need for systems, procedures, organization analysis, discipline, and related considerations. In this analysis the following questions should be satisfactorily answered:

(a) Is your organization structure up-to-date?
(b) What depth of control is required and how much can you afford?
(c) Have any new functions been added since your last analysis?
(d) How demanding are your customers?
(e) Are there too many *rush* orders?
(f) Does your system provide flexibility?
(g) Does your organization permit freedom of action?
(h) Do you have any *empire builders* in the organization?
(i) Is the proper discipline maintained—do people do what they are supposed to do?
(j) Have arrangements for replacements been made for key people due for retirement in a few years?
(k) Are decisions covering operating problems done intelligently and quickly?
(l) Are key employees' responsibilities clearly defined?
(m) Are any revisions necessary in the organization chart due to changes in the channels of authority?
(n) Have effective feedback channels of communications been established?
(o) Is every position covered by a job description and are they periodically reviewed?

The organization structure required for your production control department will be greatly influenced by your type of product and industry, product mix, mass or jobbing production, length of cycle time, floor space, size of plant, number of parts involved, number of operations, degree of complexity of products, tightness of quality standards, government requirements, single-plant or multi-plant operation, single or multiple floors, domestic and/or foreign shipments, number of distribution centers, own trucking equipment, leased or contract haulers, to whom does the production control manager report, and related considerations.

One type of a functional chart for a medium to large plant is shown in Exhibit 2-1.

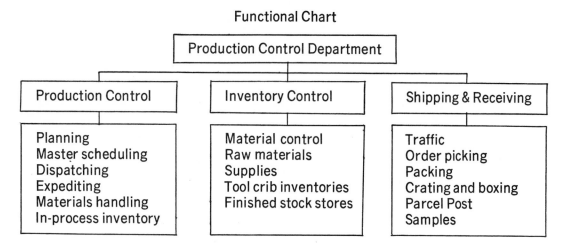

Functional Chart

Production Control Department		
Production Control	**Inventory Control**	**Shipping & Receiving**
Planning	Material control	Traffic
Master scheduling	Raw materials	Order picking
Dispatching	Supplies	Packing
Expediting	Tool crib inventories	Crating and boxing
Materials handling	Finished stock stores	Parcel Post
In-process inventory		Samples

EXHIBIT 2-1

(b) Organization Staff

After you design or redesign the organization structure, the next step is to review the capabilities of the department's personnel. In staffing, the manager attempts to find the right person for each job. To do this effectively requires the taking of a complete inventory of the incumbents of all positions and studies made of them. An established company, of course, has an organization and personnel to fill each position. Nevertheless, both organization and staffing are likely to be continuing jobs since changes are constantly taking place—employees retire, are promoted, resign or are terminated. Product-mix may be disturbed, new products added, others deleted. These processes, usually occurring intermittently, will have some impact on the organizational arrangements.

Such an analysis will reveal inadequacies, disclose misfits and incompetents. Too much emphasis cannot be placed on the need for complete objectivity during this exercise. Avoid emotional decisions, the blight of many management executives' determinations. Refrain from carrying deadweight. There are numerous examples in industry where incompetent employees are carried by others in the same section.

The following represents an actual example where the employees of the shipping department protected their likable foreman from detection by the plant manager.

Every morning the plant manager made a tour of the various departments and often stopped to chat with the respective foreman. However, on Monday mornings he failed to see the shipping department foreman. When he inquired of employees about his whereabouts he always received an evasive answer. Upon investigation of this undesirable situation, he discovered that the missing foreman was an alcoholic who usually experienced a week-end hangover and whose employees arranged to hide their boss in the department when the plant manager's visit was expected.

Also remember that some employees are better salesmen than others—do a deceptive job of selling themselves to the disadvantage of the often more competent and loyal employees, who are not so well endowed. In this same connection, do not place excessive value on the candidates for promotion or employment who are very strong in the personality and/or appearance characteristic. It is also a truism that the higher up in the echelon of management that an executive climbs, the less and less he is informed about the bad things occurring in the areas of his own responsibility. The expression—*scratch each others' backs,* is so true in industry where, in all layers of management the tendency is to protect associates' wrong doings, knowing that sometime they may need this same help themselves. It also is difficult for managers to get unbiased facts and opinions from peers or subordinates.

(c) Organization Direction

One of the most important attributes the manager of this department should possess is *drive.* In addition, he should have a strong and aggressive personality. However, these should be tempered with tact and a feeling for practicing good human relations. Softness, timidity and indecisiveness cannot be accepted in the manager of this very important position. In addition, he should report to the head of the manufacturing and/or production department. The incumbent should receive the same screening as previously mentioned. He must meet very high standards. There can be no compromise here. A weak manager would employ and foster less-than-competent subordinates. This type of personnel in such a key department could well produce loose control and an ineffective system. Competent subordinates require a strong and respected leader. The pressures on this manager are unrelenting and frustrating—it takes a strong personality to cope with them.

In one large company there were so many "emergency orders" placed by the sales people on this shipping department that it became ridiculous. No one paid any attention to them. This resulted in ignoring those that were *actually* emergency orders for important customers. Eventually, in order to bring some orderliness to what was becoming chaos, sales and production department executives reached an agreement. Only 25 customer orders were permitted to be labeled and treated as emergencies, out of hundreds of daily orders. These had to be in the shipping department office before noon each day, with delivery promised before the end of that day (if they were stock orders).

IMPLEMENTING THE PLAN

(a) Securing Reliable Sales Forecasts

The function of production planning requires reliable sales forecasts from the sales department if it is to perform efficiently. No one expects that this data will be one-hundred per cent accurate. Revisions in these estimates will be expected as time goes on but the figures presented will at least provide a basis for some planning. In one company, where product styling was a factor, the vice president of sales stated it was impossible to estimate such information. However, a recapitulation of his previous years' sales listed by various categories and compared to the first six months' actual sales for the current year, indicated that 65% of the shipments were very comparable to those of the previous years'. In other words, if this had been forecasted it would have been a great help to the production control department and to more efficient production. With experience, great improvement also could have been made in future forecasting. With this advance information the planning group could schedule the indicated production, purchasing, subcontracting, internal and external tooling and supplies. Allocation of men and machines for the fabrication of the company products then will be effectively consummated and customer requirements met.

A very close liaison should be maintained with knowledgeable personnel in the sales department. The production control department expects to be kept continuously advised of any changes in the market place, i.e., unusual economic situations, special sales campaigns, new products, price changes, credit status, changes in customer buying habits, delivery requirements, new large sales volume customers, loss of important customers, and related situations.

(b) Physically Placing Work Stations

In small companies the plant office is the usual spot for desks of personnel engaged in these activities. The manager also handles a number of functions and is usually situated within a short distance of every manufacturing operation and can exercise close surveillance from his desk.

The challenges involved in locating medium-to-large work stations are very real. The following example points the way to one solution:

In one metal working company of several thousand employees, the production control manager's office was located in the main plant office within close proximity of the vice president of manufacturing. In addition, the office of the manager of manufacturing engineering was only a short walk away. However, a production control center was situated out in the plant in the middle of all manufacturing activity. This was the nerve center of the production control department where production scheduling, dispatching, expediting and control of the movement of lift-trucks was handled.

In addition, a production control expeditor was strategically located in every large department, with his desk placed next to that of the department foreman. (See Exhibit 2-2.) Most of the paperwork covering factory orders passed through him. His duties also included the minimizing of production delays as well as providing a feedback of pertinent information channeled back through the production control center. Then, when necessary, some data was forwarded back to the production control manager's office. For the smaller departments the arrangement was to group those that were physically close and have one expediter handle several at a time. It should be understood that this is just one method and could not be used for all companies. A production control system should be tailored to fit the particular needs and facilities of each plant.

(c) Establishing Standard Procedure Instruction Manual

For the achievement of optimum results in a program of this kind, formal instructions covering the mechanics by which clerical transactions are performed should be established. In addition, forms and forms flow charts depicting the sequence of operations and assigning responsibilities for each clerical operation should be provided. This information is of inestimable value for training new employees and for aiding in the elimination of errors and for pinpointing responsibility. (See Exhibit 2-3.)

After this manual is prepared, every effort should be made to maintain it—keep it current. Some responsible employee should be assigned this task. Each key employee in the production control department should have a copy. When revisions or additions are

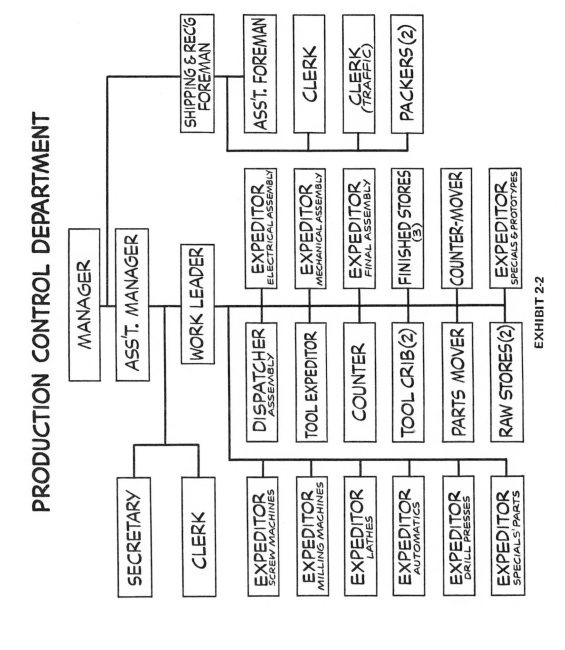

PRODUCTION CONTROL DEPARTMENT

EXHIBIT 2-2

PAPER FLOW CHART

	PRODUCTION CONTROL				PRODUCTION ENGINEERING					

Column headers (rotated): Product Engineering · Accounting Dept. · Scheduling · Tool Control · Material · Design Room · Coordination And Control · Chief Prod. Engineer · Vice Pres. Manufacturing · President

FORMS FLOW
Request For
Appropriation
Form: 10-1

Retain → [3][2][1]

FUNCTIONS PERFORMED

This Form is issued in triplicate (three white) and filled in by originator, generally by coordinator on instruction from authorized personnel in Mfg. One copy – No. 3 retained.

Two copies are forwarded to Chief Production Engineer for his approval and for his signature.

Both copies are forwarded to Vice President of Mfg. for approval and signature.

Both copies are forwarded to President for approval and his signature.

Accounting Dept. receives No. 1 copy from President's Office, so charges can be made against it.

The No. 2 copy with all required signatures affixed and with a control number assigned to it is returned to Secretary of Chief Prod. Eng. She logs R. A. No. and other data in File Book.

Coordinator receives No. 2 copy and makes a record of all transactions on it when completed, all parties concerned are informed.

No. 2 copy is received by Accounting Dept. with all original estimated cost data included and is ultimately filed with No. 1 copy.

File [2] with #1 copy

EXHIBIT 2-3

necessary it is suggested the production control manager's secretary collect these manuals, then personally insert the changes in each one, and return them to their owners. You will find that if this simple detail is not followed, certain individuals will neglect to make the required changes, resulting in many out-of-date procedures within a few months. It is recommended that other key employees, not necessarily among production department personnel, also should receive this procedure material that *particularly* concerns them.

Here is another neglected but very profitable area in plant operations for cost reduction. Too often economy programs consider only paper and printing costs and related minor considerations in their investigations. There is an inclination to overlook the generally less conspicuous possibilities for savings lurking in these daily plant operations:

(a) Poorly prepared orders received in the shipping departments, causing costly errors in customer shipments.

(b) Insufficient information regarding engineering specifications submitted by the design section, creating mistakes in the machining of parts.

(c) Poorly written route sheets prepared by the production engineering department, requiring a non-technically trained shop employee to make a technical decision involving many choices, when there should have been no decision necessary.

(d) Inadequate communications transmitted between departments because of insufficient and delayed distribution of copies of specific operating instructions, resulting in the neglect of the performance of a vital departmental function.

(e) Excessive typing time in transcribing shipping information from invoices to plant records, because of poorly planned arrangement and sequence of data on record cards.

(f) Three different forms used and handled in a clerical transaction when a single, well-designed form would have been sufficient.

(g) Illegible blueprints and route sheets requiring shop personnel to spend excessive time guessing and making inquiries about how to interpret necessary technical data.

(h) Excessive time spent by clerks, secretaries, and engineers in filing unnecessary copies of reports, forms, and related transactions.

(i) Too much space occupied by filing cabinets because of the filing and retention of unneeded clerical papers.

(j) Needless time lost by engineers, clerks and shop personnel unsuccessfully searching for required blueprints because they were misplaced.

(k) Scheduled customer shipments delayed because sales orders were lost somewhere between the production control department, where they were received, and the manufacturing departments, where the "cutting of metal" was to have started.

(l) Time wasted by employees in filling out outmoded forms covering the reporting of data no longer required.

These are but a few examples of the kinds of wasteful and inefficient practices that yearly cost some companies many thousands of dollars. Further, it is not unusual for these harmful occurrences to continue undetected and uncorrected for years.

CONTROLLING RESULTS

It must be remembered that people are one of the most important elements in the ultimate success of any system or procedure. They can make or break a system. Attempts should be made to impress all employees with the importance of the part they play in the system. Insofar as it is practicable, have them participate in the shaping and introduction of a new program or any revisions and changes that are to be made. It is a truism that people usually support any new method which they have had some opportunity to review or toward which they have made a contribution.

Follow-up of results is always necessary. The fact that you issued a directive regarding an operating situation does not indicate that everyone involved performed exactly as you prescribed. A spot check of this out in the plant to *see for yourself* may reveal some unsatisfactory conditions that do not conform to your original instructions. Communications are at best a tricky business. People are inclined to interpret instructions in the light of their own background and experience. Semantics also can play a part here. A case in point involves an experience I had in a supervisory training course where a question was stated in a true-or-false exercise, as follows:

Every effective supervisor must be a student of human behavior. Eight supervisors out of fifteen taking the course answered this in the negative—that the statement was *false.* Later, in questioning the group regarding this incorrect answer I learned that they thought the word "student" meant you had to go to college to study and learn about human behavior. They did not realize that in their everyday working experience they actually were learning about this very important subject.

Most feedback methods provide intelligence regarding *actual* results compared with the *desired* results. Then, through the use of the *control by exception* principle attention is addressed to those situations where the actual results did not compare favorably with expectations, and therefore required attention. In those operations where *actual* results compared favorably with scheduled results, no special vigilance is needed. In this manner the busy manager can give his undivided consideration to variances where definitive actions may be required.

An effective, accurate and fast feedback program is the most distinctive feature of a successful production control department. The methods to employ to insure the realization of these objectives include reports, intercom systems, pneumatic tubes, autotelegraph equipment, closed-circuit television, electronic computers, telephones, electric signaling devices and the efforts of expeditors. The slower methods also contribute through meetings, briefing sessions, personal contacts made by walking through the plant, correspondence, memoranda, union stewards' comments and reports, employee suggestions, customer complaints, and related media.

CHECKLIST FOR AUDITING YOUR SYSTEM[2]

(1) Review organization structure.

---

[2] Lewis R. Zeyher, *Production Manager's Desk Book* (Englewood Cliffs, N.J.: Prentice-Hall, Inc., copyright © 1969, pp. 18, 19, 41.

(2) Review and evaluate the effectiveness of the incumbents in all departments' key positions.

(3) Review particularly the effectiveness and qualifications of the production control manager.

(4) Check position descriptions—are they current?

(5) Check written standard practice instructions—are they complete and current? Are they religiously adhered to?

(6) Appraise scheduling efficiency—is it better than 80%?

(7) Measure inventory turnover rate—does it compare favorably with your industry?

(8) Analyze budget variances—do they continue in the same areas, and if so why isn't there some improvement?

(9) Compare employee turnover rate against the U.S. Department of Labor's yearly figures for your industry.

(10) Check disposition of old and inactive stocks—are your warehouse shelves cluttered with products that haven't moved for months, perhaps even years?

(11) Review customer complaints for the past six months, classified by causes. Have remedial actions been taken to eliminate causes?

(12) Check the department's housekeeping performance—does it meet your high standards?

(13) Review number of employee suggestions submitted, number utilized and total value of savings. How do figures compare with former years?

(14) Evaluate improvements accomplished over the past year. Could this be improved?

(15) Determine typical ordering cycle time from receipt of a sales order by manufacturing to the time first operation is started in manufacturing. This time can and should be reduced.

(16) What are you doing about employee training? Is anyone getting any coaching from you? Are any of your employees attending formal training programs?

(17) Check night shift production control activities. Does the control exercised compare favorably with the day shift?

(18) Analyze paperwork transactions—look specifically for errors, carelessness, omissions, excessive filing, duplications, number of carbon copies distributed, and related inefficient practices.

(19) Have you utilized your warehouse space economically? Are your aisles too wide? Do you have too many aisles? Do you palletize three or four tiers high?

(20) Review the current use of mechanical equipment in the processing of your paperwork—are you utilizing the most modern machines available?

(21) Review your various package designs and determine if they are the most economical available?

(22) Do you have a systematic method of periodically checking the accuracies of your inventories?

(23) Do you keep a check on machine utilization? Do you keep the fully automatic, semi-automatic and manually operated machines scheduled in that order?

(24) Do you know how many hours each week your machines are out of production due to no orders, out of material, no tooling, breakdowns, operators away from machines, too lengthy set-up times and related delays? What are you doing about minimizing or eliminating them?

(25) Review the number of emergency orders you receive from the sales department each day. Have you worked out a plan with them to keep them under some control?

(26) Make sure your material conversion factors are current.

(27) Do you keep your production over-runs under proper control?

(28) Do you have an efficient method to follow up on orders so you can determine if scheduled dates are kept? If a pattern develops do you investigate and correct?

(29) Do you verify the count of material received from vendors before authorizing payment of invoices?

(30) Do you keep all production foremen advised in advance regarding their weekly production schedules?

(31) Have you made arrangements for periodically taking samplings to determine if the theoretical conditions are being met, in the area of your responsibilities, by the actual working conditions in the plant?

(32) Are periodic audits made by outside consultants or by qualified staff members of your production control department's methods and procedures?

(33) Do you occasionally investigate your operations for excessive material and parts shrinkage, then take remedial actions?

(34) Have you a method for determining if all the tools required for a job are available and in good condition when a new job is started?

(35) Do you assure yourself that all route sheets are correct, kept current, and obsolete copies destroyed? Are you also sure the routing sequence and path indicated are followed?

3

Practical Ideas
in Plant Layout
and Material Handling

Because of their definite relationship, floor layout must be considered first when material handling problems are being analyzed. Floor layout involves the physical arrangement of equipment, machinery and buildings, and their association with people. In addition, examination should be made of all supporting services—utilities, auxiliaries, communications and control equipment. Planning should also include review of the best locations for the offices, restrooms, cafeteria, first-aid room, locker rooms, reception area and related sections. Mistakes once made in the original planning often are difficult and costly to correct. For example, in one plant the cafeteria was so poorly located that the majority of the production employees had to travel the entire length of the building to reach the cafeteria from their work stations. This occurred three times a day—lunch and two rest periods. This caused complaints from the employees as well as continued lateness of employees in returning to their individual work places.

The implementation of a well thought out floor layout plan could substantially reduce the need for some material handling equipment. Another fringe benefit is that you could more effectively utilize the equipment that is required. A thorough analysis of the movement of all plant materials followed by positive corrective actions can result in abundant savings. It has been stated that material handling costs of manufacturing industries in this country average between twenty and thirty per cent of their total labor costs. This will vary with the type of industry—the heavy industries highest, and light industries lowest. Let us look at a hypothetical plant where the yearly payroll for labor is three million dollars. Assume also that it is a plant in an industry where its handling costs are at the national average of twenty-five per cent. If an organized attack on these practices yields at least a ten per cent improvement, not an unlikely expectation, a yearly savings of seventy-five thousand dollars can be accomplished. It must be emphasized that the degree of effectiveness and savings realized of any kind of a program will largely depend on the competence and aggressiveness of the supervisor assigned to direct it.

41

FLOOR LAYOUT AND PRODUCTION FLOW

(a) Objectives[1]

Floor layout aims at an arrangement of work areas and equipment that will be *the most economical to operate and yet safe and satisfying for employees*—an arrangement of productive men, materials, machines and their supporting activities that will produce a product at a cost low enough to sell at a profit in a competitive market.

More specifically, the basic *objectives* in floor layout work include:

(1) Overall *integration* of all factors affecting the layout.
(2) Material moving a *minimum distance*.
(3) Work *flowing* through the plant.
(4) All *space* effectively utilized.
(5) *Satisfaction* and *safety* for workers.
(6) A *flexible* arrangement that can be easily readjusted.

(b) Types of Arrangement

The classic types of layout are three in number. They are as follows:

(1) Fixed Position: This is a layout where the material or major component remains in a fixed place. It does not move. All tools, machinery, men, and other pieces of material are brought to it. The complete job is done, or the product is made, with the major component staying in one location. One man or crew makes the complete assembly, bringing all parts to each assembly point. The workmen may or may not move from one location to another. Advantages are:

(1) Handling of major assembly unit is reduced (through increased parts handling to assembly point).
(2) Highly skilled operators are allowed to complete their work at one point, and responsibility for quality is fixed on one person or assembly crew.
(3) Frequent changes in products or product design and sequence of operations are possible.
(4) The arrangement is adapted to variety of product and intermittent demand.
(5) It is more flexible in that it does not require highly organized or expensive layout engineering, production planning, or provisions against breaks in work continuity.

(2) Process Flow: Here all operations of the same process or type of process are grouped together. All welding is in one area, all drilling in another, all stitching in the stitching room, and all painting in a paint shop. This layout has these advantages:

(1) Better machine utilization allows lower machine investment.
(2) It is adapted to a variety of products and to frequent changes in sequence of operations.

---

1 Richard Muther, *Industrial Engineering Handbook,* 1st ed., H.B. Maynard, ed., (McGraw-Hill, New York, copyright © 1956). Section 7, Chapter 2, p. 7-26, line 8-19; p. 7-27, line 1-50; p. 7-28, line 18-32.

(3) It is adapted to intermittent demand (varying production schedules).
(4) The incentive for individual workers to raise the level of their performance is greater.
(5) It is easier to maintain continuity of production in event of:
    (a) A machine or equipment breakdown.
    (b) Shortage of material.
    (c) Absent workers.

(3) Product Flow: Here one product or one type of product is produced in one area. But unlike layout by fixed position, the material moves. This layout places one operation immediately adjacent to the next. It means that any equipment used to make the product, regardless of the process it performs, is arranged according to the sequence of operations. Advantages of this layout generally include:

(1) Reduced handling of material.
(2) Reduced amounts of material in process, allowing reduced production time (time in process) and lower investment in materials.
(3) More effective use of labor:
    (a) Through greater job specialization.
    (b) Through ease of training.
    (c) Through wider labor supply (semi- and unskilled.)
(4) Easier control:
    (a) Of production allows less paperwork.
    (b) Over workers and fewer interdepartmental problems; allows easier supervision.
(5) Reduced congestion and floor space otherwise allotted to aisles and storage.

FACTORS INFLUENCING LAYOUT

The factors influencing any layout break down into eight groups:

(1) The *material* factor—including design, variety, quantity, the necessary operations, and their sequence.
(2) The *machinery* factor—including the producing equipment and tools and their utilization.
(3) The *man* factor—including supervision and service help as well as direct workers.
(4) The *movement* factor—including inter- and intra-departmental transport and hand-handling at the various operations, storages, and inspections.
(5) The *waiting* factor—including permanent and temporary storage and delays.
(6) The *service* factor—including maintenance, inspection, waste, scheduling, and dispatching.
(7) The *building* factor—including outside and inside building features and utility distribution and equipment.
(8) The *change* factor—including versatility, and expansion.

GUIDING FUNDAMENTALS[2]

(1) *Plan the whole and then the details.*

Begin with the layout of the site or plant as a whole, and then work out the details. First determine the general requirements in relation to the volume of production anticipated. Establish the relationship of these areas to each other considering only the movement of material for a simple, basic pattern flow. From this, develop a *general overall layout.* Only after approval of the overall layout should you proceed with the detailed arrangement within each area. This is the actual positioning of the men, materials, machines, and supporting activities which becomes the *detailed layout plan.*

(2) *Plan the ideal and from it the practical.*

The initial concept of the layout should represent a theoretically ideal plan, without regard for existing conditions and irrespective of costs. Later, make adjustments to incorporate the practical limitations of buildings and other factors.

(3) *Follow the cycles of layout development, and make the phases overlap.*

The cycles of layout development follow a sequence of four phases:

(a) Determine where the layout shall be—where the facilities to be laid out are to be located.
(b) Plan an overall layout for the new production area.
(c) Make a detailed layout plan.
(d) Plan the installation.

(4) *Plan the process the machinery around the material requirements.*

The material factor is basic. The product design and manufacturing specifications largely determine what processes to use. You must also know the quantities, or rates of production.

(5) *Plan the layout around the process and machinery.*

After the proper production processes are selected, the layout planning begins. Consider the demands of the equipment itself—weight, size, shape, movement to and away, and the like. The space and location of the production processes or machinery (including tools and equipment) are the heart of the layout plan.

(6) *Plan the building around the layouts.*

Where machinery, service equipment, and layout are to be more permanent than the building, the building should be set around the most efficient layout.

(7) *Plan with the aid of clear visualization.*

The experienced layout specialist knows that aids to clear visualization are a key to his work. They help him gather his facts, and they help him analyze.

(8) *Plan with the help of others.*

Layout is a cooperative affair. The best layout will not be obtained unless the cooperation of all persons concerned is built into it. Their ideas must be solicited—they must be drawn into the project.

(9) *Check the layout.*

After one phase has been developed, secure approval before going too far in planning the next.

---

[2] Richard Muther, *Industrial Engineer Handbook,* 1st. ed, H.B. Maynard ed., (McGraw-Hill: New York, copyright © 1956). Section 7, Chapter 2, p. 7-34, line 39-54 partial; p. 7-35, line 1-58 partial.

(10) *Sell the layout plan.*

Often the hardest part of layout work is getting others to "buy" it. It must be remembered that the result is still compromise; it means changing people around; it will require an outlay of funds. Try to get everyone to participate; take time making ready to present the layout to the people who will be expected to put up money for it.

REVIEW THE FLOW PLANNING PRINCIPLES[3]

Even to experienced plant layout engineers, the following principles should be reviewed:

(1) Plan for movement of materials in as direct a path as possible through the plant.

(2) Minimize back-tracking.

(3) Use the line-production principle wherever feasible.

(4) Plan for incoming materials to be delivered directly to work areas when practicable.

(5) Use mechanical handling equipment to assure a constant rate of production.

(6) Combine operations whenever possible to eliminate handling between them.

(7) Combine processing with transportation whenever practicable.

(8) Plan for storage of a minimum of material in the work area.

(9) Minimize walking required of production workers.

(10) Use gravity to move materials.

(11) Place related activities near each other.

(12) Plan for process involving heavy materials to be located near the receiving area.

(13) Strive for ideal manufacturing conditions in which production activities are performed while material is moving.

(14) Move the greatest weight or bulk the shortest distance.

(15) Design the flow pattern to facilitate the manufacturing process.

(16) Allow for flexibility of process or activities.

(17) Consider the probability of future expansion or contraction of the activities.

(18) Keep all moves as short as practicable.

(19) Provide for mechanical handling to and from the work area.

(20) Deliver materials directly to the operator to reduce reaching or walking.

(21) Provide for removal of scrap.

(22) Make full use of the building cube.

(23) Consider material handling equipment requiring no fixed floor space.

(24) Provide alternate plans in case of a breakdown.

(25) Do not over-mechanize for the sake of mechanizing.

PRINCIPLES OF MATERIAL HANDLING[4]

Material handling includes activities associated with the following operations:

(a) Loading and unloading trucks, conveyors and containers.

---

[3] James M. Apple, *Plant Layout and Materials Handling,* 2nd ed., (The Ronald Press Company, New York, copyright © 1963); p. 79, line 17-32; p. 209-214 partial.

[4] Bruno A. Moski, *Production Specialists,* Alexander Hamilton Institute, Inc., New York, copyright © 1970. P. 81, line 1-28; p. 82, line 1-5 and line 17-28; p. 83, line 1-13.

(b) Lifting and lowering materials to and from work tables, containers and storage locations.

(c) Transporting materials to and from receiving, storage, work place and shipping locations.

(d) Storing materials at raw materials, work-in-process or finished goods locations.

In the mind of every production specialist there is a list of principles, guidelines or ground rules which he follows, consciously or unconsciously, as he performs his daily tasks. They help him analyze and solve the specific problems with which he is confronted.

The material handling engineer generally observes the following principles:

(a) Material handling does not increase the value of a product. Its cost constitutes an economic waste.

(b) The objective of material handling is the elimination of all handling.

(c) If material handling cannot be eliminated, it is necessary to minimize the frequency and distance of handling, as well as the use of manual effort.

(d) The cost of actual travel is generally small, in comparison with the cost of unloading, loading, lifting, lowering and storing materials.

(e) Maximum use should be made of gravity and power to replace manual effort, because of the resultant decreased costs.

(f) An uninterrupted flow of materials to production centers serves to increase production and minimize delays in manufacturing operations.

(g) Ideal manufacturing consists of each productive operation being performed while the material is progressing to the next operation.

The last principle of material handling stated: "Ideal manufacturing consists of each productive operation being performed while the material is progressing to the next operation." The closest approach to this objective may be found in some chemical process industries where the materials are fluid, and flow through piping and tanks by gravity, supplemented by pumping.

In the manufacture of mechanical and electrical products, the best examples of effective material handling are found in the automotive industry. Transfer fingers move the part from one operation to the next, while subsidiary conveyors feed component parts and minor assemblies into a main assembly conveyor and assembly operations are performed as the product passes along.

The material handling engineer is always searching to effect a continuous flow of materials through the proper selection of transfer fingers, overhead lifting equipment, and conveyors.

Where continuous flow requires an excessively high investment in equipment and intermittent handling is the economical solution, the material handling engineer considers equipment of the fork lift truck type which lifts, lowers, transports and stacks pallets containing 2,000 to 10,000 pounds of material.

HOW TO SELECT THE EQUIPMENT YOU NEED[5]

When the need for a piece of material handling equipment has been determined and the expenditure for its purchase justified the next step is to make the selection that will meet your particular specifications. Its cost must also fall within the limits called for in the justification proposal.

It is also important, when deciding upon your requirements, to consult with purchasing, production control, engineering, maintenance, production, shipping, receiving, safety director, warehousing, industrial engineer, and advanced planning supervision. The final specifications should be thoroughly examined and written up in outline form. It does no harm, either, to solicit constructive criticism from all production supervisors.

The following checklist should be used in your analysis for selecting lift trucks:

(1) *Electric, gasoline or LP gas driven?*

(2) *Standard or specially built?* Do the specifications fall within industry's standard equipment category? Remember, specially built equipment will cost more, repairs and maintenance will be greater due to higher prices for spare parts; spare parts will be in poorer supply; and it will have less flexibility than standard equipment.

(3) *Doorway height:* It is better to change the height of doorways than to order a special height of truck.

(4) *Accumulate all pertinent data:* This should cover floor strengths, ceiling heights, door dimensions, elevator capacities, nature of material to be transported, building obstructions, latest floor layout, production processes involved, number and type of machines to be serviced, space requirements including allowances for raw and in-process materials, work flow, aisles, and building columns locations.

(5) *Safety considerations:* Check for hazardous conditions that will exist because of lift truck operations.

(6) *Type of containers:* Will the new truck efficiently accommodate the various containers now in use? Will new types of containers be necessary?

(7) *Hand trucks:* Will new or additional hand trucks be necessary to complement the new lift truck?

(8) *Type of industry:* Is it heavy or light industry, food, chemicals, or paper? Are dampness, brine, acids, explosive atmosphere, shipping wheels and fragile items involved?

(9) *Racks:* Are storage racks now in use? If not, will they be required?

(10) *Material received from suppliers:* How are various materials received from suppliers? Are they crated, palletized, strapped, skidded, or loose?

(11) *Truck storage and servicing?* Where will the new truck be stored when idle? How and where will it be charged, if electric? Where and how will it be repaired, lubricated and maintained? If gasoline driven, where will fuel storage be located? If LP gas is used, where will the extra supply of fuel be kept?

5 Lewis R. Zeyher, *Production Manager's Desk Book* (Englewood Cliffs, N.J.: Prentice-Hall, Inc., 1969) p. 215, lines 2-42.

(12) *Ramps:* Will transporting of materials on ramps be necessary? Are the ramps, now in use, adequate for new truck operation?

(13) *Electrically operated doors:* Will the new truck require any electrically operated doors for efficient operation?

(14) *Training:* Will special training of truck operators and/or maintenance men be necessary?

(15) *New procedures:* Will new standard practice instructions be necessary covering operation and care of new truck?

SAFE PRACTICES[6]

(a) Lift Truck Operation

The following are suggested standard lift truck practices. It is most important that a similar list be developed and implemented for your particular type of plant and operation. The easy part is to formulate such a plan; the greatest difficulty lies in its enforcement.

(1) Lift-truck operators shall keep lift trucks clean.

(2) Only authorized persons shall drive or ride on lift trucks.

(3) Drivers shall operate at safe speeds and keep safe distances from other vehicles.

(4) Horseplay shall not be permitted.

(5) Loads shall be picked up and placed down squarely without quick or jerky starts and stops.

(6) At start of shift, drivers shall check horn, brakes, steering, and battery power or fuel and oil.

(7) Drivers shall slow down at cross aisles.

(8) Engines shall be turned off during refueling.

(9) Fuel and oil spillage shall be immediately washed away or absorbed by compounds approved for this purpose.

(10) No one shall walk under elevated loads.

(11) Rail tracks shall be crossed diagonally.

(12) Lift trucks shall be driven upgrade with load first, downgrade with load last.

(13) Drivers shall not put arms, legs, or head outside the perimeter of the lift truck while moving.

(14) Lift truck wheels shall be securely blocked when unit is left on an incline.

(15) Drivers shall carry load as low as possible, consistent with safe operations.

(16) Drivers shall move empty lift trucks with forks in lowered position.

(17) Forks shall be in lowered position when lift truck is parked.

(18) Only loads that are secure and within capacity of vehicle shall be moved.

(19) Drivers shall give right-of-way to pedestrians at all times.

(20) Drivers shall move over dock boards cautiously and only when boards are secure.

---

6 From *Modern Warehouse Management,* Creed H. Jenkins. Copyright © 1968 by McGraw-Hill, Inc. Used with permission of McGraw-Hill Book Company. P. 301, lines 22-42; p. 302, lines 1-38; p. 303, lines 28-42.

(21) Wheels of highway trucks or trailers shall be secured with proper chocking before lift truck enters.

(22) Forklift shall not be used as elevator for personnel except with an approved safe platform to protect raised person from falling.

(23) Forklifts shall be equipped with fire extinguishers and drivers shall be trained to use them.

(b) Hand Truck Operation

The following are suggested standard safe hand truck practices:

(1) Operators shall keep trucks clean, oiled, and in safe operating condition, reporting any malfunction to their supervisor for corrective action.

(2) Operators shall load heaviest objects at the bottom to keep center of gravity as low as possible.

(3) Loads shall be securely stacked to prevent objects from slipping or falling off.

(4) Trucks shall bear loads with operators providing power and guidance.

(5) If load is such that it obstructs operator's vision, a second man shall guide the other end of the load.

(6) Operators shall maintain clear vision in direction of travel.

(7) With two-wheel trucks, operators shall keep truck *ahead* when moving down an incline, *behind* when moving up an incline, and shall not walk backwards.

(8) With four-wheel trucks, operators shall push load. If trucks are equipped with handle and fifth wheel, they should be pulled for most effective steering.

(9) Operators shall move trucks at cautious and safe speeds, never running.

(10) Operators shall avoid loads and situations that cause excessive strain in moving trucks.

(11) Trucks shall be stored in designated area. Two-wheel trucks shall be stored on the chisel.

(c) Carrier Loading and Unloading

The following are suggested standard safe practices for loading and unloading of rail and trucks.

(1) Loading docks, inside of car or truck, and adjacent working areas shall be well lighted.

(2) Truck wheels shall be securely chocked before loading or unloading operations begin.

(3) Rail-car doors shall be *pushed* open, using sturdy pry bar when necessary.

(4) Carrier doors shall first be opened only slightly to inspect for objects that may fall out.

(5) Contents of carrier shall be checked for insecure load conditions before starting unloading operations.

(6) Shoring and bracing shall be removed, and floors and sides cleared of nails and other protruding objects.

(7) Lumber and other debris removed from carrier shall be immediately put in designated containers.

CHECKLIST FOR IMPROVED MATERIAL HANDLING[7]

What are some of the operations to examine where improvement and potential savings in operations costs exist? A few examples follow:

(1) Do you use palletizing in your handling operations?
(2) Can pallet loaders be used advantageously?
(3) Can you make use of automatic lifts?
(4) Can you use paper pallets or non-returnable pallets?
(5) Is available space properly utilized?
(6) Is travel distance minimized?
(7) Can use be made of hydraulic lifts?
(8) Do you receive and ship in unit loads wherever possible?
(9) Do you have materials delivered by your suppliers in such quantity and type container that they can be handled with a minimum of rehandling or "breaking down" of units?
(10) Do you assure yourself that materials are adequately protected from corrosion, loss due to pilferage, or breakage?
(11) Are all materials placed in an accessible location for using mechanized equipment?
(12) Do you make use of hydraulic ramps for shipping and receiving docks?
(13) Do you use screw, motorized, or special purpose conveyors?
(14) Can cranes, elevators, or hoists be used advantageously?
(15) Can you use upenders and dumpers?
(16) Is there a need for turntables, often employed with conveyors?
(17) Do you make the proper use of hand trucks, lift trucks, and dollies?
(18) Do you use gravity, roller systems extending to truck, coupled with roller conveyors placed inside trucks?
(19) Is it possible to make use of platform conveyors or rails to carry a whole truckload of material into a warehouse?
(20) Do you use telescopic belt conveyors to transport material inside of truck from dock or to remove the material from truck to loading dock?
(21) Are gravity drops and chutes used when practicable?
(22) Can the number of unit loads be reduced by using larger quantities in loads and by using larger equipment?
(23) Do you make a maximum use of air space for storage?
(24) Is the best use being made of high cost, prime space?
(25) Are your marshalling areas adequate?
(26) Is the equipment in use performing the functions for which it was originally intended?
(27) Can time be reduced?
    (a) By decreasing the ratio of idle time to operating time for material handlers and for expensive equipment such as highway trucks, elevators, warehouse trucks and related equipment?

---

[7] Reprinted by permission of the publisher from Special Report No. 4, *Materials Handling: Tested Approaches to Cutting Production Costs,* © 1955 by the American Management Association, Inc.

(b) By increasing the speed of handling:
(1) Through better scheduling?
(2) Through improved communications?

(28) Is there too much waiting time by workers at freight elevators?

(29) Do you use the proper storage facilities, such as bulk bins, silos, hoppers, open bins, nested bins, shelves, drawers, pans, trays, boxes, rotary bins, racks, drums, counters, portable racks, and related facilities?

(30) When receiving material at receiving department, is all material placed on nearby pallet, hand truck, or similar device, and *not* on bare floor?

4

Methods Engineering and the Principles of Work Simplification

[1] The ideal methods improvement is the one which provides a means of determining the best way to do a task before the task ever begins. This is an ideal, however, which cannot usually be attained for several reasons. For one thing, as industrial technology changes, newer materials become available, and more adequate tools are invented, so that it is always possible to improve a method in some degree provided enough time and money are devoted to this aim. Also, there are practical limits to the ingenuity of industrial engineers as of a given moment which forces a modification of their concept of the ideal to include the effect of time. Put in the form of a statement, *as of a given moment, it is impossible to design the best method under prevailing conditions: the ultimate method is never found.*

Methods improvement and work measurement are inseparable. Before a labor standard is established through *any* work measurement technique or procedure, the method to be used should practically always be analyzed for possible improvement. The degree of such analysis and subsequent improvement should, of course, be tempered by the quantity of items to be produced, their economic value and related considerations. The greater the quantity, the more methods analysis and improvement can be justified. Justification is largely a question of economics—will cost of analysis, the applicable tool and equipment cost, etc., be paid for by reduced labor, less material waste, better quality and a reduction in accidents?

In the development of methods improvements it logically follows that the principles of Work Simplification should be considered. This technique provides an excellent opportunity to involve production employees in cost reduction programs and/or employee suggestion systems.

---

[1] Delmar W. Karger and Franklin H. Bayha, *Engineered Work Measurement,* Second Edition, copyright © 1966, The Industrial Press, New York, N.Y., p. 659, lines 9-21 and 28-37.

PRINCIPLES OF MOTION ECONOMY

Motion Economy: Refers to movements or motions that are made with a minimum of physical effort, time and fatigue.

Waste Motion: Unnecessary and poorly executed movements which require more than the normal time to complete.

Motion Analysis: A study of the motions used in the performance of an operation for the purpose of eliminating all unnecessary motions and building up a sequence of the most useful motions in order to achieve maximum performance.

Classes of Hand Motions: There are five general classes of hand motions; the lower classifications usually require the lesser amounts of time and effort and consequently produce the least fatigue.

(1) Finger motions.
(2) Motions involving fingers and wrist.
(3) Motions involving fingers, wrist and forearm.
(4) Motions involving fingers, wrist, forearm and upper arm.
(5) Motions involving fingers, wrist, forearm, upper arm, and shoulder. This class necessitates disturbance of the posture.

Effective Effort: A proper set of motions well motivated and conscientiously directed toward the satisfactory completion of the task with the least amount of fatigue and exertion.

Operation Analysis: A type of analysis which centers around the method of doing the work, involving a careful consideration of materials, tools, jigs, fixtures, handling equipment, working conditions, and other factors affecting the operation.

These principles are utilized by practioners of the work simplification method. Once the analyst has a sound understanding of them he will become a competent judge of what usually constitutes a good or bad operating practice. Having discovered an operation where waste effort occurs, the analyst can then proceed to eliminate it. Material savings can also result from the effective employment of these measures.

METHODS IMPROVEMENT

Before discussing methods engineering, I would like to offer H.B. Maynard's and G.J. Stegemerten's definition of this technique:

> [2]Methods engineering is the technique that subjects each operation for a given piece of work to close analysis in order to eliminate every unnecessary operation and in order to approach the quickest and best method of performing each necessary operation; it includes the standardization of equipment, methods, and working conditions; it trains the operator to follow the standard method; when all this has been done, and not before, it determines by accurate measurement of standard hours in which an operator working with standard performance can do the job; finally, it usually, although not necessarily, devises a plan for compensating labor that encourages the operator to attain or to surpass standard performance.

---

2 Maynard and Stegemerten, *Operation Analysis,* (New York: McGraw-Hill Co., copyright © 1961) pp. 1-2.

Some tools of methods engineering include operation analysis studies, flow process charts, operation process sheets, machine-load charts, cutting speeds and feed charts, job instruction sheets, value analysis, materials standardization, MTM studies, workplace layout, motion picture analysis, working conditions, plant layout, equipment and tool analysis, work sampling, standard data charts, material handling, inspection standards, material specifications, tool design, man-machine charts, established shop burdens and overheads, machining practices and charts, finishes, auxiliary equipment, inspection gages and fixtures and testing instruments.

Some actual examples of savings resulting from methods improvements follow:

Work Simplification: Through the use of a man-process chart two operators (material handlers) were eliminated from a crew of five. This was accomplished by the rearrangement of the sequence of operations, installation of some inexpensive equipment, and minimizing the waiting time. A yearly savings of $15,000 was effected.[3]

Crew Determinations: Through time-study observations of the 150 production employees working on an overhead conveyor system a 10% reduction was made in required workers. This was accomplished by using the line-standard development formula and accurately determining crew complements for each separate operation. An annual savings of $100,000 was realized. This was accomplished without a change in conveyor speed.[4]

Conveyor Crew Assignments and Most Economical Line-Speed Chart: Through the development of the subject chart that was subsequently used by the foreman of a department of 60 employees, who manned four individual overhead conveyor systems with crews of 15 each, a 20% reduction in direct-labor cost was achieved. This department was used by other departments for replacement of absentees; therefore it was necessary to reduce conveyor speeds on each line affected to compensate for this condition. Formerly, the foreman had *arbitrarily* made these crew assignments and changes in conveyor speeds—now it was done on a more scientific basis. An annual savings was estimated to be $60,000.[5]

Material Handling: A 40% reduction in direct labor was accomplished through observation and the use of Work Simplification principles in the unloading of trailers of 55 gal. filled drums in a chemical company warehouse. This was done by replacing a single drum clamp device with twin clamps and then having the originating warehouse place the drums in the trailer in a specific pattern so that the two approaches the lift-truck made to grasp the drums were cut to one.

Other Areas: There are many other areas to investigate that should reveal cost savings possibilities, such as in heat treating processes, coolants, tool sharpening, better and faster methods of chucking, pattern design and making as well as repairing, product ejecting from machines, better ways of gripping, deburring, grinding, tumbling, sand blasting, plating and anodizing. Toolroom methods and practices are usually fertile fields for savings, estimating, use of work standards, material and perishable tool control, prototype development, debugging new machinery, installation methods, tool crib handling and stocking, purchasing of materials and supplies covering method,

---

[3] See Chapter 4, *Production Manager's Handbook of Formulas and Tables,* L.R. Zeyher, Englewood Cliffs, N.J.: Prentice-Hall, Inc., 1972.

[4] Ibid., Chapter 4.

[5] Ibid., Chapter 5.

paperwork, inventory control and investigating possibilities of better materials with necessary characteristics, but less expensive, and many other related items.

MTM ANALYSIS FOR METHODS IMPROVEMENT[6]

MTM Analysis will not improve the job but it will help point out to you where methods improvements can be made. Here are some possibilities which may lead to better methods:

- Reduce long reaches and moves.
- Eliminate body motions.
- Have both hands working simultaneously.
- Place as much work as possible within machine cycle.
- Place material so that it can be picked up with simple grasps.
- Eliminate positions or reduce class of fit.
- Eliminate unnecessary inspections.
- Improve design of part to make operation easier to perform.
- Have automatic delivery and/or asiding of parts to eliminate manual motions.

Examples of these possibilities follow (see Exhibits 4-1, 4-2).

THE QUESTIONING ATTITUDE[7]

Every supervisor should have a continuing, hard-headed, insatiable, questioning attitude, which takes nothing for granted, approaching the improvement problem without preconceived ideas. To be effective, however, the questions cannot be haphazard. They must be channeled toward four possible results, as follows:

(1) *What can we eliminate?* This could be a process, a value-adding or non-value adding operation, a delay or storage, or idle or inspection. To eliminate is to improve!

(2) *What can we combine?* The use of known faster devices may be the answer. (Here the supervisor may draw upon experiences in entirely different operations: slide bins, gravity chutes, an automatic tool, etc.) If two operations can't be combined, it may be possible to combine a transportation with an operation.

(3) *Should the sequence be changed?* Changes in sequence may eliminate or reduce non-value-adding operations, transportations, delays, storages, and inspections. Again, the use of known faster devices will often make this possible.

(4) *What can we simplify?* The time to start to think about ways to simplify is when the processes and operations have been reduced as much as possible through the elimination, combination, and/or change of sequences. In this purposeful channeling, the six basic questions of Work Simplification are used over and over again: What? Why? Where? When? Who? How? The way in which these can be pinpointed to locate improvement possibilities is shown in Exhibit 4-3.

---

6 Used with permission of the Maytag Company, Newton, Iowa 50208.

7 From *Encyclopedia of Management*, 2nd ed., edited by Carl Heyel, © 1973 by Litton Educational Publishing, Inc. Reprinted by permission of Van Nostrand Reinhold Company.

work place layout change
27% improvement

EXAMPLE OF POSSIBILITY NO. 1.

Minor changes in layout can reduce excessive distances of reaches and moves.

OLD METHOD

1. Aside part and obtain next

MOVE part to aside chute	M8B	10.6
RELEASE part	RL1	2.0
REACH to part	R12C	14.2
GRASP part	G4B	9.1
MOVE part to fixture.	M10C	13.5
		49.4

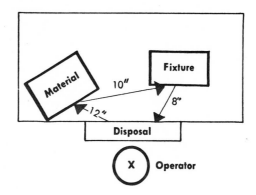

By changing the layout of the work place to have the asiding done while reaching to the next part, reach and move distances can be reduced:

THE IMPROVED METHOD
LOOKS LIKE THIS

1. Aside part and obtain next

MOVE part to aside chute	M3Bm	3.6
RELEASE part	RL1	2.0
REACH to part	mR7C	8.0
GRASP part	G4B	9.1
MOVE part to fixture	M10C	13.5
		36.2

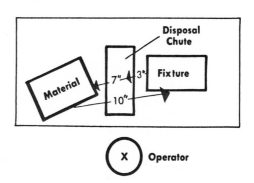

$$\begin{array}{ll} 49.4 & \text{(OLD)} \\ -\ 36.2 & \text{(NEW)} \\ \hline 13.2 & \text{TMU'S Saved or Improved 27\%} \end{array}$$

EXHIBIT 4-1

"aside part" eliminated
100% improvement

EXAMPLE OF POSSIBILITY NO. 9.

Have automatic delivery and/or asiding of parts—
eliminate manual motion.

OLD METHOD

Aside Part.

TURN BODY to left.	TBC1	18.6
Toss part to container.	mM8B	7.2
Release part.	RL1	
		25.8

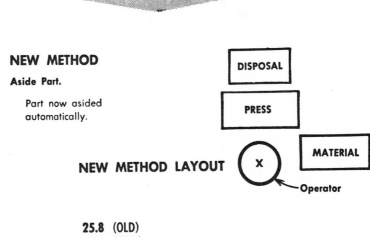

OLD METHOD LAYOUT

**By using automatic air jet to blow
part out of die,
ASIDE Eliminated.**

NEW METHOD

Aside Part.

Part now asided
automatically.

NEW METHOD LAYOUT

    25.8 (OLD)
—   0.0 (NEW)
    25.8 TMU'S Saved or Improved 100%

EXHIBIT 4-2

Six Basic Improvement Questions

Key question	Idea kickers	Improvement possibilities
WHAT is done?	What is its purpose? Does it do what it is supposed to do?	Eliminate
WHY is it done?	Should it be done at all? Can as good a result be obtained without it? Is it an absolute must?	Eliminate
WHERE is it done?	Why is it done there? Why should it be done there? Where should it be done? Can it be done easier by changing the location of person or equipment?	Combine and/or change sequence
WHEN is it done?	Why is it done then? Is it done in right sequence? Can all or part of it be done at some other time?	Combine and/or change sequence
WHO does it?	Why does this person do it? Is the right person doing it? Is it logical to give it to someone else?	Combine and/or change sequence
HOW is it done?	Why should it be done this way? Can it be done better with different equipment or different layout? Is there any other way to do it?	Simplify

EXHIBIT 4-3

INVOLVING EMPLOYEES IN COST REDUCTION THROUGH WORK SIMPLIFICATION

How Do You Do It?

Before you attempt this involvement it would be well first to create the proper employee mental condition and/or morale—a desire among them to do their best in the attainment of your objectives. Let us take the positive approach and assume your employees possess it to a satisfactory degree. Then the next step necessary is to formulate a plan of action. The full support of top management as well as their continued *active* interest are, of course, essential for success. Also, of great importance is to select an effective, courageous and aggressive leader who will be in complete charge of the programs implementation and for the final results. A step-by-step approach follows:

(a) Obtain budget approval.

(b) Train executives and supervisors in Work Simplification principles.

(c) From item (b) select the best instructors to conduct similar training courses for production employees. (These courses should consist of no fewer than 15 two-hour sessions or 4 all-day sessions.)

The basis of these courses is the theory that we *learn best by doing.* Special projects are assigned from within the supervisor's own department. Possible solutions are then analyzed and discussed in the scheduled training sessions. Various industrial engineering techniques for use in this work are explained. Some companies insist that all executives, from the president on down through the echelon of management, take the course, as well as all other employees.

Work Simplification applications are possible in all kinds of departments—office, sales, technical, production, administrative, staff, and related departments. The more heads of all departments know about this subject, the more marked will be their interest, cooperation, and understanding for cost reduction in the area of their responsibility.

An incident comes to mind in my own plant management experience where the president of the company, who had taken the course and whose expertise lay in marketing, brought to my attention on several occasions very poor assembly methods on a conveyor line. These were identified while walking past the offending work stations on his way from the company parking lot through the assembly department to his office. A methods engineer was assigned the task of examining the existing operations and subsequently developed much superior and less expensive methods. These situations became known throughout the plant and had a stimulating effect on the plant cost reduction program.

The Work Simplification Doctrine affords the following advantages:

(a) Includes full employee participation.

(b) Provides for consultive management.

(c) Stimulates human interest and enthusiasm.

(d) "Gets everyone in the act."

(e) Provides for individual creativity.

(f) Opens the door for personal recognition of accomplishment.

(g) Reduces the resistance to change.

(h) Promotes the questioning attitude.

(i) Reveals subjects for group brainstorming.

(j) Makes everyone an expert.

(k) Persuades each employee to become a member of the management team.

INTRODUCING A SUCCESSFUL EMPLOYEE SUGGESTION PLAN[8]

Outline of Plan

The following steps are recommended:

(1) Educate, instruct, stimulate, and involve all employees in the program.

---

[8] Lewis R. Zeyher, *Cost Reduction in the Plant,* (Englewood Cliffs, N.J.: Prentice-Hall, Inc., Copyright © 1965, p. 103, lines 1-15, and p. 104, lines 1-11.

(2) Use the Madison Avenue approach—advertise and publicize.

(3) Determine amount of awards—make them liberal.

(4) Establish method for submission of employee suggestions.

(5) Design and print suggestion forms and a cost analysis sheet.

(6) Provide suggestion boxes strategically located throughout the plant.

(7) Appoint a qualified "Awards Committee"—preferably three supervisors, no more than five.

(8) Establish and publicize ground rules for suggestion plan.

(9) Post specific and general plant problems that need solution.

(10) Encourage the use of plant staff technical assistance.

(11) Publicize all award winners, both in the plant and in the community press.

(12) Keep cumulative records of savings and post on plant bulletin boards. *Keep notices up to date.*

(13) Make awards for accident prevention suggestions that are adopted.

(14) Make it a practice to inform unsuccessful contributors as well as award winners. Express appreciation for their efforts and briefly explain why their suggestions were rejected; encourage them to submit others.

(15) Follow up on the installation of accepted suggestions. Exercise some surveillance over all methods changes to insure their survival. Do not permit them to be abandoned without a reasonable explanation.

(16) Investigate all valid suggestions promptly and advise contributors of committee's decisions as soon as is practicable.

*** See below.

TRUE OR FALSE QUESTIONNAIRE

As a matter of self-interest it is suggested that you take the following exercise in order to satisfy yourself that you now are familiar with the basic principles of Work Simplification. (Answers follow the questionnaire.)

*** Individuals and companies interested in learning more about employee suggestion systems should consider joining the *National Association of Suggestion Systems,* located at 435 North Michigan Avenue, Chicago,

True	False

Questionnaire

1. The principles of time and motion study are: motion economy, waste motion, motion analysis, and classes of hand motions.

2. Check the one item below that best defines *Work Simplification.*

   a. Speeding up of work.
   b. A system to make work easier.
   c. A program to methodize work.
   d. The act of making work simple.
   e. A system to make work more exciting.
   f. The organized application of common sense to find simpler and better ways of doing work.
   g. A system to eliminate work.
   h. A plan to make certain the right method is used.
   i. A system to make accounting functions simpler.

3. The following includes the five (5) classes of hand motions: (Cross out those which do not apply.)

   a. Finger motions.
   b. Head motions.
   c. Motions involving fingers and wrist.
   d. Motions involving eyes.
   e. Gripping with hand.
   f. Motions involving fingers, wrist and forearm.
   g. Motions involving fingers, wrist, forearm and upper arm.
   h. Motions involving torso and hips.
   i. Motions that include bending and twisting.
   j. Motions involving fingers, wrist, upper arm, and shoulder. This class necessitates disturbance of the posture.

4. Which one of these items correctly defines *Effective Effort:*

   a. . . . is a set of motions that results in greater production.
   b. . . . is effort requiring more physical strength.
   c. . . . is a proper set of motions well motivated and conscientiously directed toward the satisfactory completion of the task with the least amount of fatigue and exertion.

True	False

d. ... is a proper set of motions in which the best results in quality performance can be obtained.

5. Fill in the missing words:

   Operation Analysis: is a type of analysis which centers around the method of doing _____, involving a careful consideration of _____, tools, jigs, _____, handling equipment, working _____, and other factors affecting the operation.

6. Supply missing words:
   Most jobs include "_____", "_____", "_____", and "put away."

7. A rough sketch of the workplace is not neccessary.

8. Elements should be well described on paper—four or five sentences are usually necessary.

9. Every element of an operation should be questioned, including:
   (Fill in missing questions)
   a. Can it be eliminated?
   b. _____?
   c. Why was it done?
   d. Can the entire operation be discarded?
   e. Can it be simplified?
   f. _____?
   g. Will a rearrangement of the operational sequence yield a better result?

10. Decisions regarding changes in the operation being studied should be made only after consultation with those who know the operation intimately.

Answers: 1—true; 2—check item f; 3—cross out b, d, e, h, i; 4—check c; 5—the missing words in this order: work, materials, fixtures, and conditions; 6—the missing words are "make ready," and "do"; 7—false; 8—false; 9—(b) can it be combined with another? and (f) can the time be reduced?; 10—true.

5

Controlling Production with Engineered Work Standards

Few companies can exist today without satisfactory employee productivity. Low employee production performance breeds a high-cost plant operation. Too high production costs eventually result in the demise of the company. While this thought is often refuted, it is a truism that the work force has been a major beneficiary of the improvement in productivity. A concern for high productivity is not only necessary for production workers but for executives, staff, and office personnel, as well.

Productivity must become of greater and ever greater interest to employees, managers, government and company stockholders, as its effect on all our lives is enormous, but not yet fully appreciated. Some important factors in industry economically affected by employee performance include:

(1) Increased cost of capital equipment which dictates need for its most effective utilization.

(2) Rate of equipment obsolescence has increased substantially. A few years ago standard machine tools could be expected to have a useful life of 10 to 15 years. Now life expectancy of half as much can hardly be expected.

(3) Much greater sophistication of the average consumer who demands higher quality coupled with greater reliability on product performance. This may negatively influence use of some high speed equipment.

(4) Emphasis on ecology factors has required many companies to install additional expensive equipment to satisfy new government regulations. This correspondingly increases need for higher prices of their respective products.

(5) Stronger government regulations and inspection practices covering safety and health of employees. While being praiseworthy and necessary, it is still another factor increasing the cost of manufacture.

(6) More employee pension plans to which companies contribute large sums as well as more expensive coverage of those plans already in existence.

(7) Rising employee social security contributions by all companies.

(8) Continuing high cost of local, state and federal taxes.

(9) Foreign competition—our annual productivity gains in manufacturing have been below those of the other industrial nations of the world, resulting in loss of jobs in this country.

(10) It is a well known fact that the average hourly wage in this country has grown substantially more than output per man hour.

(11) In recent times more company involvement is expected by businesses in the humanitarian and social areas.

(12) Greater employee productivity improves the profit picture—profits are needed for product research, and for the purchase of more modern machinery and equipment.

To attain high employee productivity levels some form of measured work is required. Effective management control is synonymous with measurement. The use of engineered work standards supplies this need. Besides fulfilling this requirement it provides goals for both management and labor. There is an anology here between the worker and both the bowler and the golfer. They need to know the rules of these games and results are known by their individual scores. Desired performances (or scores, if you will) are indicated by management and employees should be made to realize that they will be held strictly accountable for the achievement of these desired results.

WHAT IS AN ENGINEERED WORK STANDARD?

Before a task can be measured, either by time study, methods-time-measurement, work factor or related techniques, first the method must be analyzed for possible improvement (see Chapter 4). After the best method is determined and implemented, then the task is subjected to observation by one of the above techniques.

A production standard (or engineered work standard) is a unit of measurement indicating the time necessary for an operation to be performed by an experienced operator, working effectively at a normal pace in a predetermined manner and taking the adequate allowed time for fatigue and personal needs. This is generally expressed in hours or decimal hours per unit. The standard hour, consisting of sixty standard minutes, is determined by time studies. The "normal pace" referred to is that pace accepted throughout industry as being fair and reasonable. A much less complex definition of a production standard, stripped of all the frosting, is "the normal time required by an operator to perform a given task in a predetermined manner, expressed in decimal hours per unit."

[1]Any type of manufacturing involves a conversion process. Raw materials, parts, components, and sub-assemblies are converted into finished products. These operations consume time. By use of correctly time-studied standards, the effort expended to complete this conversion process is measured. The important advantage of such standards is that all the elements in the conversion process can be measured in the same terms. You cannot compare unlike productions unless some form of a common denominator is used. It would be unfair to expect a worker to load manually two similar trucks with the same number of cartons, in the same time, when one load consists of

---

1 Lewis R. Zeyher, *Cost Reduction in the Plant,* (Englewood Cliffs, N.J.: Prentice-Hall, Inc., copyright © 1965), p. 164, lines 32-40; p. 165, lines 1-42; p. 166, lines 1-44; and p. 167, lines 1-8.

paper napkins and the other containers of metal door stops. Obviously the physical effort and handling problems are greater with metal door stops loading. A time-studied standard measures this factor and converts the effort expended and the handling difficulty into common, equivalent terms. After the proper time studies have been taken of the two dissimilar operations, production standards are developed. Each production is then expressed in standard hours per hundred pounds loaded. We now have comparable terms. They can be added, subtracted, matched and checked, one against another. Controls cannot be built upon a mixture of "apples and watermelons." To compile the total output of a plant, it must be possible to add the equivalents of many varied types of production.

WORKS STANDARDS USED AS A MANAGEMENT CONTROL

It is now generally accepted throughout industry that the average productivity of a worker not covered by some form of measured work is from forty to sixty per cent of standard. How can a foreman know how well or how poorly his department is performing unless he can compare his results against a predetermined goal? Is it possible for him to plan his work properly when he must guess the time it will take to perform a given task? If a new operating method has been developed and installed which is expected to reduce the labor required to do the job, how does he know where to "peg" this new production quota? It is generally at the foreman's level that the initial action to correct an operating problem is taken. These supervisors are also responsible for the control of their departments' costs in which employee productivity plays such an important part. Do they know the employees who are producing at a satisfactory rate and those whose rates are considerably below standard? Without the proper management control tools they can only resort to guessing, certainly not a very accurate technique. There is too much at stake in a business enterprise, and competition is too keen, to make guesses and then proceed to gamble about such important operating information. The universally accepted control technique that can be satisfactorily employed for this purpose is the production standard (work standard).

(a) List of Advantages

(1) Provides a common denominator in standard time. An operator's performance index can easily be compared with a previous week's performance or with a past month's. This can be done equitably even though he worked on different operations and was employed in other departments during this period.
(2) Provides a method of measurement and reporting the entire plant's production performance in percentage terms.
(3) Provides a means of measuring each supervisor's effectiveness in terms of his department's production performance by days, weeks, or any selected period.
(4) Provides a means of measuring each production employee's effectiveness.
(5) Provides the correct basis for overhead calculations; it is not affected by wage rates and is not affected by performance efficiencies.
(6) Can be used for the operation of budgets.
(7) Provides more accurate facts for top management planning and control.
(8) Can be used for calculating manufacturing costs.

(9) Can be used for methods improvement justifications and cost savings.

(10) Can be used for justifying the purchase of new equipment.

(11) Can be used for pricing direct labor of in-process and finished goods inventories.

(12) Can be used for pricing cost of rejects, rework, seconds, scrap, and related items.

(13) Can be used for evaluating the cost of delays and machine downtime.

(14) Can be used for determining crew size and for balancing work loads.

(15) Can be used for scheduling men and machines.

(16) Can be used for determining manpower requirements for a known volume of work.

(17) Can be used for determining overhead distribution.

(18) Can be used for estimating costs, particularly for new business.

(19) Can be used for providing information for personnel department records; can be used as an aid in appraising employee's worth and as a guide in making promotions, for highlighting those production employees who need further training and for use in meting out disciplinary actions.

(20) Can be used for installing incentive plans if a need develops. Time-studied incentives standards are the best available combination we now have both to measure capability and also to reward performance.

(21) Can be used for improving employee relations through the use of a system that provides an equitable and easily understood arrangement for establishing production quotas.

(22) Can be used for providing standard data for the establishment of synthetic standards for a new or revised operating method without the necessity for conducting additional time study analysis.

(23) Can be used for planning a reduction in manufacturing costs:

(a) For increasing production employee effectiveness by increasing productivity and thereby reducing burden expense.

(b) For increasing indirect labor and service department employees' effectiveness and reducing costs.

(c) For aiding in the elimination of operator and management delays and interruptions.

(d) For improving the utilization of equipment since irregularities that interfere with production are reduced, resulting in the enlargement of the real machine capacity. This might eliminate or postpone the purchase of additional equipment.

(e) For improving inventory turnover rates, since capital invested in inventory will be turned over more times per year.

(f) For developing more effective supervision when it is possible to manage by the use of the "exception principle." Actual production costs can be compared against standards previously established. Those in line need no immediate attention, but the costs under standard should be investigated.

(24) Can be used for measuring and controlling labor:

(a) Can establish indirect labor standards for predetermined number of direct hours by department.

(b) Excess hours over standard will be brought to the attention of supervisors for correction and follow-up.

(b) Examples of Use of Work Standards

In conveyor line operations where different tasks are performed by various groups of production employees and paced by specified conveyor speeds, crew complements are determined by analysis of their related production standards. The sum of these required man-hours is then employed to calculate the line standard.

It is after the crew assignments have been made (this can be progressive processing involving continuous line operation or a motorized conveyor system), the total standard hours for all the crews involved is then divided by the total number of pieces expected to be produced in a given period, resulting in the line standard. The development follows:

Formula[2]

$$L = \frac{T}{S \times H} \times 1,000$$

Where:

L = Line standard expressed in standard hours per 1,000 units
T = Crews' total standard hours per shift
S = Conveyor speed in units per hour
H = Scheduled hours.

Example

A conveyor line consists of eight different operations involving eight predetermined crew sizes. The conveyor speed is set at 106 units per minute and is scheduled to run 7.67 hours (allowing for two rest breaks), the production standards for each operation having previously been developed. Determine the line standard per 1,000 units.

Solution

Item	Operation	St'd Hrs. per 100 units	No. in Crew	Total St'd Hrs. Per 8 Hr. Day
1	A	0.0512	3.0	24.0
2	B	0.0637	4.0	32.0
3	C	0.0332	2.0	16.0
4	D	0.0352	2.0	16.0
5	E	0.0983	6.0	48.0
6	F	0.1002	6.0	48.0
7	G	0.0984	6.0	48.0
8	H	0.0164	1.0	8.0
		Totals	30.0	240.0

$$L = \frac{T}{S \times H} \times 1,000$$

$$L = \frac{240 \text{ Hrs.}}{(106 \times 60) \times 7.67} \times 1,000$$

$$L = \frac{240 \text{ Hrs.}}{48,800} \times 1,000$$

$$L = 4.92 \text{ St'd Hrs.}$$

---

[2] Lewis R. Zeyher, *Production Manager's Handbook of Formulas and Tables;* (Englewood Cliffs, N.J. Prentice-Hall, Inc., copyright © 1972), p. 82, lines 1-39; p. 83, lines 1-39; and p. 84, lines 1-17.

Line Standard is 4.92 Standard Hours/1,000 units produced.

Problem

Determine the production performance per cent of this department if they produced 50,000 units in an 8-hour shift while consuming 240 actual paid hours.

Formula

$$P = \frac{\frac{50,000}{4.92 \times 1,000}}{240 \text{ hours}}$$

$$P = 1.02.5\%$$

Production performance for the department = 102.5 % efficient
(100 % required)

Example

An operation in the receiving department of a factory involves unloading full cartons from trailers to the dock, opening cartons and hanging units on a moving conveyor entering plant. The empty cartons are piled nearby on pallets while a preparatory operation is performed on the recently hung units as they begin to flow through the production cycle. The conveyor line is traveling at a speed of 42 units per minute for a total of 7.67 hours per shift. A crew of four men are employed. Determine the line standard for the crew.

Operation	St'd Hrs. Per 100 Units	No. in Crew	St'd Hrs. Per 8 Hrs.
(1) Unload trailer, stack empties.	0.0419	1.0	8.0
(2) Unpack cartons, hang units on conveyor line.	0.0871	2.0	16.0
(3) Inspect, adjust and prepare units to enter production process.	0.0450	1.0	8.0
Totals		4.0	32.0

Formula:

$$L = \frac{T}{S \times H} \times 1,000$$

Solution:

$$L = \frac{32.0}{(42.0 \times 60) \times 7.67} \times 1,000$$

$$L = \frac{32.0}{19,000} \times 1,000$$

$$L = 1.68 \text{ Standard Hours/1,000 units}$$

The line standard is 1.68 Standard Hours/1,000 units.

How to Calculate Crew Determinations

Example

Formula

$$N = P \times S$$

Where

N = Number of crew required
P = Required production by crew per hour
S = Production standards in hours per 100 units.

Problem: Determine the crew required for an operation performed on a conveyor running at a speed of 40 units per minute, where the production standard is 0.0852 Standard Hours per 100 units produced.
Solution:

N = (40 x 60) x 0.0852 St'd Hrs/100 units
N = 2,400 x 0.0852
N = 24 x 0.0852
N = 2.04 operators

Crew required is two (2) operators.

KEEPING WORK STANDARDS UP TO DATE[3]

Auditing Your System

The best approach to apply here is to periodically conduct an *auditing* program which would consist of the following major steps:

(1) Review of production performance records, to determine weaknesses and to establish priorities.
(2) Time study review of selected jobs, to determine validity of standard time data values, application of standard time data and control of operating methods.
(3) Review of production reporting methods.
(4) Review of timekeeping methods.

Each of these major steps will be expanded upon, in turn.

(a) Review of Production Performance Records

These records may be classified into the following groups:

(1) Daily production reports which evaluate the performance of individual employees in terms of actual time worked on a work standard and/or incentive basis; standard hours produced during that time, and production efficiency percentages are the most desirable type of production performance records.
(2) In the absence of daily production reports, employee earnings on a daily or weekly basis must be reviewed, with the individual labor tickets scrutinized to determine specific jobs where excessive earnings have occurred.
(3) Supplementing daily production reports and employee earnings records, verbal information may be obtained from manufacturing department supervision or industrial engineering personnel, to determine specific jobs where excessive earnings have occurred.

After reviewing the above sources of information, the industrial engineering auditors are in a position to list apparent weak spots, and to establish relative priorities to correct the weaknesses, in the order of their importance.

---

[3] Bruno A. Moski, Bruno A. Moski Associates, 835 Worrell Road, Rydal, Penna. 19046.

(b) Time Study Review

Once the weak spots have been determined, and relative priorities have been established, actual time study reviews of specific jobs are necessary to determine the validity of standard time data values, application of standard time data, and control of operating methods.

It is at this point that critical damage may be done to labor relations, if the time study reviews are not handled carefully.

Even when the Labor Contract does not restrict the industrial engineering organization from taking time studies at any time, it may be very irritating, and serious labor difficulties may arise, if you boldly step in to take time studies, where jobs have been operating on an incentive basis for some time, and where there is no apparent change in method.

Rather than invite labor difficulties, it is far more preferable to conduct the auditing program in such a manner as to conduct time studies on specific jobs where method changes are apparent, or where specific incentive standards are being questioned by employees.

As an alternative, pure methods studies may be conducted, and then evaluated on the basis of standard time data or predetermined time standards.

When the opportunity does present itself to take time studies, sufficiently detailed time studies must be taken. This will permit a review of elemental time values with the basic standard time data which was used to establish the incentive standards.

A comparison of the detailed time studies with the standard time data leads to the following conclusions:

(1) The basic standard time data values are either correct or incorrect.
(2) The application of the standard time data values is either correct or incorrect.
(3) The operating methods upon which the incentive standards are based are either being maintained or have been changed.

With the above information at hand, the following corrective action must be taken:

(1) Such basic standard time values as are incorrect must be changed.
(2) If the application of the standard time data values is incorrect, instructions must be given to improve application practices.
(3) If the operating methods have been changed the incentive standards must be revised to reflect the changed methods.

When this approach is taken, the industrial engineering auditors will not only correct specific weaknesses on their priority list, but will, in the course of their investigation, unearth additional areas where similar action may be taken.

(c) Review of Production Reporting

Even though corrective action is taken with respect to standard time data, application of data, and changes in operating methods, it is still necessary to review production reporting methods to determine the validity of production quantities being recorded.

If mechanical counting or weighing devices are used, such devices must be checked to determine their mechanical accuracy, or to detect methods which may be used intentionally to overstate quantities.

If production quantities are based upon human counting methods, involving the judgment of operators or inspectors, it is necessary to introduce spot checking of quantities, in sufficient frequency to ensure that quantities are consistently recorded directly.

When spot checking indicates discrepancies, usually in connection with specific employees, disciplinary action ranging from warnings to discharge should be taken, on the basis of falsification of production records.

When prompt disciplinary action is taken in cases where there is no question regarding the facts, employees will recognize the vigilance of management in conducting spot checks, and the temptation for reporting excess quantities will be decreased or eliminated.

To minimize the necessity of spot checking, it is desirable to introduce production reporting methods which automatically pinpoint discrepancies, through routine clerical procedures.

As quantities are reported by each employee, the production dispatcher records the quantities on the corresponding job completed tickets, for the primary purpose of recording the production progress of the various jobs.

As a subsidiary by-product, however, there is an automatic method of controlling the reporting of excess quantities.

Whenever the total quantity as reported exceeds the required quantity of job lots, the production dispatcher brings the specific case to the attention of manufacturing supervision for immediate investigation and reconciliation of the discrepancy. Because of this method, which controls the situation very well, it was found that spot checking could be reduced to a minimum.

(d) Review of Timekeeping Methods

Even when time standards operating methods and production quantities all pass the test of the intensive auditing procedures, there is still the danger of inflated employee earnings as the result of inaccurate timekeeping.

Whenever it is the responsibility of the individual employee to take the initiative to report to a timekeeper, when he starts or finishes an incentive or day work assignment, there is a possibility of inaccurate reporting.

This danger is magnified whenever the Labor Contract provides for payment of "average incentive earnings" for "day work jobs." In reviewing timekeeping, the technique of work sampling may be put into effect, incurring very little risk of causing unsatisfactory labor relations.

It is a comparatively simple task to walk through a number of departments, observing the actual jobs of individual employees, and matching the jobs against the corresponding labor tickets assigned to the employees.

Where flagrant abuses exist, it may be necessary for an industrial engineering auditor to substitute physically for a timekeeper, in order to obtain all the facts first hand.

As in the case of reporting excess production quantities, when specific instances of incorrect reporting of time are discovered, it is necessary to take disciplinary action, ranging in severity from verbal warnings to actual discharges, depending upon provisions of the Labor Contract and established disciplinary practice in the specific plant.

MAINTAINING SUPERVISORY AND PRODUCTION EMPLOYEE INTEREST IN WORK STANDARDS[4] (by Appealing to Self-Interest)

Research at a number of universities has shown the success of these three principles for getting people to work together for the greatest productivity:

(1) Sharing (in the results).
(2) Cooperation (to achieve results).
(3) Participation (in setting goals).

Research has further shown that there are four steps essential to the motivation of individuals to work well together:

(1) Establishment of objectives.
(2) Letting the individual know how he is doing compared to his specific goals.
(3) Proper control by management.
(4) Three-dimensional communications between all elements of the organization.

It was also found that:
(a) Employees are motivated by a challenging job which allows a feeling of achievement, responsibility, growth, advancement, of the work itself, and recognition that has been earned by performance.
(b) Employees are dissatisfied by factors which are peripheral to the job itself, such as:
     ...Work rules
     ...Lighting, heat, air conditioning, noises, etc.
     ...Coffee breaks
     ...Clean and pleasant restrooms
     ...Titles
     ...Seniority rules
     ...Ample parking areas
     ...Wages and benefits
     ...Safe working conditions
(c) Employees become dissatisfied when opportunities for meaningful achievement are eliminated and they begin to find fault with their environment.
(d) Recognition of performance was indicated as the most effective non-financial incentive.

Suggested Practical Approaches

(1) Try to get the production worker to accept the standard as a challenge—an opportunity to beat a goal—a chance to demonstrate his superior skill compared to his associates.

---

4 Richard B. Miller, *Assignments in Management,* copyright © 1966 by Personnel Journal, Swarthmore, Penna., p.6, lines 11-25 and p. 9, lines 4-14.

(2) Periodically list the best performers on department bulletin boards.

(3) During merit reviews bring employees' production performance records to their attention.

(4) By revealing each employee's performance to him he has an opportunity "to see how he is doing."

(5) The employee who performs well in production will know that this provides him with another plus sign for promotional opportunities.

(6) The better scorers will have some of their ego needs satisfied.

(7) The use of work standards aids the company to improve its financial position, which in turn improves the employee's own job security:

(a) Better protects the employees' vested interest in the company's retirement benefits.

(b) Better protects the stability of employees' jobs...makes the company more competitive.

(c) Efficiency is synonymous with *cost reduction*. The efficiently run plant is generally the lowest cost run plant.

(d) The successful businesses of the decade that lies ahead must provide their customers with the very best in service. A company cannot offer excellent service if it is inefficiently operated.

(8) Improve your three-dimensional communications—companies must better inform their employees of the specific nature of their short- and long-range goals. They must continually try to advise employees about what is going on, by:

(a) Employee meetings addressed by top company officials.

(b) Staff meetings.

(c) Briefings.

(d) Written instructions.

(e) Bulletins.

(f) President's letters addressed to employees' homes.

(g) Company magazine.

(h) Develop reliable channels of feedback.

(i) Arrange for special committees to work on common operational objectives.

(9) Provide company sponsored courses in fundamentals of economics. (For example: why the middle income family now can afford one or two cars, compared to years ago.)

(10) Emphasize the cost of absenteeism to supervision and production employees. (Examples: machine downtime costs, all services available, supervision on hand, allotted space, payroll personnel, etc., etc.)

(11) Initiate supervisory training programs—focus on human behavior, production, waste, quality, etc.

(12) Properly indoctrinate new employees. Too often the new employee looks forward with great anticipation to his first day at the plant only to be deeply disappointed with the manner in which he is handled.

(13) Attempt to place the right employee in the job that is best for him.

(14) Management must establish a favorable climate. The proper employee morale must be developed before you can expect your employees to work diligently toward the attainment of the company's goals.

CHECKLIST FOR IMPROVING PRODUCTIVITY THROUGH USE OF WORK STANDARDS[5]

(1) Have all your direct labor jobs covered by work standards.

(2) Make an effort to have all your indirect labor jobs covered by work standards, either by time study observations or by work sampling.

(3) Conduct periodic time study rating checks to maintain consistency among your engineers. Use the Society for Advancement of Management Rating Films, (contact 135 West 50th Street, New York, N.Y. 10020).

(4) Use special allowances sparingly, and then arrange to cancel them when the need for them disappears.

(5) Chief industrial engineer should periodically sample studies turned in by his engineers.

(6) Continually review adherence to specified machine feeds and speeds.

(7) Production performance records of each employee should be recorded every week.

(8) Review production performance records, to determine weaknesses and to establish priorities.

(9) Periodically review production reporting methods.

(10) Continually examine timekeeping methods.

(11) Production employees should be held strictly accountable for their performances.

(12) Plant manager should periodically review unsatisfactory employee production records with their respective foreman who should be held accountable for results.

(13) Assure yourself that the channels of communications between production and engineering management personnel are clear and effective. Changes in methods should be promptly reported.

(14) Commend production workers who continue to maintain good performances.

(15) Consider giving additional training to those employees who have trouble meeting their standards.

(16) Periodically sample production counts for accuracy.

(17) Periodically check machine and work stations to look for retained production pieces being saved by operators for bad days. This is particularly important where incentive pay is involved.

(18) It is important that each production employee is instructed in the method employed by management in arriving at his production performance figures.

(19) Beware of any indication of retrogression in the plant weighted average production performance as compared to earlier periods. Should this occur, immediately investigate, analyze, and then take corrective actions.

(20) At least once every two years have an outside qualified industrial engineer or consultant audit your production standards. This is in addition to your own company audit.

(21) Occasionally make either a four- or eight-hour production delay study to check on correctness of questionable standards and methods.

(22) By the use of "spread sheets," periodically analyze machine downtime by departments and by machines, then initiate any required improvements.

5 Lewis R. Zeyher, *Cost Reduction in the Plant*, (Englewood Cliffs, N.J.: Prentice-Hall, Inc., copyright © 1965), pp. 181-182 partial.

(23) When making up your standard data for any particular operational element, continually seek out too loose or too tight time study values and eliminate before selecting the final figure.

(24) Assure yourself that the best method is employed at machine or work station before time study observations are begun.

(25) It cannot be overemphasized that the engineered work standard system *must* be continually checked, analyzed, and reviewed for it to be successful. The careful maintenance of such a program is just as important as its successful installation. When such a program eventually fails, it is generally the result of management neglect and careless maintenance.

6

Improving
Your Inventory
Turnover Rate

In many companies excessive and/or unbalanced inventories represent vulnerable areas for cost reduction attacks. Companies neglecting to keep a checkrein on their physical inventories, i.e., raw materials, work-in-process, finished goods and supplies, do so at their peril. Inventory losses are considered to be one of the primary direct causes of business failure.

The annual carrying cost of inventories is estimated to range from 10 to 30 per cent of the manufactured cost of the inventory. Therefore, at the annual carrying cost of 25 per cent, a $100 product would be worth $125 ($100 X 1.25%) by the end of the year. In a three year period, using the same type of calculation, the product's worth would have just about doubled.

An additional worry for the plant manager is the very real conflict of interest between the sales department and the treasurer's office. The typical sales manager wants a lot of everything on the warehouse shelves. He cannot face the possible loss of a customer sale because the required style, color or size is not immediately available. At the same time, however, the treasurer is complaining to the plant manager that the company's inventory costs are excessive and need trimming—too much money is tied up on the warehouse shelves. Not to be forgotten is the emergence of a new cost-element—manufacturers, at times, being forced to assume the burden of carrying their customers' inventories.

Still another factor is the accelerating construction cost of building warehouses or just adding floor space to existing buildings. Let us not forget, floor space is expensive and there is no relief in sight. Yet, some managements continue to use prime space as though it were but a very minor overhead expense. In this connection, a few actual examples of the exercise of poor executive judgment follow:

(a) In one large oil company where the sales department was in a dominating position, requests for additional tank storage and warehouses flowed directly from sales executives to the engineering department. Sales personnel determined the size and locations of these buildings with little regard for the economics involved. These costs continued to grow until top management became alarmed and a special study, in some depth, was made. It was found, in many instances, that the overly optimistic sales forecasts resulted in unnecessary capital expenditures when anticipated sales volumes failed to materialize. In other situations, where sales volume was expected to increase, say 30 per cent over the previous year's volume, an increase in floor space of 30 per cent was likewise requested. Proper consideration was *not* given to increasing the frequency of truck shipments from the refinery to warehouses.

(b) This incident involves a warehouse storing all kinds and sizes of tires, when one day, a company salesman enthusiastically remarked to the division manager that he had just sold a tire to a very happy customer. He said the customer had unsuccessfully tried to buy this unusual size tire at twelve different competitors' service stations. Upon questioning the salesman, the division manager determined, much to his chagrin, that the tire was for a fifteen year-old model motorcycle. This reflected the great difference in their respective thinking, the salesman pushing sales while neglecting consideration of costs, while the division manager, also interested in sales volumes, coupled his sales thinking with cost considerations. The twelve competitive service stations apparently were, in this instance, better inventory managed than the company who carried obsolete sizes in stock.

This company eventually placed the responsibility for approval of additional warehouses and/or just additional space to existing buildings with a newly created planning department, reporting directly to the executive vice president.

CALCULATION OF INVENTORY TURNOVER RATE[1]

What is inventory turnover? It is the number of times that a company sells and ships products equivalent in value to the average monthly manufactured cost of its physical inventory. Turnover rates are computed by dividing the annual rate of usage for finished goods, work-in-process, raw materials and supplies, by the average inventory on hand during the period being measured (usually 12 months). These are calculated on the basis of the manufactured cost. For example, if a company sold $10,000,000 of product in any one year when its average monthly inventory was $2,000,000, both calculated on a manufactured cost basis, then the result is a turnover of five times a year. Different industries reflect varied standard turnover figures. The variations in the length of the manufacturing cycle in each different industry largely influence and determine these distinctions. It is true, of course, that as previously mentioned, the degree of effectiveness of management in the same industry can produce a full range of turnover figures, from a desirable high frequency to an unacceptable low one. Occasionally some unusual operating condition or unforeseen external problem of supply, price, transportation difficulty, strike, flood, blight or similar situation could affect these figures and consequently should be taken into consideration.

Inventory Turnover Rate Calculations

(a) *Textile Mill* manufacturing a consumer product with a wide
    range of styles, sizes and colors:

> Yearly sales volume (manufactured cost) = $8,000,000
> Average monthly inventory (manufactured cost) = $3,300,000
> Inventory Turnover: $\dfrac{\$8,000,000}{3,300,000} = 2.4$ times

---

[1] Lewis R. Zeyher, *Cost Reduction in the Plant,* (Englewood Cliffs, N.J.: Prentice-Hall, Inc., copyright © 1965), p. 184, lines 1-35; p. 185, lines 7-41; and p. 186, lines 1-13.

Comment: This mill should have had an average inventory of approximately $1,300,000 or a turnover of approximately 6 times a year.

(b) *Electronics Manufacturer* producing a series of measuring instruments consisting of assembly operations:

Yearly sales volume (manufactured cost) = $1,300,000
Average monthly inventory (manufactured cost) = $390,000
Inventory Turnover: $\dfrac{\$1,300,000}{\$390,000} = 3.5$ times a year.

Comment: This plant should have had an average inventory of approximately $180,000 or a turnover rate of approximately 7.5 times a year.

COST OF CARRYING INVENTORY

This varies with the type of industry as well as each company's particular sales and operating policies. There are also other important considerations such as lead time required in ordering raw materials and supplies, length of time consumed in the manufacturing cycle, number of different sizes, materials and styles fabricated, curing cycles, necessity for accelerated aging processes of finished product before final testing and jobbing or mass production type of business. It is generally agreed, however, that annual carrying costs of inventory may vary from 10 to 30 per cent of the manufactured cost of inventory.

These items are generally considered in determining the annual cost:

(1) Interest on the capital invested.
(2) Insurance.
(3) Housing (floor space occupied).
(4) Keeping housing in repair.
(5) Looking after inventory:
   (a) Handling cost.
   (b) Taking physical inventory.
   (c) Clerical costs.
   (d) Depreciation costs for material handling equipment.
(6) Deterioration and spoilage.
(7) Repairs.
(8) Obsolescence.
(9) Pilferage.
(10) Transportation time—large inventories require longer distances traveled by warehouse personnel in transporting product, supplies, materials and components; also causes delay for company trucks.
(11) Plant protection.
(12) Labor losses—time lost by personnel searching and looking for specific product items which may be hidden under or back of other products, awkward to secure and requiring double handling; these operating obstacles could all be caused by excessive inventories.

Let us now examine some actual examples described previously—textile, electronics and jobbing metal working companies. Assume the annual cost of carrying each of their inventories was approximately 20 percent; then, by maintaining them at too high levels, they would suffer these estimated losses:

Type of Industry	Estimated Amount of Excessive Inventory	Annual Interest at 7%	Yearly Total Loss at 20%
Textile	$2,000,000	$140,000	$400,000
Electronics	210,000	14,700	42,000
Jobbing Metal Working	108,000	7,600	21,600

These are worthwhile savings to make. It requires effective management, with excellent control, to eliminate these losses. A casual approach to this operating problem will accomplish very little. A well-planned program, aggressively executed, is the only way to bring about the maximum realization of your objectives. One company with an annual sales volume of approximately twenty million dollars was able to save $175,000 on interest alone, just by increasing the turnover of the inventory by one time a year.

USUAL CAUSES OF HIGH INVENTORIES[2]

Excessive inventories can be brought about by:

(1) Manufacturing too many products or lines for size of company.
(2) Speculation in merchandise; that is, by buying heavily in anticipation of a rise in prices which often fails to materialize. Remember, you are *not* in the *gambling business.*
(3) Poor judgment in future markets; that is overbuying.
(4) The production or handling of a product which is off style or not in public demand.
(5) Unknowingly having prices which are competitively high.
(6) *Not* keeping the inventory neat and up to date.
(7) Poor production control practices.
(8) Poor manufacturing methods and procedures.
(9) Lack of a firm hand with the personnel responsible for implementing the system you have, by not insisting they strictly adhere to the policies established.
(10) Having finished inventories controlled by the sales department.

How Do You Reduce High Inventories?

Typical Example: One rule-of-thumb method to apply in determining if your company is carrying excessive inventories is to use the following test:

The average manufactured cost of your inventory should not exceed 75% of the net working capital.

This test may not work in every instance but it has actually been successfully applied to a number of manufacturing companies. In one outstanding example it was applied in a textile mill, whose sales were in the $10,000,000 range. The resulting comparison indicated an excess of $3,000,000 in inventory. Most of this was in finished goods inventories where the sales department insisted on carrying too many styles and too many colors in stock. Just a few years before the company had added a new and very modern warehouse which now was inadequate. In fact, an alert top management should have

---

2 J.K. Lessor, ed., *Business Management Handbook*, revised ed., (McGraw-Hill: New York, copyright © 1954), p. 149, lines 1-7.

recognized this situation without applying any type of formula or test. The warehouse foreman continually complained that he had too much stock to the point where he was compelled, on occasions, to move stock two or three times in order to get the specific style he needed for a customer's order.

Due to the fact that most of their financial resources were tied up in finished goods, this company eventually was forced to liquidate the company.

In an analysis of another company—a jobbing type of metal working company—the following was indicated in their financial data:

Manufacturing cost, average inventories $800,000
Net working capital 700,000

Inventories	Manufacturing cost	Per cent
Work-in-process	$560,000	70
Raw materials	160,000	20
Finished stock	80,00	10
Totals	$800,000	100.0

$$\frac{\$800,000}{\$700,000} = 114\%$$

$$114\% - 75\% = 39\%$$

$800,000 x 39% = $312,000 excess inventory according to the test.

Cost of carrying excess inventory—(usually is between 10 to 30% of manufacturing cost), in this example use 20%.

0.20 x $312,000 = $62,400 annually (interest charges alone, @ 7.0%, equal $21,840)

In this particular instance, space was in short supply so by reducing this excessive physical inventory more space would become available. This reduction in material handling would also result in substantial labor savings.

ANALYSIS OF EXCESSIVE INVENTORIES

Let us now examine the three categories of inventories. The biggest item is *work-in-process*. This is a bit unusual because in most types of industries, the largest item is in finished goods stock. However, in a jobbing type business work is performed by individual job orders. Once an order is finished it usually is immediately shipped to the customer so that the invoice can be mailed and customer payment consummated.

The company had 150 pieces of equipment of various types and capacities. It was assumed that work was not moving through these machines and being processed as quickly and efficiently as it should.

This suggested the application of Phil Carroll's formula— [3]

Inventory Parking Ratio:

$$R = \frac{C}{T} - 1$$

where:

R = Parking rate (sitting time)
C = Customer cycle time
T = Operation time per lot

---

[3] From *Practical Production and Inventory Control,* Phil Carroll. Copyright © 1966 by Phil Carroll. Used by permission of McGraw-Hill Book Company, New York, p. 225, lines 3-11.

Naturally, it would not be practicable to apply this to every order in any given period, but it could be done on a sampling basis. A few big jobs, some simple jobs and some complicated ones could be selected and the formula applied. Weaknesses disclosed on these would, no doubt, be true of many others. One of these applications follows:

Given: Customer order cycle time 25 days (600 hours) for a lot of 200 units consuming a total of 14 operations, of which 4 are productive and 10 unproductive times. The unproductive operations include inspection, temporary storage, transportation and delays. The productive operations took 133 hours and the unproductive 467 hours. Solution:

$$R = \frac{C}{T} - 1$$
$$R = \frac{600}{133} - 1$$
$$R = 4.5 - 1$$
$$R = 3.5$$

The answer indicates that the product sits, or is parked 3.5 times as long as it takes to make it.

Obviously, something is wrong here and remedial actions should be initiated. A few suggested actions follow:

(a) Shorten inspection time—improve quality, make operators more responsible for quality of their work.

(b) Improve scheduling and expediting of production—reduce temporary storage time.

(c) Check on transportation methods and times.

(d) Eliminate or minimize delays.

(e) Shorten set-up times.

(f) Improve machine maintenance—reduce mechanical failures during production runs.

(g) Eliminate material shortages.

(h) Consider automation or conveyorized line.

(i) Install production standards.

(j) Place customer order entries under the production control department.

(k) Periodically check time consumed by customer orders before reaching production.

(l) Minimize "rush" or emergency orders—they only *delay* all other orders.

FURTHER DEVELOPMENT OF REMEDIAL ACTIONS TO IMPROVE TURNOVER

(a) Shorten Inspection Time

First, it is important that all employees know exactly who is responsible for quality—the inspector or the production operator. Many an argument has ensued on this question, sometimes resulting in spirited discussions on the factory floor, interrupting production. There must not be any doubts here—responsibility must be fixed and everyone concerned properly instructed.[4] The following rules are recommended, unless there are compelling conditions to the contrary:

(1) The responsibility for deciding whether a *process should commence operation* rests with production. "Setup acceptance" is a production responsibility.

(2) The responsibility for deciding whether a *process should continue operation* rests with production. "Process acceptance" is a production responsibility.

(3) The responsibility for deciding whether the *product is satisfactory* to go to subsequent operation (or to the customer) rests with inspection. "Product acceptance" is an inspection responsibility.

(4) The responsibility for *defects produced but not accepted* rests with production alone.

(5) Responsibility for *defects produced and accepted* is joint—with production for making, inspection for accepting them.

If you give inspection responsibility for deciding whether the machines should run or stop, you will reduce scrap on some jobs. But you pay the price of relieving the production people of responsibility for making it right in the first place. That price is too high.

You can give production responsibility for deciding whether the product is acceptable or not. But this can lead to shocking results. For instance, the production foreman may very well be tempted to meet his schedule problems by slighting product quality. Furthermore, if all he has to do is accept the product there is no real incentive to correct the conditions that are causing the poor quality. If defects do get out to the customer the manager must be careful to call both production and inspection to account. Production must have no escape from the responsibility for making it right in the first place, inspector or no inspector. Where or not you agree with the above principles of how to divide responsibility between production and inspection, you should decide these responsibilities at *top levels. Do not* leave them to be settled by default at bottom levels.

(b) Improve Scheduling and Expediting—Reduce Temporary Storage Time

Scheduling—The primary function of production control is to direct, guide and coordinate the flow of raw materials. This starts with their receipt and continues through the various manufacturing processes to shipment of the finished products to customers. The scheduling of these raw materials starts with the receipt of a customer order. Scheduling means the process of establishing starting and finishing times for performing individual operations. By the use of efficient and reliable feedback methods intelligence regarding the successful completion of your instructions can be obtained and analyzed. This is the point where an aggressive manager can expedite production. Delays that reoccur can be permanently eliminated—weaknesses in your system can be discovered and strengthened—incompetent personnel can be replaced and discipline enforced.

---

[4] Reprinted by special permission of *Factory,* November 1952. Copyright, Morgan-Grampian, Inc., November 1952.

Expediting[5]—"Expediters," "follow-up" men, or "stock chasers" are sometimes an integral part of the production control procedure, although more frequently they are necessary only because the production control system does not function perfectly. Expeditors are primarily job pushers. They push orders through the plant faster than they would otherwise go. This applies only to particular orders and not to all orders. Some specific tasks they perform include:

(1) Locating lost orders.
(2) Finding delays—referring them to his superior.
(3) Keep selected orders moving.
(4) Oversee special orders for important customers.
(5) Find lost material.
(6) Make sure jobs are on specific machines and are being processed.
(7) Sees that material is moved quickly from operation to operation, even if he has to move it himself.
(8) Check on delays covering lack of tools.
(9) Work closely with dispatchers.
(10) Work on given lists of the most urgent orders.

(c) Check on Transportation Methods and Times

This includes a surveillance of both internal and external transportation. Internally covers transporting of raw materials, components, tools, supplies and related items within the plant. Assure yourself that they are delivered to the designated work station at the required time, in an undamaged condition. Too many unnecessary delays occur here and should be eliminated or minimized.

External transportation relates to the handling of vendor's deliveries promptly, including warehousemen availability when trucks dock so truckers will not be compelled to wait. Paperwork should be taken care of expeditiously. Shipments to customers from warehouse should be handled efficiently as the company cannot expect payment until the customer receives the product. Too often, when following up customers' orders, the production foremen will state that the order is finished and waiting to be packed for delivery to shipping department. The customer order, however, is *not finished until it is shipped*. In addition, every attempt should be made to eliminate the rush during the last days of the month.

Example

Warehousing Costs Related to Product X Activity and to Storage[6]

Elements	A Costs related to activity	B Costs related to storing
Interest	. . .	$1.20
Freight, inbound	1.00	. . .

---

[5] Franklin G. Morre, *Production Control*, (Mc-Graw Hill: New York, copyright © 1951), pp. 268-270 partial.

[6] Creed H. Jenkins, *Modern Warehouse Management*, copyright © 1968 by McGraw-Hill Book Company, p. 22, lines 24-41; p. 23, lines 1-30.

Elements (*cont.*)	*A* Costs related to activity (*cont.*)	*B* Costs related to storing (*cont.*)
Labor:		
Receiving	0.22	. . .
Upkeep	. . .	0.48
Space	. . .	1.92
Insurance	. . .	0.10
Taxes	. . .	0.50
Loss and damage	0.03	0.01
Obsolescence	. . .	0.02
Totals	$1.25/unit	$4.23/unit

The unit cost of carrying inventory when related to turnover is determined by using the following formula:

$$\text{Unit Cost} \quad A = \frac{B}{\text{turnover/year}}$$

Examples of how turnover affects inventory carrying cost per unit are shown below:

Turnover per year	Equation	Inventory Carrying Costs per unit
1.0	$1.25 + $\dfrac{\$4.23}{1.0}$	$5.48
2.0	$1.25 + $\dfrac{\$4.23}{2.0}$	$3.37
4.0	$1.25 + $\dfrac{\$4.23}{4.0}$	$2.31
6.0	$1.25 + $\dfrac{\$4.23}{6.0}$	$1.95

To determine the total cost of warehousing materials, as opposed to inventory carrying costs shown above, simply add the unit cost of the shipping operation and the outbound freight to the unit inventory carrying costs. For example:

Shipping operation	$0.40/unit
Freight, outbound	2.00/unit
Inventory carrying cost	5.48/unit
Total warehousing cost	$7.88/unit

As turnover increases, unit cost for carrying inventory decreases. As shown for product X, for a year it is shown as $5.48 per unit (27.4 percent) for a turnover of once a year, which decreases to $1.95 per unit (9.8 percent) for a 6.0 times per year. Assuming that all items in a product line are supplied through the warehouse, the turnover rate becomes a very important index of inventory performance. However, under a different distribution plan, turnover may be a completely meaningless or even misleading measure of performance.

7

Plant Engineering
and Preventive
Maintenance[1]

Most of the material in this book covers efficiency performance and management control techniques, which deal primarily with people. There are other systems for measuring plant performance. These deal with machines, utilities and plant efficiencies. These techniques provide additional methods for measuring plant operating performance and constitute an area that should be more fully explored in any cost reduction program.

Here, basic costs, not dollar costs, will be used. By basic costs are meant such things as man-hours of labor, kilowatt-hours of electric energy, gallons of water, and cubic feet of gas per unit product. These values remain stable regardless of the time period involved, and by the use of appropriate conversion factors can be changed to dollar costs when so required. This data provides the basis for measuring and plotting plant efficiencies for the individual plant or for comparison between plants in a multi-plant operation.

So that plant efficiency can be determined, and appropriate action can be taken to improve this efficiency with the end result in mind—*reduce plant operating costs.*

Do you know, for instance what your maintenance costs were for the past year? Do you know whether your costs are up or down from the previous year? Finally, do you know the significance of the increased or decreased cost? The cost alone is meaningless unless you can relate it to production, because a 10 per cent increase in costs with a 30 per cent increase in production will actually show a decrease in cost per unit produced.

In this chapter we hit only the high spots of both plant engineering and preventive maintenance. Volumes have been written on each of these functions, and therefore many phases of these disciplines, due to space limitations, necessarily will be omitted.

---

[1] John Molnar, *Plant Operation Manual,* (Englewood Cliffs, N.J.: Prentice-Hall, Inc., copyright © 1967), p. 1, lines 13-22; p. 6, lines 26-33.

RESPONSIBILITIES OF THE PLANT ENGINEER[2]

Maintaining buildings, equipment, and grounds is an important function of maintenance management. The necessity for adequate maintenance of the facility—whether it be a manufacturing, research and development, service, or administration facility—is rarely, if ever, questioned. What constitutes adequacy, or the required level of maintenance, however, is often a matter of opinion. Equally important, but seldom questioned, is the degree of effectiveness that the maintenance manager and/or plant engineer obtains from his maintenance resources. A maintenance budget, or the total amount spent for the maintenance activity, is not a good indicator of either the amount of maintenance service rendered or how effectively the managers of the maintenance activity utilize their resources.

The total amount of maintenance services required, total dollars budgeted or spent for the maintenance activity, and maintenance management effectiveness are interrelated. Whether top management decrees by its action that the budget shall be the result of needs or that amount of service shall be the result of the moneys available, it nevertheless behooves the maintenance manager to utilize his resources as effectively as possible.

Strictly speaking, most maintenance departments are called upon to perform or contract for considerably more than the term "maintenance" connotes. They often have to erect new buildings or partitions, handle involved rearrangements of equipment, manufacture equipment and parts, design equipment or components, and the like. Because these indirect maintenance functions are usually performed by the same skills and types of labor as the maintenance functions, however, they can be managed by the same managers using the same techniques and procedures.

Effective maintenance management requires the manager to understand and utilize many of the tools of modern management.

MAINTENANCE MANAGEMENT

Master Rules:

At one time, one of the major firms in the United States adopted eighteen rules for good maintenance management. Subsequently, the United States Navy adopted these same rules. Because they have proved to be sound over the years, they are repeated here as a guide to policy determination.

(1) *Set Up a Responsible Organization.* A separate maintenance control group with overall control of procedures, the conduct of inspections, and analysis of maintenance information.

(2) *Use a Work-Order System.* A work-order system is vital to maintenance control. A written work-order procedure requires that every maintenance job be requested on a

---

2 From *Maintenance Management,* Sylvan L. Kapner, *Handbook of Business Administration,* ed. H. B. Maynard, copyright © 1967. Used with permission of McGraw-Hill Book Company. P. 7-50, lines 1-16, and 21-29.

standard form that becomes the basis for equipment records, job analysis, work scheduling, and work measurement.

(3) *Keep Equipment Records.* An accurate inventory and a permanent record of maintenance work performed are essential.

(4) *Analyze and Plan Jobs.* The importance of an analysis of each repair order should be stressed. A separate planning organization is used which leaves supervisors free for direct supervision and personnel problems.

(5) *Make a Weekly Forecast.* Schedule each week's work by no later than the middle of the previous week. Generally about 75 per cent of the work included in the weekly forecast can be performed as specified.

(6) *Prepare Daily Schedules.* Daily schedules for the next day are to be prepared by the supervisors prior to 3 p.m. each day to assure that maintenance men are not required to wait for assignments every morning.

(7) *Set Up a Manpower Control.* Manpower control includes a backlog control of manpower requirements that indicates when the crew is too large or too small for the work ahead in each function, area, or shop.

(8) *Set Up a Preventive-Maintenance Program.* The emphasis should be on doing maintenance work at the best time for all to assure that manpower is continuously busy instead of working in surges.

(9) *Use Budgetary Control.* A maintenance budget is prepared on an annual basis and broken down into monthly subdivisions. The annual budget is fixed; the monthly budget varies to meet changing situations.

(10) *Provide Material Control.* Material control involves the establishment of accurate maximum and minimum amounts for all stored items, material, and replacement parts as well as firm adherence to an established distribution and issue system.

(11) *Plan Plant Shutdowns.* Determine the expected life of various critical components in each equipment group and then plan the shutdown frequency so that overall downtime will be at a minimum.

(12) *Set Up Major Overhaul Procedures.* Determine the best method for overhaul of any piece of equipment, including a description of the tools, parts, and manpower requirements.

(13) *Develop Standard Practices.* These refer to minor repetitive jobs or shop work.

(14) *Use Engineered Work Measurement.* The intent is to evaluate labor performance by recording the amount of actual time taken on a series of jobs and comparing it with standard times established through engineered work measurement.

(15) *Improve Equipment.* Improvement of equipment is a long-range objective aimed at making maintenance easier by improving design, materials, or manufacture. Standardization of design is also essential.

(16) *Train Supervisors.* All levels of maintenance supervision should be trained to understand and use maintenance controls. An important part of the training is to emphasize that maintenance controls have the strong support of management.

(17) *Train Maintenance Men.* Training is essential for new men and for new installations, and when increased effectiveness of experienced maintenance personnel is desired.

(18) *Analyze Performance and Costs.* Analysis of performance and costs consists of continuing self-criticism of the total maintenance effort.

Contract Maintenance. In every maintenance operation, sooner or later a decision has to be made on whether to attempt to maintain a certain type of equipment or to contract it out. Several general rules that will help guide you in these decisions are as follows:

Consider contracting the maintenance...

(1)   Where specialized equipment is required.

(2)   Where the equipment under consideration is not directly involved with the production of the company's product or service, or where it can easily be circumvented.

(3)   Where specialized skills are required.

(4)   Where the estimated man-hours per year are low.

(5)   Where maintenance can be tied to leasing equipment more economically than purchasing the equipment.

Organization

The planning of an organization for a small plant will differ considerably from that of a large plant. However, even the plant with fewer than fifty production employees can justify a simplified plan for an organization. Usually the key man in the smaller plant is a shirt-sleeve type individual knowledgeable in electricity, but who is expected to also handle other kinds of repairs and general maintenance chores. Plumbing, carpentry, welding and related special skills are employed, as needed, or purchased on a contractual basis. Then as the company grows, individuals experienced in these crafts are gradually employed and added permanently to the department.

In the large plants all kinds of organizational structures will be found. The supervisor of this department (plant engineer, maintenance superintendent or foreman) should report directly to the executive responsible for production. In one plant of seven hundred employees the plant engineer reported directly to the production superintendent, who, in turn, reported to the vice president of manufacturing. All the production foremen reported to the superintendent. This arrangement worked out very well. In a plant of fifteen hundred employees, where some heavy machinery was used and a steam power plant was required (for process steam and for heating), the plant engineer reported to the works manager, who, in turn, reported to the vice president of manufacturing. In addition, the machine shops, that employed forty employees, came within his responsibilities. In plants requiring manufacturing engineers (discussed at some length in Chapter 1), the foreman of the machine shop or toolroom logically would report to this position. It is practically impossible to draw a hard line regarding such arrangements because of the many variables present. Such factors as type of product, complexity, job shop or mass production, heavy or light machinery, food, metal, plastics or process industry must be taken into consideration. As part of good organization practice a standard procedure instruction manual should be prepared and maintained. In addition, complete job descriptions should be prepared and *kept up to date,* for all personnel.

TOOLS FOR MEASURING PLANT EFFICIENCIES[3]

(a) Data Required

The first step in establishing a program for measuring plant operating efficiencies is to separate the controllable from the non-controllable costs. While it is true that all costs are controllable within certain limits, it would not be sound economic practice to devote too much time to small or to relatively fixed costs. For instance, real estate tax is a noncontrollable expense, but a thorough study may show that unproductive real estate may be disposed of, thereby reducing the tax. Nevertheless, this item is still non-controllable.

Since many industries have seasonally fluctuating outputs, the costs and product output cannot be merely monthly subdivisions of annual figures. They must represent actual costs and output on periods no larger than the month.

Secondly, suitable product units, consistent with the product line, must be established. The following is an example of the more common industries and representative units:

(1) Food processing: can, case, 100 cases, barrels.
(2) Chemical industry: pounds, gallons, barrels, tons.
(3) Steel industry: finished product in net tons.
(4) Automobile industry: units produced.
(5) Tobacco processing and manufacture: cigarettes (finished product)—packs, cartons, cases. Cigars—packs, boxes, cases. Tobacco—pounds, 1,000 pounds, tons.
(6) Textile mills: yards of material per standard width.

Finally, the number that is obtained when the basic cost is divided by the product unit should be convenient for general understanding, i.e., extremely large or small numbers should be avoided.

For instance, a particular food processing plant requires about 51,500 BTU's of heat to produce one case of food.

BTU's available for plant processing — 95,017,500,000
Cases produced   —   1,845,000
Yield . . . . 51,500 BTU's per case per month.

However, the monthly total BTU figure is unwieldy and should be reduced and recorded in 1,000 BTU's/case.

(b) Establishing Utilities Costs

The next category after labor is energy. It is used to mean only that which is needed to drive machines and equipment, and excludes, for instance, oil or water which is used in

---

[3] John Molnar, *Plant Operation Manual,* (Englewood Cliffs, N.J.: Prentice-Hall, Inc., copyright © 1967), p. 7, lines 8-15, and 27-44; p. 8, lines 1-7; p. 9, lines 1-5; p. 10, lines 1-11 and figures 1-2, 1-3; p. 11, lines 1-42; p. 12, lines 1-40; p. 13, lines 1-43; p. 14, lines 1-13; p. 15, lines 37-43; p. 16, lines 1-27; p. 139, lines 21-44; p. 140, lines 1-40.

the finished product. This becomes product material and must be separated from energy. However, do not ignore it; class it and control it under materials.

The first step in preparing to measure performance and costs of plant utilities is to list all categories of energy that your plant uses.

(1) Electricity   (5) Gasoline
(2) Oil   (6) Water
(3) Coal   (7) Steam
(4) Gas

Second, construct, in tabular form, annual usage reported on a monthly basis, with one row showing quantity of units produced during a period. See Exhibit 7-1.

	JAN	FEB	MAR	APRIL	MAY	JUNE	_ _ _	TOTAL
ELECTRICITY-KWHRS								
OIL-GALLONS								
COAL-TONS								
GAS-CU. FT								
GASOLINE-GALLONS								
WATER-GALLONS								
STEAM-POUNDS								
PRODUCT-CASES								

EXHIBIT 7-1: Monthly Report Showing Energy Usage and Product Output [4]

While this will give an adequate idea of total utilities usage fluctuations as related to production variation, the curve presents the most graphic picture. Plot the quantity of utilities and the quantity of product units produced along the ordinate against time in 12 months along the abscissa. This will provide a composite picture so that fluctuations can be compared.

Third, and this is possibly the most difficult assignment to this point, separate the utilities usage into fixed and variable quantities. Although the technical personnel may not be available to perform this breakdown, a sample is presented. In this case, electrical energy is taken and separated by use and area.

Electricity	Office	Mfg. Area	Warehouse Area
Lighting	640	1,200	800
Power	0	160,000	220
Heating	0	12,800	0
Heating & A.C.	11,200	4,000	3,200
Total	17,600	178,000	4,220

Utilities Assignment Sheet—Kilowatt-Hours
Total .... 199,800 Kw-hrs.

---

4 *Plant Operation Manual,* John Molnar, Prentice-Hall, Inc., copyright 1967, page 10.

Once this sheet is completed, the fixed portion of electricity is readily established and it should be subtracted from the total monthly usage to determine that portion assignable to production. It is this quantity that should be used (in Exhibit 7-2). It is obvious, however, that the fixed portion merely raises that curve and does not contribute to the variation. Therefore, in the simpler form the total usage may be used, but for those who require extreme accuracy, the above table is required. This same type of table can be established for all the different utilities used.

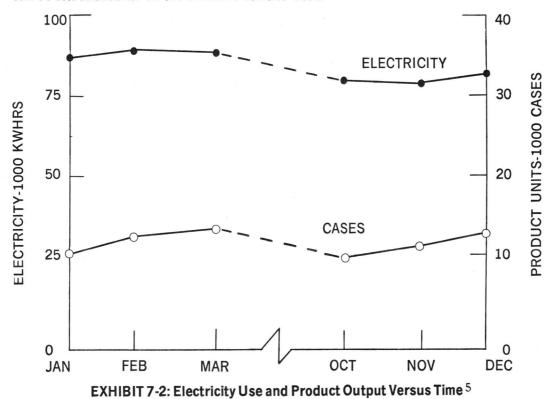

EXHIBIT 7-2: Electricity Use and Product Output Versus Time [5]

(c) Measuring Machine Efficiency

So far only part of the operating expenses in producing a product have been covered, i.e., *men* feeding materials into machines which consume *energy* to produce a *product*. Machine efficiency is also an important segment of total plant efficiency, and too often it is ignored.

In the case of the machine, we are primarily interested in efficiency, i.e., output divided by capability. Note carefully that the denominator is not input but capability. Therefore, a machine that is capable of 300 units per minute, but produces only 150 units in that period, is operating at 50 per cent efficiency.

Machine efficiency calculations for individual machines are relatively simple, but they should be calculated in order to determine whether or not operation is improving.

---

[5] *Ibid.*

The real problem is with the series production line. A typical example is a process line in the food industry where the flow of product is as illustrated below:

(1) Case unloader
(2) Bottle washer
(3) Filler
(4) Pasteurizer
(5) Labeler
(6) Packer
(7) Palletizer

Of course there are many conveyors that handle the product or container as it makes its way from the case unloader through the palletizer. These are not considered as part of the machines because their contribution to inefficiency is usually insignificant.

In order to be in a position to improve efficiencies on a product line the entire line must be studied simultaneously. For the example shown above, construct the following table:

Machine	Unit Produced	Unit Capability	Efficiency Percent
Case Unloader			
Bottle Washer			
Filler			
Pasteurizer			
Labeler			
Packer			
Palletizer			

Production Line Efficiency Table

When this table is completed it will be a relatively simple matter to determine where the faults lie which cause the lowest efficiencies. Second, this table will quickly show if any part of the line is too slow or too fast for the rest of the line.

You must analyze your lines and individual machines in order to be able to construct the proper table for efficiency evaluation. Once the table is constructed you merely fill in the blank spaces and then calculate the efficiencies. The next step is to plot the efficiencies so that a progressive comparison can be established. This will show whether or not your efficiency is improving, and you can establish a firm goal for the future.

(d) Measuring Individual Operating Efficiencies

In measuring individual operating efficiencies, include both men and machines. Sometimes it will be difficult to separate man from machine because the man operates the machine. In most cases, the individual operating responsibility can be assigned properly to either one or the other.

There are two types of operations involving men and machines. In the first type, the man serves primarily as an observer. This is true, for example, in the case of the bottle filling machine into which bottles are automatically fed and from which they emerge, having been automatically filled. The man's responsibility here is to start the operation, clear jams and faults, and observe during normal functioning periods. While at first this appears a clear-cut machine operational function, it is not entirely so.

In a two or three shift operation, carefully log the daily production of the machines so that shift comparison can be made. In this manner the variable machine can be eliminated and the men's productivity can be measured. Where production records show that one shift continually lags behind the others, visual observation of the operator performance must be made. This may reveal the trouble spot. Also, try the competitive approach. Plot the efficiency of the operation in terms of output per capability on a per shift basis so that each operator can see his competitors' efforts. Rotating the operators' shifts may sometimes help to increase efficiency.

Measuring the individual efficiency of operators performing the same function on different machines often is meaningless, because here the prime objective is machine efficiency.

In the second type of machine operation, the man feeds the machine. The case packer is an example of this, for here cans or bottles are automatically fed into the machine but the man hand feeds the cases and actuates the filling operation. The efficiency of the operator can and must be measured. Again, plot the output per capability on a daily basis.

The simplest area of measuring individual efficiency is in operations of the job shop variety. Here the man picks the material, performs some function, and passes it on. In this case man establishes capability and his efficiency is his output per capability. Sometimes individual performance is as meaningful as individual efficiency, and it is easier to handle.

Measuring individual efficiency will be useful, providing increases can be effected. Here, as in all cases of measuring efficiencies, after the information has been tabulated and the curves plotted, appropriate action must be taken.

(e) Measuring Plant Efficiency

One dictionary definition of efficiency is "the ratio of the work done by a machine to the amount of fuel consumed." Efficiency, by definition, is output over input, which is the reciprocal of basic costs as defined earlier.

Previously, it was shown that one food plant required 51.5 K BTU's per case of food produced. This number was obtained by judiciously manipulating the size of the component numbers to yield basic costs in practical values. Therefore, efficiency becomes:

$$\frac{1}{51.5} \times 100 = 1.94\%$$

Actually, the basic cost figures could have been any number, depending upon whether BTU's, 100 BTU's, or 1,000 BTU's were used. This, of course, would affect the number obtained when efficiency is calculated. The most important single significant feature of calculating and plotting in curve form the efficiency of any portion of plant operations is that it will produce a curve where the rise signifies improvement, whereas with basic costs, improvement will appear as a decline on the curve.

In some cases you will note that your efficiency may be initially above 100 per cent, or will later rise to above 100 per cent, but this merely means that your basic cost figures were not correctly adjusted.

This same company has a basic cost of 5.68 pounds of coal per case, which yields a coal utilization efficiency of:

$$\frac{1}{5.68} \text{X } 100 = 17.1\%$$

These figures when plotted in curve form, produce results consistent with accepted concepts in efficiency reporting.

Where do you start to measure plant efficiency? As stated in the introduction, the analysis is based upon the smallest possible subdivision. This means that you start with the individual machine and work up through the line to total plant machine efficiency. The same method applies to utilities usage. There is more than one reason for this: First, it is far easier to analyze a single machine or line, a single operator or department, than the entire plant as a whole; and second, the responsibility for plant operation must lie with the first line supervisor.

Cost Reduction Checklist for Both Machine and Energy

(1) Does the machine operate at maximum rated speed?
(2) Does the speed cause excessive waste, or damaged product?
(3) If so, could simple adjustment cure this fault?
(4) If not, has the manufacturer been consulted?
(5) Can the machine be fed continuously at maximum output?
(6) In a production line, is there provision for accumulation of the machine's output when short-time stops occur downstream?
(7) If not, this start-stop operation could create excessive wear on the machine and also create product damage.
(8) Do you have an effective preventive maintenance program?
(9) Is it scheduled during off-production periods?
(10) Is the machine adjusted for maximum energy utilization efficiency?
(11) Is the drive motor or mechanism properly rated to the load requirements?
(12) Is there product spillage or loss at the machine station?
(13) Is it planned to coincide with off-production periods?
(14) Is your lubrication program automatic?
(15) Is the lubricant of the proper quality and as recommended by the manufacturer?
(16) Is any machine in a production line so critical that down-time on it cripples production?
(17) Do you permit machines to run idle for prolonged periods?
(18) Do you know energy consumption per unit produced?
(19) Can this be improved?

While this is by no means an all-inclusive list for all industry, a checklist is a must for any program of performance evaluation. A checklist is necessary for the proper operation of equipment.

Look at the above list as a starting point for your operation and add to it the specific items for your particular machines. You may be amazed how quickly you can develop an effective list that could well increase the efficiency of your plant. If you already have a list, then review it. If not, then develop one. Finally, the list must be distributed to all responsible individuals for maximum utilization.

A cost reduction investigation means more than a quick 15 minute tour through the plant with the comment, "Everything looks in order." It requires a thorough study, an effective checklist, a formal efficiency report, and a continuing follow-up. Cost reduction does not come automatically; it requires diligent work.

Determining Down-Time Cost

There are a number of ways to determine and establish down-time costs for any operation. There is usually one method appropriate for the particular operation. But, regardless of the method used, down-time costs must be determined. These costs vary with the type operation; they may vary directly with down-time, increasing uniformly with increased time, or they vary at some increased rate with respect to time.

Down-time means idle men and machines, and results in lost production. Since production loss is different for different operations, down-time must be investigated for the different production operations.

(1) Job Shop. There are two types of operations involved here: (a) components are produced for stock to be used later in the assembly of a product, (b) components are produced in a continuous production line operation where the components are used as they are produced.

In the first case, down-time costs are relatively simple to determine: they are the sum of the direct and indirect costs. Direct labor costs are those actually required to produce the component. Indirect (overhead) costs are those costs incurred which cannot be charged to the product. Indirect costs are usually expressed as a per cent of direct costs, e.g., 125 per cent indirect costs mean that for every $1.00 direct labor cost there is an additional cost of $1.25, or since direct cost is a hundred per cent, 100 per cent + 125 per cent = 225 per cent. Where labor cost is $3.00 per hour the total operating labor cost is $6.75 per hour.

$$\text{Down-time Cost/Minute} = \frac{\text{Labor Cost x Overhead}}{60}$$

For total down-time, multiply the above by the number of minutes of idle time. Calculate down-time cost for 10 minutes at the above rate.

$$\frac{\$3.00 \times 225\%}{60} \times 10 = \$1.125 \text{ Down-time Cost}$$

In the second case a somewhat different approach is taken. Suppose that an entire production line employing 30 people must be shut down for ten minutes. Here the labor cost of the entire line must be used. For instance, with an average labor cost of $2.50 per hour, a shutdown of this line costs approximately $28.10 per minute. A ten minute delay because of the lack of effective communications will cost $281. This is now quite a significant loss.

The intangible losses are difficult to measure. Operating on a tight production schedule, these 10 minute losses over a month's period could cause shipping dates to slip by one day. What effect would this have on the present order? On future orders?

(2) Continuous-Operation Production Line. In a food processing plant, food spoilage must be taken into account in addition to the labor cost for product line down-time. This loss could be more than just the food loss cost; it could mean a complete loss of the particular product when one ingredient becomes unavailable.

The best method for determining down-time costs with any production line operation is to use the tabular system. (See the following table.)

Machine Operation	Unit Rate Per Minute	Cost Per Minute	Lost Time	Total Cost
Case Unloader				
Bottle Washer				
Filler-closer				
Pasteurizer				
Labeler				
Case Packer				
Palletizer				

Production Line Loss Cost Table

A similar table can be established for any production line by following this simple step-by-step procedure:

(1) List all machines or operations that are serially connected.
(2) Determine the unit rate per minute for each machine.
(3) Calculate the cost per minute for each machine.
(4) Log the lost-time in minutes for each machine down-time. This is best done on a per shift basis.
(5) Calculate the total lost-time cost per machine and for the total production line.

The method for determining the lost-time cost for the continuous-process operation is very much the same as for the above. It requires establishing a step-by-step procedure as outlined and developing a suitable table. With this system, any production operation can be properly evaluated and lost-time costs established.

PREVENTIVE MAINTENANCE

How to Control Your Maintenance Problems[6]

Every company has repairs and maintenance problems. If these problems to a limited degree are predictable, they are to a similar extent also controllable.

What is the difference between the ordinary run-of-the-mill type of shop maintenance and the more formal, planned type of preventive maintenance? The best of plans will not entirely eliminate an occasional machine breakdown during a scheduled production run. In spite of this, however, a well-planned program will prevent many costly and untimely breakdowns. A plan for periodically inspecting specific parts of equipment, to search for unusual wear or to look for the possible malfunction of a moving part, will often reveal the need for remedial action. By anticipating these problems you detect many of them before they become serious and troublesome. A major breakdown is more costly and inconvenient to repair than a minor adjustment or the timely replacement of a worn, inexpensive part.

6 Lewis R. Zeyher, *Cost Reduction in the Plant,* (Englewood Cliffs, N.J.: Prentice-Hall, Inc., copyright © 1965), p. 57, lines 1-5, 11-19; p. 58, lines 1-4; p. 59, lines 1-38.

The Advantages of Preventive Maintenance

(1) Improves customer relations through improved production scheduling.

(2) Results in less costly repairs.

(3) Produces better quality products.

(4) Affords more efficient maintenance work planning and coordinating.

(5) Results in better and more economical spare parts ordering and supply.

(6) Gives more efficient assignment of work to the special as well as limited skills and crafts available.

(7) Improves maintenance work force productivity.

(8) Results in better and more convenient building repairs.

(9) Gives more convenient major overhauls of equipment.

(10) Takes equipment out of production at more convenient periods.

(11) Makes better use of outside services.

(12) Provides adequate machine records.

(13) Improves paperwork handling.

(14) Standardizes maintenance methods.

(15) Encourages use of maintenance production standards.

(16) Provides for written procedures.

(17) Prompts the systematic evaluation of performances and results.

(18) Establishes better organization and lines of authority.

(19) Elicits cooperation of line supervision.

(20) Provides for faster emergency service to production foremen.

(21) Better accommodates budgetary control procedures.

(22) Reveals shoddy work.

(23) Fixes worker responsibilities.

(24) Aids in planning for plant shutdowns.

(25) Reduces machine down-time.

(26) Highlights excessive cost areas.

(27) Reduces costs of replacement parts, and facilitates standardization of equipment.

(28) Encourages use of incentive systems.

(29) Forecasts workload vs. manpower.

(30) Reveals need for better machine designs.

(31) Aids in justification for new capital equipment.

(32) Improves maintenance communications.

(33) Reduces frequency of "quickie" repairs.

(34) Facilitates effective supervision.

(35) Places a firm control in the hands of management.

NOTE: For additional information on methods to use to install this system, refer to the Prentice-Hall, Inc., book, *Cost Reduction in the Plant,* by L.R. Zeyher, Chapter 6.

8

Quality Control
and Inspection
Practices

The personnel of this department perform as service advisors acting as guardians of product integrity, as well as aiding other departments in eliminating manufacturing defects. They also are responsible for making all company personnel quality conscious so that spoilage and rejects can be reduced. In the performance of these very important duties their activities will reach into all phases of manufacturing in addition to maintaining contacts with other staff departments.

IS YOUR QUALITY CONTROL FUNCTION TOO EXPENSIVE?

This department supplies a service and does not add any value to the product. It contributes to overhead expense and as a staff function, its performance is difficult to measure. Questions that continually arise include: how many employees should this function require, or are more employees needed so that product quality can be improved, or do you think we are overmanned? These are difficult questions to answer. Too many variables exist—each plant has its own personality. Such elements as employee morale, complexity of company product, government contracts or consumer goods production, old or modern building and equipment, sophisticated or inexperienced management, are but a few elements to consider.

Examine the Costs

Very few companies know the total monthly cost of their particular system. Further, they have never segregated all the elements of these costs, so that they can be properly dissected, analyzed, and then effectively challenged. To do so, would undoubtedly uncover many areas where savings could be accomplished without impairing the potency of your system.

There are three general classes of costs [1] entering into economy studies involving

---

[1] Eugene L. Grant, *Statistical Quality Control*, 3rd. Ed. (New York: McGraw-Hill Book Company, copyright © 1964 by McGraw-Hill, Inc.), p. 516, lines 15-46; p. 517, lines 1-35; p. 518, lines 27-41; p. 519, lines 1-42.

quality of conformance. In using the word quality, it is necessary to recognize the distinction between quality of design and quality of conformance. In the sense that a Lincoln is considered to be a better automobile than a Ford, or a Cadillac a better quality one than a Chevrolet, the word *quality* is used in the sense of quality of design. The designers of the higher priced automobiles have included certain more costly features aimed to secure greater comfort, better appearance, better performance, etc.

In the sense used in this chapter, quality of conformance relates to whether or not the quality characteristics of a product correspond to those really needed to secure the results intended by the designer. Used in this sense, margins of safety written into design specifications are often aimed chiefly at securing quality of conformance. Where such margins of safety are used with this objective, design specifications and acceptance specifications are properly viewed as interrelated matters.

Decisions involving quality of conformance may relate to the amount and type of inspection, to production methods and objectives, and to margins of safety used in design specifications. In making economy studies to guide such decisions, it is helpful to divide the costs influenced by the decisions into three general classes. These may be somewhat loosely referred to as (1) production costs, (2) acceptance costs, and (3) unsatisfactory-product costs.

In this usage, the expression *production costs* is intended to refer to those costs involved in the production of the article under consideration. Different design specifications may require different materials, different labor skills, different amounts of labor time, and different machines. For example, increased strength requirements for a part may change the material to be used; closer tolerances on dimensions may call for use of newer or different machines. This general class of costs properly includes *spoilage costs,* i.e., the production expenses on all product discarded as not meeting specifications minus any receipts from the disposal of this discarded product. It also includes *rework costs* necessary to make product acceptable and screening costs, if any, on rejected lots.

The *acceptance costs* include not only testing and inspection costs but also the costs of administering the acceptance program.

The expression *unsatisfactory-product costs* is intended to refer to those costs resulting from the acceptance of product that turns out to be unsatisfactory for the purpose intended. In this sense the word *cost* should be interpreted as including a reduction in revenue as well as an increase in expense. It should be recognized that some or all of the product that is technically defective in the sense of failing to meet design specifications is not necessarily unsatisfactory for the purpose intended whenever the common practice is followed of including a margin of safety in the specifications. This distinction between product that is really unsatisfactory and product that is satisfactory even though nonconforming to specifications is an important one in any discussion of the economics of quality decisions.

Of these three classes of costs affected by quality decisions, unsatisfactory-product costs are inherently the most difficult to evaluate. Doubtless the greatest difficulty occurs in the consumers' goods industries, where the product goes to a great many different customers who make no formal acceptance tests. It is hard to predict the consequences to the manufacturer of consumers' goods when some stated percentage of his product fails to give satisfactory service to its purchasers, and it is even more difficult to place a money value on these consequences. Where the consumers' product carries a guarantee, past customer service costs can be used as a guide to judgment and changes in these costs can be carefully watched and related to changes in design specifications and in inspection and acceptance procedures.

The most favorable circumstances exist for securing reliable information on unsatisfactory-product costs when all of the product goes to one user. This user may be another department in the producer's organization, or it may be a single purchaser who is responsible for the design specification.

SOME ECONOMIC ASPECTS OF DECISIONS ON THE AMOUNT AND TYPE OF INSPECTION

Sometimes it is economical to do no inspection at all, sometimes 100 per cent inspection is the most economical, and sometimes sampling inspection of one type or another is better than either. The objective should be to select that amount and type of inspection that will minimize the sum of the production costs, acceptance costs, and unsatisfactory-product costs influenced by the decision regarding inspection. Once this viewpoint has been adopted, certain conditions are evident that are favorable, respectively, to no inspection, to 100 per cent inspection, and to sampling inspection.

Where submitted product is consistently satisfactory for the purpose intended, it is likely to be most economical to have no inspection whatever. In this case, there are no unsatisfactory-product costs to be reduced by inspection. Neither do there appear to be production costs such as spoilage and rework to be reduced by diagnosis of control charts or through the pressure for process improvement exerted when product is rejected. Sometimes, however, as in the case of overfill of containers, concealed opportunities may exist for reducing production costs; such opportunities might be disclosed by variables sampling inspection using control charts.

Low unsatisfactory-product costs per unit of such product may also make it economical to do no inspection whatever. For example, where unsatisfactory product is readily discovered and eliminated in a subsequent production operation, it may be cheaper to tolerate a moderate percentage of such product than to eliminate it by inspection.

Where submitted product is consistent in quality but nearly always contains a substantial percentage of unsatisfactory product, 100 per cent inspection may be the most economical alternative. Here the choice is likely to be between 100 per cent inspection and no inspection for acceptance purposes; with a statistically controlled product, sampling inspection cannot be expected to separate the relatively good lots from the relatively bad ones. The higher the percentage of unsatisfactory product submitted and the higher the unsatisfactory-product, the more favorable the conditions for 100 per cent inspection as compared with no inspection. The higher the unit cost of inspection and the less the effectiveness of 100 per cent inspection in eliminating unsatisfactory product, the more favorable the conditions for no inspection.

In making economy studies regarding the amount and type of inspection, it should be recognized that sampling inspection schemes may possibly reduce unsatisfactory-product costs in two ways. One way is by the rejection or rectification of the relatively bad lots of product, thereby making the proportion of unsatisfactory product approved less than the proportion submitted. The other way is by reducing the proportion of unsatisfactory product submitted; sampling inspection may improve quality through diagnosis of causes of quality troubles and through the exertion of effective pressure for process improvement. This improvement of product quality may also reduce production costs, particularly costs of spoilage and rework.

If this possible contribution of sampling inspection to the improvement of product quality is neglected, the following general statement may be made: The economic field for sampling inspection is where submitted product is usually good enough for no inspection to be more economical than 100% inspection and where submitted product is occasionally bad enough for 100% inspection to be more economical than no inspection.

DETERMINING THE BEST ORGANIZATION FOR YOUR PLANT[2]

It is a truism that quality must be *built* into a product; it cannot be *inspected* into it. It therefore follows that the responsibility for quality ultimately lies in the hands of the manager of production. The supervisor of quality control, who reports to the production manager, is on an equal plane with the other staff positions on the organization chart. By reporting to the top manufacturing executive, this supervisor is given the prestige and backing required for making final decisions in regard to product quality.

Compare the typical organization charts of two different metal working plants—one, Exhibit 8-1, an electro-mechanical assembly, jobbing-type shop with five hundred production employees; and the other, Exhibit 8-2, an electronic component and assembly-type shop with two hundred production employees.

This department generally has four classes of inspection:[3]

Class	Inspection Functions Performed by:
(1) Tool and gage	Tool and gage inspectors
(2) Process Inspection	Patrol inspectors
(3) Lot Sampling	Final inspection
(4) Acceptance Sampling	Receiving inspectors

In addition, the department has a staff function of Quality Control Engineering, which responsibilities are performed by the Quality Analyst.

Quality Responsibilities

(1) Tool and Gage Inspection. The function and responsibilities of this class of inspection are as follows:

(a) The inspection of all tools, gages, etc., whether fabricated internally or externally (outside vendors).

(b) Inspection of first piece parts, both fabricated and outside vendors.

(c) Inspection of last parts produced in the main shop.

(d) Inspection of experimental tooling, parts, etc., that may be required.

(e) Maintain adequate gage control, by the inspection of all gages and inspection equipment after usage.

---

2 Lewis R. Zeyher, *Production Manager's Desk Book,* (Englewood Cliffs, N.J.: Prentice-Hall, Inc., copyright © 1969), p. 51, lines 27-33.

3 Lewis R. Zeyher, *Cost Reduction in the Plant* (Englewood Cliffs, N.J.: Prentice-Hall, Inc., copyright © 1965), p. 29, lines 3-39; p. 30, lines 1-6.

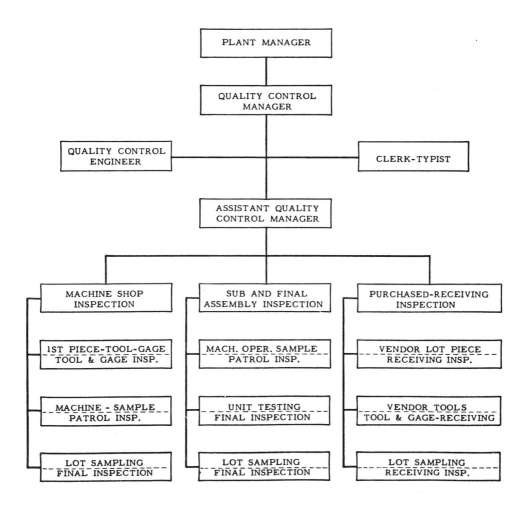

QUALITY CONTROL DEPARTMENT FUNCTIONAL
ORGANIZATION CHART

EXHIBIT 8-1

(2) **Process Inspection.** The functions and responsibilities of this class of inspection are:

(a) To perform periodical machine inspections and to record inspection results on inspection forms provided at each machine.

(b) To advise the production operator when defective work has been found.

(c) To see that all rejected material is removed from the machine and properly identified as to the reason for rejection.

QUALITY   CONTROL   DEPARTMENT

```
                              ┌──────────────┐
                              │   MANAGER    │ ◄──── Reporting to V. P. of Manufacturing
                              └──────────────┘
                 ┌──────────────────┐        ┌──────────────────┐
                 │ QUALITY ANALYST  │────────│ CHIEF INSPECTOR  │
                 └──────────────────┘        └──────────────────┘
```

RECEIVING INSP. (INSP. CRIB)	GAGE INSP.	FLOOR INSP. (PLANT-1)	FLOOR INSP. (PLANTS-2-4)	TOOL INSP.
WORK LEADER		WORK LEADER	WORK LEADER	INSPECTORS
RECEIVING	FIRST PIECE	FIRST PIECE	PROCESS	PROCESS
RECEIVING	FIRST PIECE	PROCESS	PROCESS	PROCESS
FINAL	FIRST PIECE	PROCESS	PROCESS	PROCESS
FINAL	FIRST PIECE (NIGHTS)	PROCESS	PROCESS	PROCESS
FINAL	PROCESS (NIGHTS)	FINAL	FINAL	PROCESS
	PROCESS (NIGHTS)	FINAL	FINAL	

EXHIBIT 8-2

(3) Lot Sampling. The functions and responsibilities of this class of inspection are:

(a) Remove from the production lots a quantity of parts and, based on the results of the inspection, accept or reject the entire lot.

(b) See that all rejected and reworked material has been corrected by taking samples from the lot and inspecting for the defects called out in the original rejections.

(4) Acceptance Sampling. The functions and responsibilities of this class of inspection are:

(a) Refer to single sampling plan shown in MIL-Standard, entitled "Sampling Procedures and Tables for Inspection by Attributes," or similar tables, and remove quantity of parts from the lot. Then based on the results of the inspection of the samples, accept or reject the entire lot.

(b) Perform 100 per cent screening of rejected lots and see that acceptable parts are identified and sent to stock and rejected parts returned to vendor.

NOTE: The staff function of Quality Control Engineering will be discussed in a separate section which follows.

Quality Engineering[4]

This responsibility generally rests with the quality analyst, an engineering position reporting directly to the supervisor of the department. In the fulfillment of this responsibility he engages in two major activities:

(1) New-Design Control

(a) Provides pre-production services to design engineering and manufacturing engineering in analyzing the "quality-ability" of new products and production processes and in debugging quality problems.

(b) Performs the planning of inspection and tests to be carried on when production is under way on the new product. This is to establish continuous control of in-process quality.

(c) Designs modern inspection and testing equipment—genuine quality control equipment rather than mere mechanized sorting devices.

(2) Incoming Material Control—to assist in the establishment of good quality relationships with suppliers by:

(a) Planning the periodic rating of the quality performance of present suppliers.

(b) Evaluating the quality capability of potential suppliers, thereby aiding purchasing.

(c) Establishing quality certification programs, which places the burden of quality proof on vendor.

Other duties include preserving adequate records, training inspectors, providing advice to supervisors, maintaining discipline, initiating quality improvement programs, keeping records of scrap and rework costs by departments, keeping vendors' performance records, improving communications, checking on working conditions of subordinates and maintaining the proper rapport with the personnel of all plant departments concerned with quality control procedures.

INSPECTION PROCEDURE

The flow chart inspection system presented in Exhibit 8-3 depicts only one method— your plant may require an entirely different approach. As indicated earlier in this chapter, each system must be tailored to your particular situation. There is *no one* standard plan that will fit every plant's situation.

---

[4] Lewis R. Zeyher, *Production Manager's Desk Book* (Englewood Cliffs, N.J.: Prentice-Hall, Inc., copyright © 1969), p. 52, lines 19-41; p. 53, lines 1-2.

RECEIVING INSPECTION PROCEDURE

MATERIAL AND RECEIVING REPORT

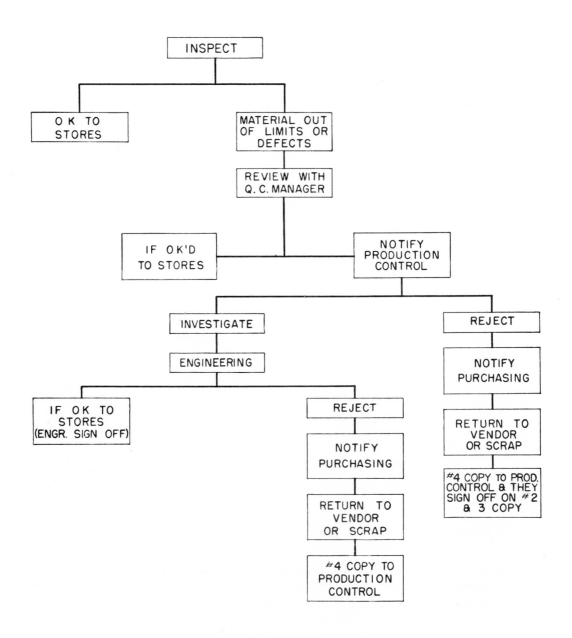

EXHIBIT 8-3

Notes on Inspection Procedure

(1) Statistical sampling plan is used which will economically control the quality of the product.

(2) For each operation in the manufacture of a part, the first piece fabricated, after the machine is set up to run the lot, requires the approval of the First Piece Inspector before the job is run. At suitable time intervals an inspection of the parts being run is made by a Process Inspector. In some cases, depending upon the type of operation and part, an inspection (sampling or detailing) of each batch will be made before passing the product on to the next operation. Critical parts are inspected 100 per cent. In general, standard gages are used unless special ones are furnished.

(3) A final inspection is made of all finished parts and assemblies. The final inspector covers the checking and inspection of all other operations on parts not covered by previous inspections and ascertains that all previously required inspections have been performed.

(4) Spare parts are inspected before packing and an inspection is made of packing just prior to sealing.

MAKING AN EFFECTIVE ANALYSIS OF COSTS[5]

Before you can organize and implement a program for improving your quality control function, you must determine the specific nature of your total quality control inspection costs. In consultation with the plant manager and the chief accountant, the following operating cost items should be investigated:

(1) Maintenance of the quality control department.
(2) Scrap.
(3) Rework.
(4) Handling customer returns.
(5) Machine down-time due to defective materials, tools, or poor maintenance.
(6) Servicing customer complaints.
(7) Spoilage.
(8) Special tests.
(9) Outside endorsements.
(10) Special packaging.
(11) Training.
(12) Quality maintenance of patterns and tools.
(13) Paper transactions.
(14) Maintaining test equipment.
(15) Selling "seconds" at lower than regular price.
(16) Excessive service adjustments and warranty problems.
(17) Uneconomical feeds and speeds, due to impractical specifications of finish or related requirement.
(18) Unrealistic specifications.
(19) Poor vendor performance.

---

[5] Lewis R. Zeyher, *Production Manager's Desk Book* (Englewood Cliffs, N.J.: Prentice-Hall, Inc., copyright © 1969), p. 34, lines 5-32.

(20) Due to inadequate tooling for the job required.

(21) Printing and duplicating—forms, records, procedures.

(22) Meetings.

(23) Review Board's time (if you maintain one).

(24) Telephoning.

(25) Accounting.

There are others, depending on the type of product and industry. There is little doubt that the costs of some of the above items are difficult to measure or even to estimate. An awareness of them, however, could bring about some improvement. (See Exhibits 8-4, 8-5, and 8-6 for suggested forms.)

A CHECKLIST FOR COST SAVINGS THROUGH BETTER QUALITY PERFORMANCE[6]

(1) Know what your quality control costs are.

(2) Have all the elements of your quality costs properly segregated.

(3) Clearly define the objectives of your quality control function.

(4) Be sure your senior plant executive receives adequate quality control reports.

(5) Be certain your employees know what all the benefits of quality control are.

(6) Obtain organization charts of your quality control department. Keep them up-to-date.

(7) Keep job descriptions of all your quality control department personnel.

(8) The quality control function should report to the senior executive of the plant.

(9) Conduct tool and gage inspection.

(10) Conduct process inspection.

(11) Conduct lot inspection.

(12) Conduct acceptance sampling.

(13) Obtain a quality analyst.

(14) Have your top plant executives assign all quality responsibilities on the factory floor.

(15) Prepare a standard procedure instruction manual covering all procedures and instructions of your quality control function.

(16) Keep a record of your production operators' quality performance.

(17) Provide your production foremen with their scrap and rework costs each month.

(18) Definitive disciplinary actions should be taken regarding employees with bad quality performances.

(19) Have your quality analyst provide pre-production service to design engineering and manufacturing engineering for new products.

(20) Conduct a scheduled checking and maintenance program for your test equipment.

(21) Keep a vendors' performance record.

(22) Keep your vendors periodically informed about their quality records.

(23) Be sure your quality control department works closely with your purchasing department in evaluating the quality capability of potential suppliers.

(24) Prepare a quality certification program.

---

6 Lewis R. Zeyher, *Cost Reduction in the Plant* (Englewood Cliffs, N.J. copyright © 1965), p. 37, lines 14-41; p. 38, lines 1-43; p. 39, lines 1-29.

TOOL & GAGE INSPECTION ROOM

PROPOSED LAYOUT-19' X 20'

SCALE $\frac{3"}{8} = 1'$

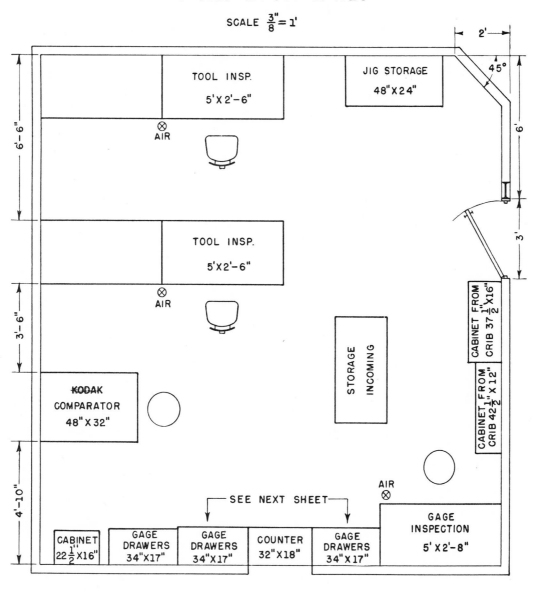

EXHIBIT 8-4

QUALITY CONTROL DAILY SCRAP REPORT

DATE _____

CUSTOMER	PART NO.	PART NAME	DEPT.	QUANTITY REJECTED	QUANTITY ON OPERATION	REASON	REMARKS	CORRECTIVE ACTION TAKEN
A	A-5931	Piston	Buffing	19	24	03	Undersize	
B	46A41254	Flywheel	Lathe	1	269	01	Undersize	
C	46A51254	Flywheel	Lathe	1	268	02	Deep undercut	
D	30F81732-3	Drum	Lathe	1	299	02	Tool marks	Badly bent before attempt to straighten
E	1-A-64	Playback Arm	Burr	19	231	03	Broken during straightening	
F	9718899	Sleeve Clutch	Drill	2	65	02	Hole too deep	Order complete
G	138432-2	Cam Shaft	Lathe	26	500	02	.499 dia. eccentric	All parts finished on operation concerned
H	46G41203	Base	Drill	1	274	02	Holes off location	
I	306070	Sleeve	Vendor	60	1600	53	Cracked ends	Vendor's error

REASON CODE:

01 Setup man
02 Machine Operator
03 Bench Worker
04 Assembly Man
05 Supervision
06 Insufficient Instruction
07 Short Count
08 Careless Handling

11 Inspector—Receiving
12 —Process
13 —Component Part
14 —Assembly
21 Operation Record—Missing Operation
22 —Wrong Sequence
23 —Cancelled Operation
31 Stores Handling—Trucking

32 —Containers
33 —Storage Bins
34 —Rust
51 Blueprint
52 Tools
53 Defective Material
54 Engineering Change
60 Other

EXHIBIT 8-5

QUALITY CONTROL DAILY REWORK REPORT

DATE _____

CUSTOMER	PART NO.	PART NAME	DEPT.	QUANTITY REJECTED	QUANTITY ON OPERATION	REASON	REMARKS	CORRECTICE ACTION TAKEN
A	A-5922	Piston	Buffing	9	155	03	Breakthru	
B	A-5931	Piston	Buffing	9	62	03	Breakthru	
C	A-8336	Attenuator	Eng.	104	655	54	Run fillet on flange	Engineering change as wished by customer
D	A-8254	Cavity Assy.	Drill	14	70	02	Holes off location	Blocks to be inspected before soldering
E	DC-1087	Connector	Drill	81	346	02	Bent in drilling	Dull Drill was used Inspector & Operator both shifts cautioned
F	A-5922	Piston	Plating	52	148	03	Poor Plating	Poor contact on plating bars - corrected
G	A-5931	Piston	Plating	1	61	03	Poor Plating	Plating Foreman

EXHIBIT 8-6

(25) Have your inspectors provide for on-the-spot shop-floor analysis of defects when practicable.

(26) Be certain your inspectors feed back facts about defects from floor so corrective actions can be taken elsewhere.

(27) Have your plant organize an effective quality improvement program.

(28) Arrange to have your production employees adequately trained in the specific remedies to apply to their jobs so defects can be minimized.

(29) Make sure your supervisors have been properly trained in how to instruct their subordinates in quality improvement.

(30) Encourage employees to offer suggestions on quality improvement, and do something about these suggestions.

(31) Be sure aggressive efforts are made by your management to keep employees informed of progress regarding quality performance.

(32) Recognize and reward exceptional quality performances on the part of production employees.

(33) Be certain organized efforts are made to sustain quality interest after a formal program is concluded.

(34) Prohibit the use of marked-up prints to be used in the shop.

(35) Discourage the practice of your supervisors' maintaining private print files.

(36) Eliminate the utilization of make-shift tooling cn the production floor.

(37) Prepare an effective method of keeping altered or damaged tooling out of production.

(38) Prohibit the practice of your engineering department approving sub-standard work but then not approving the revision of the print.

(39) Minimize the practice of modifying completed manufactured parts, usually during assembly operations.

(40) Conduct a program of checking for and eliminating use of shabby and unreliable inspection equipment.

(41) Assure yourself that your inspection department has a uniform method established for properly identifying acceptable work.

(42) Make sure your methods for isolating defective work are adequate for your type of industry.

(43) Insist on only required tolerances coupled with adequate controls instead of unnecessarily tight tolerances due to loose controls.

(44) Assure yourself that you have adequate handling and storage facilities to protect the quality of your product in the plant.

(45) Review occasionally the adequacy of your product packaging to insure its safe arrival at destination.

(46) Assure yourself that all your supervisors have the proper attitude toward quality.

(47) Make sure your employees are properly informed regarding the nature of your customers' quality complaints.

(48) Be certain you employ the practice of having your suppliers verify their final inspection rather than requiring your company inspectors to perform a receiving inspection for them.

(49) Prohibit the practice of the engineering department issuing ambiguous, incomplete, and inaccurate drawings and related information to other operating departments.

(50) Do not tolerate the practice of some supervisors and employees to intimidate inspectors, and have an effective method of revealing the identity of those responsible.

(51) Make sure your inspection records and reports are accurate and complete.

(52) Arrange for your system to reveal and properly identify the cause of defective work and to eliminate it subsequently.

(53) Insist that your top management have the company quality control system periodically auditied by internal as well as external sources.

(54) Periodically have your plant executives apply work-sampling techniques to test the effectiveness of your quality control program.

(55) Conduct a continuous training program for your quality control personnel with emphasis on new personnel.

(56) Be sure you have a program of developing better quality control and inspection methods.

(57) Periodically conduct a plant survey looking specifically for possible improvements in working conditions for both operators and inspectors in lighting, heat, ventilation, and workplace.

9

Warehousing—
Determination of
Location and Control

One of the most neglected areas for potential cost reduction is in warehousing operations. Many companies who have aggressively explored this field of the functions of receiving, storing, and shipping, have accomplished many worthwhile savings. In addition, this area lends itself well to engineered cost controls thereby providing for more efficient management.

In this chapter we cover the high spots of operations found in site selection, cost elements of construction, design factors of facilities, warehouse planning processes, measuring performance and controlling costs.

DETERMINING GEOGRAPHIC LOCATION AND SITE[1]

Proper selection of warehouse locations is essential to an effective distribution system. The difference between carefully selected locations and random selections could well mean the difference between a successful warehouse system and one that is doomed to failure. Improper locations could result in many serious problems, such as poor service to customers, high operating costs, excessive loss due to theft, and high freight costs. The selection of warehouse locations is too often based on the desire of the warehouse and sales managers to live in a certain place, or on an exceptionally good buy in real estate. Such personal and incidental reasons should remain secondary to those that have a direct bearing on the success of the warehousing operation. Some of the main considerations in selecting warehouse locations are listed and discussed here.

(1) Delivery-Time Requirements

There is a wide range in the delivery-time requirements for different product lines. To be competitive, some products must reach the customers within a few hours after

---

1 From *Modern Warehousing Management,* Creed H. Jenkins. Copyright © 1968 by McGraw-Hill, Inc., used with permission of McGraw-Hill Book Company. P. 39, lines 3-39; p. 40, lines 1-16, 35-39; p. 41, lines 1-41; p. 42, lines 1-43; p. 43, lines 1-36; p. 44, lines 1-27 partial; p. 45, lines 13-21; p. 46, lines partial; p. 47, partial; p. 48-64 only items listed; p. 69, lines 11-31; p. 70, lines 9-12; p. 71, lines 3, 16-19, 31, 40-4; p. 72, lines 10-34.

placement of the order. Other types of products have a normal delivery time of 1 to 2 weeks. The specific delivery-time requirements for the particular products to be warehoused should be established before warehouse locations are determined.

(2) Customers

Warehouses should be centrally located with regard to the markets that are to be served. Knowing who and where the customers are is essential to a proper choice of the warehouse location. This information should be supplied by the sales or marketing organization. Provisions should be made for potential new customers as well as for existing customers. Research should be conducted to determine factors and trends that will effect changes in the present conditions. Marketing conditions are characteristically dynamic, even ever-changing. A good location for a warehouse one day could be literally all wrong the next, if the warehouse's purpose were to service one large customer and that one customer went out of business or moved. Even when the warehouse has a broader customer base, the hazard of potential market change may make the warehouse location obsolete. Since warehousing depends on customers, the best that can be done is to try to anticipate what the customers will do. Some of the clues to changing markets are listed here.

(a) **Population Trends:** Examples are the movement from the farms to the cities, from the East to the West, from the steelmaking and mining areas to the electronics, space, and research centers.

(b) **Industry Trends:** Examples are changes from surface transportation to air, from overalls to pants, from iceboxes to refrigerators, from heavy metals to light metals, and from tubes to transistors.

(c) **Recreation Trends:** Examples are changes from movie theaters to home television and from black and white to color television, the comeback of bowling and billiards, and the increase in foreign travel.

(d) **Business Management Trends:** Examples are increased use of data processing, telecommunications, and specialists of all varieties; and the increased growth of big companies with more and more centralization.

These and other such trends change the flow of goods and therefore can influence every phase of warehousing. Markets and business in general will continue to change. Warehouse management must do its best to anticipate the changes and use them to its advantage when possible.

(3) Distribution Centers

When locating a warehouse or a system of warehouses, management should look first to the distribution centers of the nation. Certain cities are natural centers for marketing and distribution. Locating in or near these cities will greatly reduce the risk of warehouse investment. Some cities have a much greater proportion of their business and real estate related to warehousing than do others. This is so because they are geographic centers of industry or population, or because they serve as a hub or gateway for rail, truck or water shipping. Another reason, quite unrelated to the natural flow of goods, is that certain cities and states induce warehousing to locate within their boundaries by establishing favorable tax conditions. For these reasons and others, including the promotional efforts of interested parties, a large part of the economy of certain areas depends upon warehousing. Other localities that may have greater population or be centers of a specific type of industry will have little or no warehousing. Some of the major marketing and warehousing centers of the nation are:

Seattle	Houston
Portland	New Orleans
San Francisco	Atlanta
Kansas City	Miami
Dallas	State of New Jersey
	Great Lakes Region
	(Chicago in particular)

This is by no means all-inclusive. For instance, it does not include certain major distribution centers for specific types of commodities and specific types of warehousing. It includes only localities that have long been recognized as important general warehousing centers. The list is not static, either. New centers will emerge and add to, or take the place of, those that are now most prominent.

(4) Industrial Parks

Within the major distribution centers, and many of the lesser centers, industrial parks or communities are located. These parks consist of certain defined areas, generally in the suburbs of a large city, that are developed and promoted to attract light industry and warehousing. The promotors of these areas obtain local zoning ordinances and establish specific ordinances of their own to attract and hold the type of business they are after. Although these industrial parks are developed with the primary interest of making money for the landowners and promoters, the parks do provide many real advantages for warehouse locations. Consequently, they are becoming widespread throughout the nation. It is becoming more and more unusual to build a warehouse in an area all by itself. Warehouses and light industry locate together in clusters whether the name of industrial park is adopted or not.

Some of the advnatages of the industrial-park type of location are listed here:

(a) Carrier Service: Because an industrial park generally has many businesses that have to ship and receive, carriers can economically provide regular and reliable service to the area. If payloads cannot be picked up from one customer, they probably can be from one or several others in the area. The industrial park provides a ready-made market center for common carriers' services. On the other hand, if a warehouse were to locate by itself away from other businesses that provide freight, it is quite likely that carriers would not provide such good services, because it would be uneconomical for the limited and uncertain amount of freight available. Even rail lines are able to provide better switching services when many businesses requiring this service are located in the same area.

(b) Common Interests: The purpose of industrial parks is to provide an area where the zoning and services will attract and hold certain types of business. Most industrial parks today are set up to attract warehousing and light industry. One of the advantages of a community that is made up of this type of business is that many interests are common to all. Although the businesses may be competitive in some ways, they have certain similar requirements that can be filled when several companies are doing similar types of business. One business establishment standing alone has its own strength and resources to draw on, while many working together will be much stronger.

Some of the common interests that are best satisfied in an industrial type of community are:

Police and security-patrol protection
Street cleaning and repair services
Truck and rail services
Low property tax assessments
Favorable zoning controls
Good restaurants in vicinity
Availability of labor supply
Increased strength in labor negotiations
Availability of equipment-repair services

(c) Protected Investment: Another important consideration in selecting a warehouse location is to find one that is good now and that will continue to remain good. The industrial-park type location offers some assurance of this. Because of common interests discussed before, there is a greater likelihood that the community will not change into one that will be undesirable for warehousing. The united pressures that can be brought to bear to maintain favorable conditions serve to protect the individual investments. A warehouse that is located alone in an area has much less chance of maintaining the desired environment.

(d) Financing: Whether the warehouse is to be leased or purchased, some type of financing will be involved. If it is to be leased, the owner's financial plan will probably be for the lessee to make payments out of future earnings. The terms of the lease are very important to him as well as to the lessee. Generally, the best rate can be agreed upon if it is a long-term lease. However, the risk for the lessee increases with the length of the lease. If the warehouse is located in an area that is favorable to warehousing and has a good change of remaining favorable, the risk is greatly reduced. The modern type of industrial park generally provides this kind of situation.

If the warehouse is to be purchased, the same risks are involved; however, the additional problem of initial financing is encountered. Banks and other lending institutions want the best security possible for their loans. If the warehouse is in a prime industrial park which is located in one of the nation's distribution centers, the location is considered desirable. A desirable location will make it easier to get a good loan on the property. The loan company can afford to give the best rates and the maximum coverage in such a case because their risk is minimal.

DETERMINATION OF MOST ECONOMICAL SHIPPING TERMINAL BETWEEN TWO SOURCES
(Actual Situation)

A large corporation operated two plants that basically produced the same products. One plant was located in Mississippi and the other in New Jersey. A management study of both plants was made and recommendations submitted to top management to close the New Jersey plant and move all operations to the Mississippi plant. The supporting data is listed below:

Supporting Data and Exhibit

(1) Supervisory attitudes at New Jersey plant poor.

(2) Low production employee productivity.

(3) Low volume and high cost plant operation.

(4) Production costs per unit favored the Mississippi plant.

(5) New Jersey plant had surplus production facilities resulting in under-absorption of burden expense.

(6) Mississippi plant's percentage of gross profit to sales was almost twice as great as New Jersey plant's percentage.

(7) New Jersey's organizational structure was top-heavy with supervisory and staff personnel in relation to sales volume, duties and responsibilities of positions.

(8) Maintenance and engineering costs were high and labor poorly controlled.

(9) New Jersey plant facilities were old and in some instances obsolete—buildings were in need of repair and were out-of-date.

(10) The air polution problem was greater in the New Jersey plant than in the southern plant.

(11) Sewage disposal was a major problem in New Jersey, less so in Mississippi.

(12) On a straight-line mileage and customer volume basis, there were only fourteen states closer to New Jersey terminal than to Mississippi plant with sales volume of New Jersey plant only 10 per cent of the total U.S. sales.

(13) Mississippi's terminal production costs were much lower.

(14) Insurance savings considerable by moving to Mississippi.

(15) Additional advantages to be gained by this move included:

(a) Mississippi terminal location was closer to the fast-growing western, southwestern, and southern states, industrially and in population. (See Exhibit 9-1.) These areas forecasted growth potentials far greater than the eastern states.

(b) This location also provided more room for plant expansion.

(c) More modern plant and a demonstrated superior management team.

NOTE: This recommended move was consummated with excellent results in all operating and financial areas. Additional advantages also occurred that had not been forecast or foreseen.

COST ELEMENTS OF CONSTRUCTION

The two main considerations in selecting the right warehouse structure are the initial capital outlay (or financial commitment, if the building is leased) and the continuing operating expenses. It would be false economy to save money in the building construction if this were to cause greater loss in operating expenses. On the other hand, it would be as great a waste to put more into the building than was necessary. The objective is to reach an optimum balance between initial and continuing costs. The best way to do so is to determine, analyze, and evaluate all the elements that affect these costs. The more important of these elements are indicated in the following:

Determination of Most Economical Shipping Terminal–Geographically

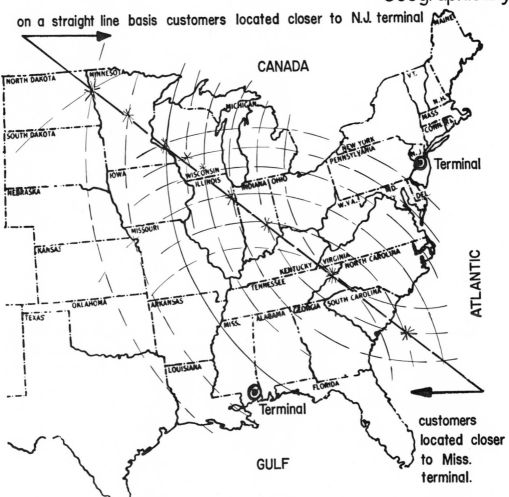

EXHIBIT 9-1

(A) Site Selection

(1) Rail service   (4) Building code
(2) Truck service   (5) Neighborhood
(3) Cost of land   (6) Advertising

(B) Construction Cost Factors

The cost of the building should include all permanent expenditures related to complete and efficient structure. If an existing building is leased or purchased, the cost of alterations must be considered; however, the discussion here will mainly be directed toward the construction of a new building. Many factors involved in such a venture would also apply to the acquisition of an existing building.

The following represents the cost elements encountered in new warehouse construction: (should more detail be required see Creed H. Jenkins' *Modern Warehouse Management,* published by McGraw-Hill Book Company, New York, N.Y.)

(1) Professional fees
(2) Evacuation, foundations, grading
(3) Electric wiring
(4) Sprinkler system
(5) Heating system
(6) Ventilating system
(7) Security
(8) Air conditioning
(9) Communications system
(10) Rest rooms
(11) Water cooler
(12) Lunch room

Facility-Design Factors

(1) *Rail-dock requirements*
   (a) Enclosed rail-dock
   (b) Dock level
   (c) Dock dimensions
(2) *Truck-dock requirements*
   (a) Recessed truck docks
   (b) Dock level
   (c) Covered outside dock
   (d) Dock plates
(3) *Building size*
   (a) Height
   (b) Width-length ratio
   (c) Configuration efficiency

(D) Building Materials

(1) Steel
(2) Aluminum

    (3) Brick and concrete block
    (4) Tilt-wall concrete
    (5) Wood

(E) Building Code Restrictions
    (Items of Typical Building Restrictions)

    (1) Space occupancy
    (2) Landscaping
    (3) Business regulation
    (4) Parking area
    (5) Storage areas
    (6) Partly finished construction
    (7) Evacuation
    (8) Building materials
    (9) County building code

THE WAREHOUSE PLANNING PROCESS

Step 1—Establish the Objectives

Objectives for Overall Warehouse Operations

- To provide minimum-cost warehousing, even though service may be sacrificed.
- To provide minimum-cost warehousing while maintaining the desired level of service.
- To provide better service than competition, regardless of costs.
- To provide competitive service at the lowest possible cost.
- To maintain a level of housekeeping and storage that will provide a "showcase" for the company's products.

Specific Layout Objectives for Storage Layout Program

- To utilize space to the maximum.
- To provide for the most efficient material handling.
- To provide the most economical storage in relation to the costs of equipment, space, material damage, and handling labor.
- To provide maximum flexibility to meet changing storage and handling requirements.
- To make the warehouse a model of good housekeeping.

Step 2—Gather the Facts

The main facts relevant to layout planning are the exact dimensions of the warehouse, the inventory plan in detail, and the planned sales volume for each item to be warehoused.

Step 3—Analysis

With the facts collected which relate to the physical dimensions of the warehouse, the dimension of racks, the specifications of handling equipment, and the inventory plan, analysis can begin.

Step 4—Formulate the Plan

Most successful layout programs make use of some form of building plan drawn or otherwise prepared to a reduced scale, such as 1/4 inch to 2 feet. Movable templates representing racks and other equipment are also useful in determining the best layout.

Step 5—Implement the Plan

Implementation of a warehouse layout—shifting stocks, erecting racks, lining aisles, bringing in new stocks, etc.—should be scheduled like any other warehouse work as to timing and manpower requirements. The layout will be accomplished more effectively if it can be carried out during a time when there is no shipping and receiving activity.

A good warehouse layout, with a master control drawing and prints for working copies, should provide the following:

(a) An effective means for the manager to control where materials are stored.
(b) A miniature view of the entire warehouse to plan the best storage and handling programs.

Step 6—Follow-up

Unless a concerted effort is made to maintain the layout to meet changing requirements, it will soon become ineffective. A good layout is not something that once done stays done. It must be maintained continuously.

A tool essential to this maintenance and follow-up is the master layout drawing. The master drawing should be changed only with the authorization of the manager. The actual storage should conform to the master drawing; any change in the storage should be planned on the drawing first. Mistakes are easily observed and corrected on paper. They are more difficult to detect and much more costly to correct when dealing with actual materials storage.

WAREHOUSE ORDER PICKING AND ASSEMBLY DISCIPLINES[2]

Several basic disciplines are used to select the items needed to make up a shipment, marshall them, and dispatch them to shipping.

(1) The Area System

The merchandise is stored, with the inventory of each item together, the items arranged in some logical pattern. The order picker circulates through the warehouse picking each item in turn until the order is complete; the order is then transported to a packing and dispatching area for shipment. The system is self-marshalling, since each order is accumulated individually as the picking proceeds.

(2) The Modified Area System

The system operates as does the area system, except the inventory is divided between working stock and reserve stock. A secondary work force or process is employed to replenish working stock from reserve stock.

---

[2] John F. Magee, *Physical Distribution Systems* (New York: McGraw-Hill, Inc. Copyright © 1967). P. 80, lines 31-37; p. 81, lines 1-41; p. 82, lines 1-11.

(3) The Zone System

Each picker or group of pickers works within a specified warehouse or merchandise zone. The order is "exploded," that is, divided down by zone, and each portion is sent to the appropriate zone for selection and transport to a marshalling area where the order is assembled for shipment. Each zone operates according to the area or modified area zone.

(4) The Sequential Zone System

Each portion of the order is picked in the appropriate zone, and the order is transported from zone to zone in sequence as it is assembled. One order after another can be started into the sequence of zones.

(5) The Multiple-Order, Explosion, or Schedule System

A group of orders is collected, and tickets or other indication of items required to fill the group are prepared and sorted by zone. The items from each zone are selected and transported to the marshalling area, where the items are sorted by order, and the order assembled. This system requires careful control to assure that all the items for an order, and only those, are brought together. Generally, each order is assigned a time at which all items are to arrive in the marshalling area and a position in the area in which they are to be put as they arrive; the material handling system is set up to collect items from each picking zone on a set time schedule and sort them to the right location in the marshalling area.

The area system is undoubtedly the most common system in use. It is simple to manage and control. However, it becomes unwieldy when the number of orders or the number of items is large. The zone system is an effort to meet this difficulty by breaking the total order-filling system into a series of areas operated in parallel (the zone system) or in sequence (the sequential zone system). When the area system, or a modification, is mechanized, the capacity of the system is hard to adjust to accommodate changes in load.

The multiple-order or schedule system is better adapted to circumstances where large numbers of items are managed and a very large number of small orders, few items per order, must be processed. While it is more complex to manage, the schedule system has great flexibility and capability to expand or contract under load variations.

MEASURING WAREHOUSE PERFORMANCE AND CONTROLLING COSTS[3]

(a) Measuring Warehouse Performance

The application of engineering time standards to shipping, receiving and warehousing should be considered. Handling times and space utilization standards can be used to great advantage in lowering costs and improving operating efficiencies. Exhibit 9-2 depicts a performance-control report for handling time and space utilization. The report covers only four product lines and two warehouses, but the same

---

[3] From *Modern Warehousing Management*, Creed H. Jenkins, copyright © 1968 by McGraw-Hill, Inc. Used with permission of McGraw-Hill Book Company, p. 108, lines 35-41; p. 109, Exhibit 16; p. 242, lines 22-41; p. 243, lines 1-14 and Exhibit 28.

WAREHOUSE PERFORMANCE REPORT

Month and Year _____

HANDLING TIME
Standard versus Actual Hours

PRODUCT LINE	LOS ANGELES Warehouse			SEATTLE Warehouse			TOTAL This Month			YEAR-TO-DATE		
	St'd.	Act.	%	St'd.	Act.	%	St'd.	Act.	%	St'd.	Act.	%
A	400	500	80	100	150	67	500	650	77	1,800	2,100	86
B	300	350	86	200	200	100	500	550	91	1,400	1,500	93
C	460	600	77	150	140	107	610	740	82	1,650	1,900	87
D	150	200	75	200	220	91	350	420	83	1,000	1,400	71
Total	1,310	1,650	79	650	710	92	1,960	2,360	83			
Year-to-Date	3,720	4,650	80	2,130	2,250	95	---	---	---	5,850	6,900	85

SPACE UTILIZATION
Standard versus Actual M Sq Ft

PRODUCT LINE	LOS ANGELES Warehouse			SEATTLE Warehouse			TOTAL This Month			YEAR-TO-DATE		
	St'd.	Act.	%	St'd.	Act.	%	St'd.	Act.	%	St'd.	Act.	%
A	18M	20M	90	12M	16M	75	30M	36M	83	78M	97M	80
B	6	8	75	8	10	80	14	18	78	50	75	67
C	26	34	76	4	4	100	30	38	79	90	98	92
D	4	8	50	14	15	93	18	23	78	55	75	73
Total	54M	70M	77	38M	45M	84	92M	115M	80			
Year-to-Date	158M	210M	75	115M	135M	85	---	---	---	273M	345M	79

EXHIBIT 9-2

type of report is applicable to warehousing systems involving many different product lines and many warehouses. The same kind of report is also appropriate for a single warehouse operation. Such a report can provide management with valuable insight into its warehousing operations.

(b) Controlling Costs

The forecast of operations should take into consideration the following influences on warehouse expenditures:

(1) Types and quantities of products to be warehoused. This is commonly referred to as "product mix."
(2) Major repair projects for buildings and equipment.
(3) Major stock-rearrangement projects.
(4) Equipment additions and deletions.

(5) Space additions and deletions.
(6) Personnel requirements.
(7) Wages and salary adjustments.
(8) Travel and entertainment plans.

This forecast of operations should then be converted into an expense budget by assigning estimated costs to a prescribed classification of expenses. Estimates of costs should be based on the best information sources available, which include historical data, engineered standards, and the warehouse manager's educated guesses.

Refer to Exhibit 9-3 for an example of an operations and expense budget for a medium-size warehouse. When the budget is approved by the warehouse manager and his manager, a copy is given to accounting to use in reporting actual expenses against budget. This performance report contains the same expense accounts as those used in the approved budget.

SUMMARY EXPENSE BUDGET
Warehouse Operations Division

(Forecast of Monthly Expense by Quarter)

Warehouse_____   Year_____

	AVERAGE MONTHLY TOTALS				AVERAGE MONTH FOR YEAR
	1st Qtr.	2nd Qtr.	3rd Qtr.	4th Qtr.	
Operating Forecast					
1. Shipping volume, in M units	100	175	200	150	156
2. Storage inventory, in M units	400	300	250	300	312
3. Space: office, in M ft	2	2	2	2	2
4. Space: storage, in M ft	53	53	53	53	53
5. Salary personnel	4	4	4	4	4
6. Direct labor hours	1,330	1,630	1,630	1,400	1,497
7. Lift trucks	4	4	4	4	4
Expenses Account					
1. Salaries	$ 3,500	$ 3,700	$ 3,700	$ 3,800	$ 3,675
2. Wages	5,700	6,900	6,900	6,000	6,375
3. Equipment depreciation	600	600	600	600	600
4. Equipment rental					
5. Equipment operation	200	300	300	200	250
6. Equipment repairs	200	600	200	200	300
7. Building depreciation					
8. Building rent	3,600	3,600	3,600	3,600	3,600
9. Building repairs	700	100	100	100	250
10. Packing supplies	100	180	200	160	160
11. Office supplies	50	90	100	80	80
12. Travel and lodging	200	50	50	40	85
13. Communications	250	350	350	250	300
14. Utilities	200	100	100	200	150
15. Property taxes	700	700	700	700	700
16. Miscellaneous	200	200	200	200	200
17. Total	$16,200	$17,470	$17,100	$16,130	$16,725

Approvals:_____   _____

EXHIBIT 9-3

10

Taking Optimum Advantage of the Industrial Engineering Function

A well-staffed and competent industrial engineering department can play a vital role in the administration of a production facility. If the skills of its personnel are properly utilized, this department could well be the most potent force on your management team. If its potential is effectively exploited you will have gone a long way toward the achievement of your production objectives. In most instances this function exists primarily to provide specialized services to the production division.

SCOPE OF INDUSTRIAL ENGINEERING FUNCTION

What are the responsibilities generally assigned to this department in a medium to large plant?

Floor Layout

Plan floor layout of machinery, equipment, benches, offices, warehouses, tool cribs, parking lots, factory additions and new plants.

Methods Engineering[1]

Involves the close analysis of all operations in order to determine the quickest and best procedure for performing each necessary operation. Briefly, the purpose of methods engineering is to establish and improve standards of accomplishment. Such standards are essential to the modern administrator, whether his responsibilities lie in agriculture, a bank, a drug store, a government department, a hotel, a school, or an industry. In these and other instances, the aim is to obtain the optimum return possible from investment in equipment and personnel.

---

[1] Winston Rodgers, "Methods Engineering," *Industrial Engineering Handbook*, H.B. Maynard, Ed., 1st Ed. (New York: McGraw-Hill, Copyright © 1955). Section 2, Chapter 1, lines 2-7.

Measuring Work[2]

This involves the utilization of such work-measuring techniques as time study, methods-time-measurement, work-factor method or estimating to determine the time necessary for an operation to be performed by an experienced operator, working effectively at a normal pace in a predetermined manner and taking adequate allowed time for fatigue and personal needs. On the basis of this information production standards are established for control purposes.

Material Handling

Aid in determination of the need for material handling equipment for a specific use. Then assist in the selection of the correct piece of equipment after this decision is made.

Job Evaluation

This responsibility is usually assigned either to the industrial engineering or personnel departments. This involves writing up job descriptions for each job in the plant and office and subjecting them to an evaluation procedure. From this analysis, wage and salary rates are determined.

Standard Procedure Instruction Manuals

This responsibility is assigned either to the industrial engineering department or controller's office. This involves the preparation, maintenance and control of written instructions and procedures covering all systems, forms, regulations and procedures of the company.

Paperwork Analysis

This involves the review of all paperwork operations with the objective of improving as well as streamlining them. New forms and procedures are constantly being introduced, while at the same time the old procedures and reports continue undiminished, even though the need for some no longer exists.

Cost Reduction Programs

The industrial engineering department is in the best position to spearhead an attack on excessive operating costs. While periodic, special cost reduction programs should continue to be initiated, it should not be forgotten that this is a continuous, day-to-day responsibility of this department.

Aid in Training Programs

This is an ideal department to use for employee training courses, depending, of course, on the program's training objectives. There should be considerable involvement here.

---

2 Lewis R. Zeyher, *Production Manager's Desk Book* (Englewood Cliffs, N.J.: Prentice-Hall, Inc., copyright © 1969), p. 46, lines 1-7; p. 47, lines 1-36; p. 48, lines 1-44; p. 49, lines 1-47; p. 50, lines 1-24.

Waste Control

Determine methods that can be employed to control waste and to increase material yields. Are they effective? Could changes produce greater yields?

Ratio and Delay Studies

Where production performances are continually below standards, time-study engineers should conduct four- to eight-hour delay studies. These will uncover the operating deficiencies that require attention. Follow up on compliance with resulting recommendations.

Product Design

Industrial engineering knowledge and thinking can have a great influence on product designs. How deeply involved do the engineers get with your product development department? They should sit in on planning sessions and their advice should be sought, particularly in regards to cost factors. The personnel of the subject department should play an important role in product design development.

Safety and Accident Prevention

An engineer from this department should be a member of the plant safety committee and actively participate in their programs.

Union Stewards' Training

In union organized plants this department should provide a training course in time study and industrial engineering appreciation. It is generally worth the time expended.

Aid in Preparing Arbitration Cases

This department can provide invaluable engineering services to help the personnel department prepare for arbitration cases. All technical data required should be developed and thoroughly discussed with other interested members of management before the arbitration meeting.

Employees' Suggestion System

The manager of this department should either act as chairman of the Employees' Suggestion System or a subordinate should be a member of the Committee. The methods engineers should also be available to assist production and office employees with any technical advice required in the submission of their suggestions.

Justifying the Purchase of New Equipment

The personnel of this department should be available to assist department foremen and related management personnel in the necessary mathematical calculations required in their justification proposals for buying new equipment.

Work with Accounting Department in Establishing Budgetary Controls

This department should cooperate and assist the personnel of the accounting department to develop, install, and maintain an effective budgetary control system, particularly those based on engineered standards. They should also encourage and aid supervisors in establishing special controls for their individual departments and help them in maintaining accurate controls.

Cooperate with Purchasing Department in the Utilization of Value Analysis Principles

Purchasing department and industrial engineering personnel can make up a potent force for analyzing company products to determine a cheaper way to get desirable quality, acceptable performance and still retain, if not improve upon, existing sales features.

Assist Supervisors in First Detecting and Then Minimizing Production Bottlenecks

Industrial engineering personnel are in an advantageous position for detecting production delays and bottlenecks. While their responsibilities do not include the right to take definitive remedial actions, they can act as the eyes and ears of those supervisors who can take required actions.

Assist Production Supervisors in Making Crew Determinations

Where conveyors are widely used and labor crews are required industrial engineers are specifically trained to make these determinations on an economical basis. They should always be available for these assignments.

Participate in Short and Long Range Planning

Industrial engineers are uniquely well equipped to participate in establishing short and long range planning goals and programs, as well as to follow up on progress.

Estimating Production Cost for New Jobs

Due to the availability of production figures, standard data, efficiency records, knowledge of machines, product elements and equipment, as well as training and skills in this area, the senior men of this department are usually used for estimating assignments.

Other Duties

Due to their broad knowledge of the company's facilities, products and organization, engineers in this department are often utilized for many and varied assignments. Just a few follow: put in charge of taking the annual physical inventory, visiting important customers on product quality problems, estimating damage claims, packaging design and problems, assisting in computerization of management controls, checking on incentive pay grievances, selling new methods to foremen, help manufacturing engineering in the modernization of plant machinery and equipment plans, aid production control regarding use of certain materials and substitution of same with cheaper and better substances, and related activities.

ORGANIZING THE INDUSTRIAL ENGINEERING FUNCTION FOR THE SMALL COMPANY

Research has shown that industrial engineering principles can be used to advantage in any size company and all types of industry. In support of these research findings a personal experience can be recalled where the plant manager of a chemical plant of one hundred employees remarked that his type company could not use industrial engineering practices, such as time-and-motion study and/or the principles of Work Simplification. Later, a study in some depth of the operations of a similar plant proved him incorrect. In an analysis of the over-simplified version of *make ready, do, and take away* operations in manually charging reactors, the *make ready* and *take away* elements turned out to be loaded with labor-saving possibilities, using Work Simplification principles.

In organizing this function in the small plant, one competent time study engineer can do an effective job. He should logically report to the man in charge of production. If the company employs a chief engineer or manufacturing engineer, he could report to the incumbent of either of these positions. In fact, I have seen successful arrangements, in very small plants, where the time study engineer or industrial engineer reported to the chief accountant or even to the personnel manager. I do not personally favor this practice. The particular kind of organization chosen, of course, depends on many other considerations prevailing at the plant, i.e., mass production or jobbing type, complex product or simple consumer type product, hard or soft goods industry, heavy equipment or only light assembly, etc.

It should be emphasized that optimum effectiveness can best be expected when top management *knows how to make proper use* of this discipline's great potential for operations improvement. Too often competent industrial engineers' talents are *not fully exploited*. Under these conditions the more ambitious engineers leave for challenging positions with other companies.

FOR THE LARGE COMPANY

Here we have an almost limitless number of organizational structure arrangements. The plant with production employees in the five hundred to two thousand range could have an organizational structure similar to that depicted in Exhibits 10-1 and 10-2. The number of engineers required in each category shown in these exhibits would depend on the many factors discussed previously. The plant with 100 per cent coverage of measured day-work or incentive pay plan naturally would require more engineering personnel than if there were only 50 per cent coverage. Likewise, a *process* flow type plant would require less personnel in this department than the *product* flow type plant. In addition, in some of the larger plants the subject department is sometimes used as a catchall for all kinds of duties and tasks, some of which are not exactly industrial engineering related.

Where appropriate, the organizational structure depicted in Exhibit 10-3 could be employed.

In a company with seventy plants across the country, and which was organized on a three regional area basis—Eastern, Central and Pacific Regions—the industrial engineering department's organizational structure was based on a similar regional area plan. The head office staff, located at the corporate office in New York City, reported to the vice-president of manufacturing and each of the three regional offices had their own chief industrial engineer with a small staff. All plants also had their own chief industrial engineer with staffs depending on the size of each plant. These plants ranged in size from several hundred to three thousand employees and the chief industrial engineers reported directly to the plant managers. At the same time, they bore a staff relationship

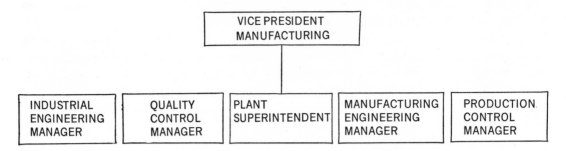

EXHIBIT 10-1

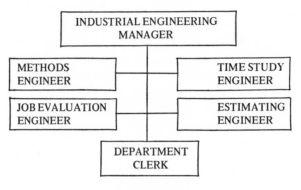

EXHIBIT 10-2

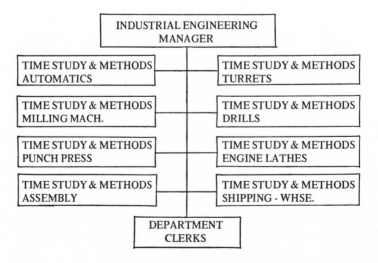

EXHIBIT 10-3

with their respective regional chiefs, who, in turn, bore a similar staff relationship with the corporate staff chief located in New York City.

This corporation was very highly industrial engineering oriented. All operations were covered by production standards and budgetary control. Standard procedure instruction manuals included all company policies and procedures. Positions were all covered by job descriptions and wage and salary administration programs.

At this point it should be remembered that there is no universal organizational structure in which every industrial enterprise can be housed, any more than there is a universal manufacturing structure in which every production process can be housed.

Organizational practice consists in knowing organizational truths, and in applying them with intelligence to the circumstances of particular cases. It cannot be overemphasized that the principles of organization must be applied in the light of particular circumstances.

There are generally two things defined by an organization:

(1) Responsibilities of members; and
(2) The relations among members.

The relations among members of an organization should involve the process of *self-coordination.* This means the solution of problems arising between members in different chains of responsibility, without intervention of supervision. Good administration requires that the bulk of such problems be disposed of by self-coordination, but it also requires that important differences be disposed of by resort to supervision.

MAINTAINING PROPER RELATIONSHIPS BETWEEN THE ENGINEERING (STAFF) AND THE (LINE) FUNCTION[3]

How Do You Go About Getting Cooperation from Your Associates?

The secret of getting along well with other foremen is much the same as winning cooperation from your employees: find out what they want most from their work, then satisfy those desires. Except that with associates, it's not so much a problem of providing satisfaction as it is of *not blocking* their goals and ambitions.

Face up to the fact that, to a degree, you and your associates are competing—for raises, promotions, praise, popularity, and a host of other things. If you compete too hard, or compete unfairly, you won't win much cooperation from your fellow supervisors. And your chances of getting ahead often depend upon your ability to run your department in smooth harmony with those departments that interlock with yours.

To win friends among your fellow supervisors means intelligent sacrifice. Occasionally you'll have to put aside your wish to make your department look good so that you don't put Ralph, foreman of the department, behind the eight ball. Willingness to lend a hand when another foreman falls behind and avoiding hair splitting when allocating interdepartmental charges and responsibilities will help.

Above all, let fellow supervisors run their own shows. *Don't try to give orders in their departments* or encourage disputes between your workers and theirs.

---

3 Lester R. Bittel, *What Every Supervisor Should Know,* 2nd Ed., (New York: Mc-Graw-Hill Book Company, copyright © 1968), p. 209, lines 26-38; p. 210, lines 1-8 and 16-25.

How Can You Get Along Best with Line People?

Generally speaking, staff people in your plant are almost entirely dependent upon production supervisors for cooperation. And in this case, cooperation will breed cooperation. If you cooperate with people, their jobs are made infinitely easier. Their supervisors judge them by their success in getting your assistance and upon the degree to which they accept and act upon your advice. So if you can cooperate with line people, you're actually helping them to get more satisfaction from their work. And you can be pretty sure that they'll go a long way toward helping *you* make a good showing on your job.

CHECKLIST FOR IMPROVED PERFORMANCE

(1) Scope of department's function—the responsibilities and accountabilities of the department should be clearly defined and well understood.

(2) Effectiveness of each employee—is each one effectively performing his duties? Everyone should pull his weight. Take remedial actions where required.

(3) Work assignments—assignments should match skills as closely as practicable. Tasks should be accomplished in the scheduled time and supervisors held accountable.

(4) Examine human relations posture—new personnel should be properly indoctrinated by their supervisors. They should be cared for, encouraged and adequately remunerated.

(5) Keep procedures up to date—make every effort to keep all standard operating procedures up to date. Revise, modify, eliminate, delete and strengthen them as conditions dictate. Assure yourself that they are religiously followed.

(6) Time study rating consistency—periodically check the rating consistency performance of time study engineers. (The Society for Advancement of Management Rating Films are the best for this purpose.)

(7) Cost reduction—check on the extent of cost reduction applications, and determine if the estimated savings were realized. If not, why? Take remedial actions.

(8) Industrial engineering nomenclature—every technique has its own language. A formal and well-written list of commonly used engineering terms should be widely distributed among the personnel concerned. Assure yourself that such a list exists, is up-to-date, and well understood.

(9) Attendance—your supervisors should keep adequate records, covering their employees' attendance and tardiness. Take disciplinary actions with those whose records are unsatisfactory.

(10) Meetings—periodic scheduled meetings should be held, both for department supervisors and for leadmen. Minutes should be kept and be well distributed. Special assignments can be made to participants and deadline dates for completion indicated. An occasional meeting of all the department employees is recommended. Employees from other departments should be included when the subject of meeting is of importance to them.

(11) Overtime—keep a close control of overtime and assure yourself that the practice is not being abused.

(12) Types of engineering services offered—review the services provided the production and office departments. Are the skills you offer being unwisely utilized? For example: is your senior industrial engineer performing janitorial services for an employee of the office? An analysis of past practices may justify the promulgation of a standard list of engineering services offered and permitted. Establish guidelines.

(13) Coverage for night shift—provisions for engineering services for night shifts are often neglected. Examine and determine if condition exists here and then take required actions.

(14) Indirect labor work measurement—check the extent of your work measurement of indirect labor. At least 90 per cent of all operations should be covered. Some plants report 100 per cent.

(15) Aid in training programs—this is an ideal department to use for employee training courses, depending, of course, on the program's training objectives. There should be considerable involvement here.

(16) Servicing production standards and incentives—check the degree of servicing extended the various production departments. This should cover surveillance of methods, production standards and/or incentive pay rates. Are changes made as required? Are the specified machine feeds, speeds, cuts and finishes being followed?

(17) Waste control—determine methods employed to control waste and to increase material yields. Are they effective? Could changes produce greater yields?

(18) Ratio and delay studies—where production performances are continually below standards, time study engineers should conduct four- to eight-hour delay studies. This will uncover the operating deficiencies that require attention. Follow up on compliance with resulting recommendations.

(19) Requisitioning engineering services—review the procedure established for requisitioning these services by other departments. Is it working effectively and is it too loosely or too tightly controlled? Take the necessary remedial actions.

(20) Supervisory following-up practices—examine the methods employed by supervisors and key employees to check on the progress of projects. Do they have a workable system? Do they use check points, charts and various acceptable types of scheduling techniques?

(21) Standard data—review department policies, covering standard data accumulation. Is this program on schedule? Is it being properly and efficiently handled? Are time study observation break-points clearly defined? Are rating factors consistent? Make required changes.

(22) Promotional opportunities—review the records over a period of years and determine the extent and type of promotions made in subject department. This department offers great potential for promotional opportunities in practically every department of the company. Is the potential being effectively exploited? Make adjustments and recommendations to superior for improvements in policies.

(23) Assignment of priorities—determine methods employed to assign priorities of engineering assignments and special projects. Do they have a system? Is it working satisfactorily? Are the required completion dates changed frequently?

Are they loosely controlled? From an analysis of the answers to these questions remedial steps will be suggested.

(24) Measure work, either by yardstick or micrometer—how is this decision made? Should dozens of time study observations be conducted on a certain job when one short, single study would be adequate? Should the operation be broken down into twenty elements when ten are sufficient? Is this practice properly controlled? The results of your study should dictate the definitive, remedial actions to take.

(25) Salesmanship of new methods—often a good idea fails to be implemented because of the lack of persuasiveness and poor approach of its sponsor. Have your engineers been trained in sales techniques? Was the presentation effectively performed? Was the timing right? Generally this area of departmental operations could be greatly improved by further instruction and training.

(26) Product design—industrial engineering knowledge and thinking can have a great influence on product designs. How deeply involved do they get with your product development department? Do they sit in on planning sessions? Is their advice sought? Do the design engineers anticipate and consider manufacturing cost factors? The personnel of this department should play an important role in product design development.

(27) Safety and accident prevention—an engineer from this department should be a member of the plant Safety Committee and actively participate.

(28) Union stewards training—union organized plants should provide a training course in time study and industrial engineering appreciation. It is generally worth the time expended.

(29) Temporary production standards—put a time limit on the life of a temporary standard. Do not permit them to be in use over too long a period. The time factor will vary according to circumstances.

(30) Handling methods and specification changes—your procedure should be designed to highlight the need for these changes. Re-studies should be made, records revised and old specifications rendered obsolete. Promptly inform all interested parties of these adjustments.

(31) Aid in preparing arbitration cases—this department can provide invaluable engineering service to help the personnel department prepare for arbitration cases. The supervisor of this department, in conference with the production manager, should develop all the technical data required. This information should be double checked.

11

Employee Training and Improving Your Three-Dimensional Communications

Developing people is fully as important a part of the supervisor's job as getting out the day's work, and the higher up in the echelon of management he climbs, the more important this responsibility becomes.

It also is a truism that a manager is only as good as the people who work for him. Any improvements in the operating effectiveness of a supervisor's work force is like putting money in the bank. He cannot expect to achieve outstanding operating results if his department is composed of a number of inefficient and poorly trained employees.

A company never stands still. It either improves in its performance each year or it retrogresses. The latter course generally results in failure and eventually all plant operations cease. Similarly, a plant department cannot stand still—it must move ahead. Continued improvement in operations is imperative. A supervisor is expected to develop his skills as an effective manager, particularly his ability to improve subordinates' performances. Here we will discuss the many facets of the training process. Later in this chapter communications will be covered.

WHAT ARE THE SUPERVISOR'S RESPONSIBILITIES FOR TRAINING?

A supervisor's responsibilities include the task of continuously appraising operations, looking specifically for opportunities for improvement. One productive area lies in providing for more and better employee training.

It is the usual practice of supervisors, when breaking in new employees or teaching a new task to an old employee, to assign them to an experienced operator. The operator-instructor may not have had any training in the theory of the learning process or in the techniques of teaching others. While it may not always be practical to select the best qualified employee for a specific teaching assignment, these decisions should be made with the proper care and forethought when such a judgment is permitted.

A well-selected and properly motivated employee, with high morale, offers the best potential for learning new skills. Likewise, the supervisor who is employee-centered will achieve the best results with his training activities. An effective instructor must be a good leader. He should have the ability to convey an impression of helpfulness rather than dominance—guidance rather than control.

Turning over the breaking in of a new employee or the teaching of a new task to an old employee does not relieve the supervisor of his ultimate responsibility and accountability to his superior for results. He has the final responsibility to make it possible for subordinates to do their own work most effectively. He also has a responsibility to the entire company organization.[1] An executive, be he the president or a plant supervisor, can never delegate accountability. Though he vest his assistant with full responsibility and complete authority, the executive nevertheless cannot escape final full accountability for the results. His only recourse for seeing to it that things go right is through supervisory participation—maintaining enough contact with every job so that he is "on top of it" by "keeping his hand in."

How can a busy supervisor "keep his hand in" regarding his employee training responsibility? One method is to periodically *sample* or *spot check* some of the operational areas where employee training has just been concluded to observe results. This also provides the supervisor with an opportunity to show a personal interest in the trainee's progress. All employees appreciate this attention, but it is particularly important with new employees.

KEY FORCES INFLUENCING TRAINING[2]

What Is Learning?

Learning involves change. It is concerned with the acquisition of habits, knowledge, and attitudes. It enables the individual to make both personal and social adjustments.

Any change in behavior implies that learning is taking, or has taken, place. Learning that occurs during the process of change can be referred to as the *learning process*.

Learning that occurs as the individual observes or talks with others, reads, reacts mentally, or attempts to solve a problem is viewed as *process*.

Learning involves making new associations and developing new ways of doing things. It enables the individual to satisfy interests and to attain worthy goals.

The changes that are taking place during learning may be expected to be evidenced in the learner's behavior and to become a part of his total personality.

These changes may include the acquisition of items of information, the mastery of simple skills, the mastery of more complicated mechanical performance or of difficult abstract material, and improved emotional or social adjustments.

---

1 James C. Harrison, Jr., "How to Stay on Top of the Job," *Harvard Business Review* (Boston, Mass., November-December, 1961, copyright © 1961 by the President and Fellows of Harvard College), p. 108, lines 5-13.

2 Copyright © 1963 by David McKay Company, Inc., from the book *Readings in Human Learning* by Lester and Alice Crow. Published by the David McKay Company, Inc. Used with permission of the publishers.

Aspects of Learning

The individual consciously engages in much mental activity and strives for definite learning results.

As he engages in his daily activities, he often unconsciously acquires:

> *new attitudes*   *modes of thought*   *forms of behavior*

But many of these experiences are steeped in attitude qualities and may exercise a powerful influence upon his:

> *thinking*   *conduct*   .   *relations with others*

Various aspects of learning are included in:

... acquisition of motor skills
... acquisition of factual information
... formulation of attitudes
... formation of behavior habits

Something is learned through every experience. The readiness of the learner, the kind and the nature of his responses, and his reaction to success or failure determine, in part, the nature and extent of the learning that occurs.

Types of Abstract Learning

(1) Memorization of learning material with little or no understanding of the ideas involved.
(2) Formation of simple concepts.
(3) Discovery and understanding relationships in more complex situations.

Learning is demonstrated when the individual can *repeat verbatim* any learning content or when he can *demonstrate understanding* by reporting in his own words the ideas contained in the material studied.

Examples of Types of Learning

(1) *To repeat verbatim* is rote learning.
(2) *To demonstrate understanding* is logical learning.

   Note: logical learning is best—also achieves longer retention.

Factors Inherent in Learning

Learning as commonly conceived means not only change but improvement. However, instances can be cited to demonstrate that bad habits rather than good habits can result from improper learning.

The instructor is the key person in the formal learning situation. It is his responsibility:

(1) To provide the experience that will facilitate learning.
(2) To motivate individual learning.
(3) To provide a learning situation which will enable an individual to develop his learning capacity to the fullest.

What are the influences that affect the nature and extent of learning in any situation?

(1) interests
(2) attitudes
(3) social sensitivity
(4) health status
(5) degree of emotional tension

When these factors are favorable the individual has the greatest chance for learning success. For example, the introduction of the *success* factor can arouse interest in learning and promote positive attitudes that encourage the learner in his pursuit of an education.

Significant Factors of Skill Mastery

Competence in a skill is achieved only through learner activity. The learner is conscious of his own muscular movements. Hence motor learning is associated with kinesthetic sensations.

(1) Awareness of Goal: It is important that a learner be aware of the goal toward which he is striving and know the amount and kind of activity needed to reach that goal. These understandings help the learner recognize errors and improve his performance. Hence the power to discriminate among responses has a significant effect upon the attainment of skill competence.

(2) Observation of Model: Much can be discovered about skill competence by observing, analyzing and understanding the performance of a highly skilled person who serves as a model. The initiation of an excellent model has value throughout the learning process but is especially helpful when the learner has reached the stage of adequate performance, provided he is interested in attaining greater than average competence in it.

(3) First Attempts: Initial attempts at mastering a skill usually are awkward and imperfect. The learner may become so discouraged by his first failures that he may appear to have developed a mental "block" that will cause further learning in the skill area to be mediocre in quality, if not impossible.

Teaching Aids (Suggestions, Clues, Hints, Etc.)

It is one thing to understand terms and facts, and it is another to apply them properly. To begin with, the trainee must have the inclination actively to operate on information he receives and to seek the relationship between such information and the environment.

A man may observe hundreds of professional basketball games in which great skill is abundantly displayed without any appreciable effect upon his own motor behavior.

(Let us pause here to examine the meaning of *motor learning.* Essentially, skill is the performance of a task. During his lifetime, an individual engages in many tasks, such as various forms of locomotor activity, riding a bicycle, driving an automobile or flying an airplane, speaking, playing a musical instrument, pitching a baseball, typing or any other form of activity that requires muscular coordination and motor control.)

Motor Control and Coordination

The acquisition of competence in any skill is based upon the development of motor control. The *primary* pattern of motor development is gross bodily movements, in which most or all the large muscles are involved, as in walking, jumping, running, skating or swimming. In the *secondary* pattern, coordination and control of the smaller muscles are needed, e.g., writing, drawing, and working with tools or other implements. The learning of most skills requires the coordinated movements of both gross and fine muscles.

Teaching and learning are not collateral terms, because learning is influenced by many conditions, of which teaching is only one—and neither a necessary nor a sufficient one at that. Thus, trainees can learn without being taught (that is, by teaching themselves); and even if teaching is manifestly competent, it does not necessarily lead to learning if the trainees concerned are dull, inattentive, unmotivated, or not sufficiently knowledgeable.

Learning Curves: Educational psychologists accept the concept of a learning curve in which gradual increments in learning are plotted against successive trials, and place great stress on the importance of overlearning for long-term retention. This latter position is actually adopted by the vast majority of teachers, coaches, parents, and students who follow the maxim "Practice makes perfect." Careful consideration should be given to the impact on learning of intelligence and aptitudes. The effects of interests, attitudes, and motivation also are factors.

In the final analysis, all learning is self-initiated. Hence any forces that can induce the learner to utilize and combine appropriate stimuli from the environment will be valuable aids to continue learning.

Overlearning: Practice or constant repetitions of learning material is referred to as overlearning. It is possible that incorrect as well as correct responses can be overlearned. Hence drill or practice must be correct or accurate. The learner needs help in recognizing and discarding incorrect responses as soon as they occur, and substituting the correct for the incorrect. Moreover, if unimportant details of the learning situation are stressed and consequently overlearned, they may interfere with the fixing through practice of more needed responses.

Length of Practice Periods: The rate at which an individual practices a task is an important factor in skill development. The length of time needed to gain proficiency in a skill varies with individual ability and interest, as well as with previous learning.

Distribution of Practice Periods: The distribution of practice periods depends partly upon the age and ability of the learner. Distributed practice yields more effective mastery than does mass practice. This principle holds for the learning of most skills, from the simple to the complex.

Spacing of Practice Periods: The spacing of practice periods has been found to be important. Too short rest periods may fail to relieve fatigue; too long rest periods may interfere with the learner's desire to improve his performance. For each area of skill learning there probably is an optional distribution of practice and rest periods to obtain rapid and effective progress.

Not all employees will learn at the same rate of speed. Those who learn quickly can easily become bored if the pace is not fast enough—the slower learners may become discouraged and frustrated if they cannot keep up the required pace.

Research repeatedly bears out that the greater a trainee's personal participation is, the higher his motivation will be.

For many industrial purposes, *individual differences in ability* are far more important than varying degrees of experience.

KEY POINTS IN TRAINING

In Carl Heyel's book, *The Supervisor's* [3] *Basic Management Guide,* under the caption "On-the-Job-Training," he lists the following key points:

(1) FEEL. When putting a micrometer on a piece of stock, the key point is "how tight"—a matter of "feel." It can be imparted only by actual demonstration.

(2) KNACK. When riveting, an important point is to know when to *listen* to the riveting. The sound will change when the pieces are solidly together.

(3) TIMING AND PLACING OF HEAT. When welding, there are among others two main "key" points: (a) apply the metal *ahead* of the weld, and (b) get the metal to the right heat. These are a matter of observing the color and behavior of the metal.

(4) HAZARD. When using a knife, a "key" point is to "cut away from you." When lifting a load with an overhead crane, a "key" point is to pull the chains or cables taut, then hesitate for a moment to check the hitches, before lifting the load.

(5) SPECIAL MOTION. When catching hot rods rushing out of rolling mills, the key point is to swing the flowing rod quickly in an arc away from you before inserting the end in the next set of rolls.

(6) SPECIAL INFORMATION. On some kinds of electric wiring the "key" point is to attach the identified negative wire to the tinned screw, and the positive wire to the brass screw.

(7) KNACK OF JUDGING SOUND. In mines, the strength and safety of the roof is determined by tapping the roof rock with a steel bar. The "sound" as the bar strikes the roof tells the story. Judging the sound is the "key" point.

Carl Heyel also suggests the following regarding *learning:*

(a) *Motivation:* Rate and effectiveness of learning are tied in with motivation. No matter how good an instructor you are, you will not get satisfactory results with an indifferent employee. Motivation will differ as between older and younger workers, men and women, married and unmarried, social and racial factors, and the like ... *know your people.*

(b) *Reinforcement:* People learn best when they see some evidence of progress. This,

---

3 Carl Heyel, *The Supervisor's Basic Management Guide,* 3rd. Ed. (New York: McGraw-Hill Co., copyright © 1965 by McGraw-Hill Co.), p. 260, lines 23-32; p. 261, lines 26-29; p. 262, lines 1-12; p. 167, lines 26-31; p. 128, lines 1-33; p. 169, lines 1-33; p. 170, line 1-31.

of course, is simply a continuance of motivation. Psychologists term this *"rein-forcement"* - the feeling that what they are doing is getting them a part of or closer to the reward they are seeking.

This matter of encouragement and reinforcement is extremely important in the learning process, and has been found to be much more effective than criticism, punishment, or threat of punishment when mistakes are made.

(c) *Individual Differences:* The rate of learning varies considerably among different individuals, and learning does not take place at a uniform rate for the same individual. If you are dealing with a group, you will have to adopt instruction speed to the rate of the slowest learner, unless you spend extra time with him individually. Often you can help meet this situation by providing the more capable ones in the group with more challenging exercises or practice work. (See Exhibit 11-1.)

(d) *Meaningfulness:* A "position transfer" in learning (using the psychologists' term) takes place most readily when what is being learned has some meaningful relation to the employee's past experience, or to well-defined tangible goals. Therefore in teaching, avoid abstractions as much as possible—translate what you are teaching into "real" terms by showing practical relationships to the learner's previous experience and to the present job situation. (A case in point here is the example of a High School mathematics instructor who had difficulty in interesting his male students in his Algebra instructions, with the students claiming that it had no practical value to them. After he became aware of this, he demonstrated how the knowledge of logrithms was used in navigation. Their interest was stimulated and he had no further trouble.)

(e) *Learning by Doing:* Learning speed increases when people become as totally involved in the process as possible—when they not only read about what they know and

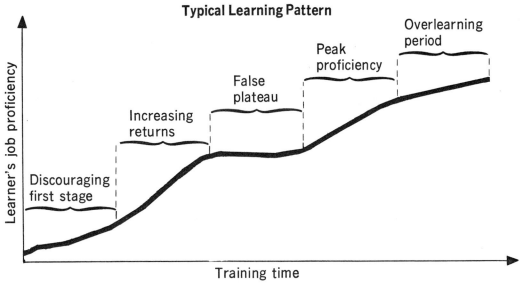

EXHIBIT 11-1: Hypothetical Learning Curve [4]

---

[4] George Strauss and Leonard Sayles, *Personnel: The Human Problems of Management* (Englewood Cliffs, N.J.: Prentice-Hall, Inc., copyright © 1960). By permission of Prentice-Hall, Inc.

do, but also hear an explanation, and see the job performed—and, best of all, when they get the "feel" of the job by actually doing it themselves. Therefore don't rely so heavily on films and other teaching aids as to short cut learning by doing. Of course, this implies that there is someone there to watch for mistakes and prevent incorrect work patterns at the very start.

(f) *Learning Units:* "Learning is improved when the learning units are small enough to be digestible." This provides for the reinforcement mentioned previously, making it possible to sense progress by consecutively mastering pieces of the whole. Units that are too large are discouraging in the first instance, and may be simply too unwieldy for ready remembering or for practical learning by doing. But conversely if the job is broken into pieces which are too small, they may appear like disjointed bits, difficult to fit into the whole process.

(g) *Practice for Specific Skills:* Beyond doubt, practice is extremely important in the acquisition of skills. However, for most tasks repeated experiments have shown that short periods of practice interspersed with brief periods of rest result in more efficient learning than continuous practice. It is not possible to give any specific prescription, beyond saying that practice periods should be short, but not so short as to break up a task into artificial or meaningless units. Within reason, the longer the rest period, the more rapid the learning of a skill—but very long rest periods will bring diminishing returns. In general, it appears to be much more effective to have short practice periods interspersed with frequent short rest periods than to have long rest periods and long practice periods.

(h) *Learning Patterns—"Learning Curves":* Psychologists use the term "learning curve" to indicate the way the rate of learning changes with practice. Measures used include the number of mistakes made in repeated trials, or the speed of performance after days or weeks of practice. In many experiences of skill acquisition, the learning curves will show level portions, or "plateaus," perhaps halfway to the time when the curve levels off at the attainment of maximum proficiency.

TYPES OF ABSTRACT LEARNING

Rote Learning: Examples are: memorizing the multiplication tables, learning a new language, memorizing a poem, learning a ritual, becoming familiar with a musical score, etc.

Logical Learning: Examples are: solving problems, making decisions, employing mathematics to solve a problem, developing solutions to human relations problems, and using your reasoning powers to settle disputes and issues.

Reasoning Types of Test Questions (circle correct one)

(a) Vacuum cleaner is to broom as automobile is to: (A) brush, (B) carriage, (C) eraser, (D) airplane.

Answer   A   B   C   D

(b) Which one of these is most unlike the other three? (A) typewriter, (B) clock, (C) pen, (D) pencil.

Answer   A   B   C   D

(C) Land is to lake as frame is to: (A) House, (B) Wall, (C) Picture, (D) Lot.

Answer   A B C D

(d) Which one of these words is most unlike the others? (A) thin, (B) cloth, (C) paper, (D) wood

Answer   A B C D

(e) Two trains start one hour apart from the station and in the same direction. The first is running at the average rate of 20 miles per hour, and the second is running at the average rate of 30 miles per hour. In how many hours will the second train overtake the first?

Answer   1 2 3 4 5 6 7 8

(a) A Ⓑ C D
(b) A Ⓑ C D
(c) A B Ⓒ D
(d) Ⓐ B C D
(e) 1 ② 3 4 5 6 7 8

TRAINING PROCEDURES — RULES FOR THE FORMATION OF ASSOCIATIONS[5]

(a) Frequency of repetition influences the number or strength of associations.
(b) Attention and inattention are important mental sets for learning.
(c) Distributed or spaced repetitions are superior to massed accumulated repetitions for most standard learning conditions.
(d) Whole learning generally is favored over part learning.
(e) Recitation or active repetitions are superior to another read.

What Is Associative Learning?

Job activities that depend most heavily upon pure *associative learning* are those that require memorization.

Associative learning takes place in all types of learning, and it is through this that man's behavior is modified by experience. However, some learning situations are almost entirely dependent upon the process of connecting experiences with one another. We experience objects with our sense organs and we experience responding to the stimulation they produce. When any of these experiences becomes linked with any other, so that one of them arouses or recalls another, associational learning has taken place.

The term *conditioned response* also is used to designate a movement rather than an idea that is aroused by a sensation.

Although all forms of learning involve formation of associations, only some may be said to be confined to this aspect of learning. Job activities that depend most heavily upon pure associative learning are those that require memorization. Examples of routine learnings are: spelling, recalling telephone numbers, learning to read a new language, etc., and all aspects of job information that do not require understanding or judgment.

---

5 *Psychology in Industry,* 3rd ed., by Norman R.F. Maier. Copyright © 1965 by Houghton Mifflin Company. P. 378, lines 31-39; p. 379, lines 8-11, 18-25; pps. 385-387, italicized paragraph headings only.

The following represents a good example of *associative learning:*

A guidebook for Sea Scouts contained this suggestion—laymen often find it difficult to remember the difference between the *port* side of a boat and the *starboard* side. Also, which colored light is displayed on what side? Look at the comparison shown in Exhibit 11-2.

Facing the bow of a ship (to the layman, the front)

Left Side	*Right Side*
Port side	Starboard side
Red light	Green light

Note: the *less* numbered lettered words are all on the left side of boat when facing the bow, and the *greater* numbered lettered words are all on the right side.

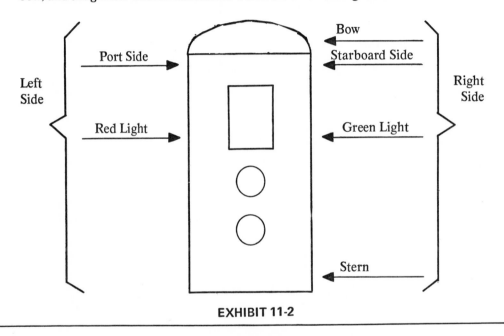

EXHIBIT 11-2

MULTIMEDIA INSTRUCTION TECHNIQUES[6]

Multimedia instruction techniques include:

Linear Instruction
Audiovisual Presentations
Films
Laboratory Exercises
Textbooks and Workshops
Reference Material
Learn-by-Doing Sessions
Spaced Quizzes
Person-to-Person Tutorial Assistance

---

6 *High Achievement Multimedia Training Courses.* Used by permission of Maynard Research Council, Incorporated. Copyright © 1970, 300 Alpha Drive, Pittsburgh, Pa. 15238. P. iii, lines 12-30.

Audiovisual presentations, films, texts, and linear instructions enable the trainee to absorb the vital subject matter with relative ease.

Each course has many checkpoints to ensure that the trainee fully understands the material he has studied. He moves to the next stage of learning only when he passes a checkpoint correctly.

To hold the trainee's interest, lessons vary in length and employ different instructional techniques.

The above briefly describes courses provided by the Maynard Research Council, Incorporated, of Pittsburgh, Penna. These courses are available at Maynard Training Centers located in major cities of the U.S.A. and abroad.

How Does This Unique System Work?[7]

Instead of a classroom set-up, each trainee works by himself in a carefully designed booth. There are several kinds of teaching equipment which he operates himself. Most courses include color slides and related sound tapes, written programmed instruction material, sound color films, laboratory experiments, workshop practice, texts, and reference material.

The lessons vary in length and techniques so that the trainee is obliged to switch from one type of teaching aid to another. Because of this, he is rarely bored.

Although Maynard's training technique does not require a full time teacher, it does not do away with the human factor. A counselor is almost always involved. He meets with the trainee on a personal, one-to-one basis to answer questions and discuss any problems.

Why is this new kind of training especially effective? The following reasons are probably most important.

Flexibility: The new training method is an extremely flexible tool. Since each person works individually, one or more can be trained at any time. There is never need for a whole group of key people to be away from their jobs at the same time or for an extended time. Nor is it necessary to delay training when only one needs it.

The flexibility of individualized training also allows each trainee to proceed at his own learning speed. Rates of learning vary with the person—a detail that strict training methods cannot consider. In this new approach to training, however, a course can take as long as the individual needs. The trainee competes only against himself. This can still be a powerful incentive, yet rarely a destructive or problematic one. For instance, the older employee tends to freeze up when he is put into a classroom situation with younger and possibly more aggressive men. If he is allowed to train by the individualized method, this situation is omitted. He has no need to worry about falling behind or to feel embarrassed by age or a slower learning speed. This method of training lets the particularly fast learner speed ahead at his own best rate.

Other advantages include uniformity, learning-by-doing and lower training costs.

---

7 *Individualized Approach to Management Training.* Used by permission of *Automation,* September, 1968 Issue. Copyright © 1968 by Penton Publishing Co., Cleveland, Ohio 44113. Lines 92-171.

IMPROVING YOUR THREE-DIMENSIONAL COMMUNICATIONS[8]

Top and middle management, office, sales, and plant employees continue to complain about the inadequate communications each receives. A plant manager accidentally discovers a long-festering and unattended employee problem and reproaches members of his staff for failure to bring it to his attention. Supervisors repeatedly complain that top management fails to inform them of its plans. Few managements can be proud of the effectiveness of their three-way communications—the uninterrupted flow of information, *up, down* and *across*. The information conveyed must be accurate, unbiased, complete, understood, and promptly transmitted.

Examples of Downward, Upward and Across Communications

Downward Communications: The local paper of a small city, where the factory of a nationally known company was located, released a headline story complete with a large photograph of the plant stating that the building had been sold. The next day the main topic of discussion among the employees was the reported sale of the plant. Rumors circulated that the company was selling out and planned to close the plant permanently. Some production employees did not even report for work that morning, but immediately began searching for new jobs. Fortunately, several supervisors picked up these rumors and passed them up quickly through the various echelons of management to the general manager. He took immediate action. Word was sent to all department heads that all machinery was to be shut down five minutes before noontime and work would cease. The manager then delivered a brief explanation to all employees over the company intercommunications system. He told them the plant was not closing. The only change was that the company, who leased the plant, in the future would pay their rent to a different owner. He assured them their company had a long-term lease on the property and work would continue. This prompt action instantly squelched the unsettling and untrue rumors.

Upward Communications: A plant manager in a nonunion company who had served in his new position for only a few months, had established a friendly, approachable relationship with the employees. He often stopped to chat with various operators and one day he stopped to talk to a turret lathe operator located just off the main aisle of the plant. The conversation was generally about fishing, hunting or bowling, but this time he asked the manager if he would object if he made a complaint. He then proceeded to describe a deficiency in plant operations that, if ignored, would have created a major upheaval in management-employee relations. The manager immediately initiated an investigation. The results of this brought about changes in certain supervisory responsibilities, modifications of organization, corrections in some department policies, restudies of past established practices, the retraining of some staff personnel, and a complete overhauling of all the attendant procedures. By prompt and vigorous action, the inefficient and unfair production employee conditions were corrected.

In this case the channel of communications was an old and loyal production employee. The right channel should have been the supervisor of this department, who,

---

8 Lewis R. Zeyher, *Cost Reduction in the Plant* (Englewood Cliffs, N.J. Prentice-Hall, Inc., copyright © 1965), p. 111, lines 36-40; p. 112, lines 23-39, 1-22.

when questioned, admitted that he had prior knowledge of this undesirable situation. Although his position did not include the authority to take the drastic measures required in this instance, it was his responsibility to pass along this information to his superior. His excuse for not doing so was his fear of involving the staff associate who was responsible for the trouble.

If effective communications had prevailed, this problem would have been referred immediately to the attention of the plant manager (the one production executive who had it within his authority to take required action), and the problem would, consequently, have been handled in a much shorter time. The irritant to the production employees would have been removed shortly after its origin with much less fanfare and trouble than did finally transpire.

Communications Across: [9] The second shift supervisor of a three shift operation in a chemical plant complained that the first shift supervisor failed to inform him about the incompleted maintenance work on a reactor during his shift. Further work was required during the second shift in order to complete the job. Not knowing this important bit of information, it was incorrectly assumed that the reactor involved was ready for charging. The loading operation was started with disastrous results. This expensive error would have been avoided if there had been better communications between the two supervisors. In an effort to eliminate this type of problem in the future, the plant manager purchased a number of inexpensive tape recorders so that each supervisor could conveniently leave messages for the succeeding shift supervisors. This proved to be a very productive investment.

The Process of Communication[10]

Telling: At one time most managers looked upon communications as the process of *telling*. They told others what they wanted them to know, what they wanted them to think, and what they wanted them to do. In so doing, they thought they were communicating. But in spite of their telling, they found that people still did not understand. Later, communications was regarded as a two-way process—one person talked to another and got feedback to find out if he was understood. But research shows that two-way communication is inadequate, as is our conventional approach to the subject. We have established that communication is also a four-way process. It involves asking, telling, listening, and understanding.

Asking: As managers, we often overlook the key activity necessary to get the communications process under way: that of asking other people for the information we don't have but feel that we need. This applies at all levels. The professional manager does not wait to be told. He asks. He asks his subordinates for their advice and suggestions on common problems. He asks to find out about their points of view and to make sure they understand his. The manager asks his superior for the information and advice he

---

[9] Lewis R. Zeyher, "Improving Your Three-Dimensional Communications" (Swarthmore, Pa.: *Personnel Journal,* May, 1970, Volume 49, No. 5). Copyright © 1970 by *Personnel Journal,* Inc. P. 415, lines 39-59.

[10] Louis A. Allen, *The Management Profession,* (New York: McGraw-Hill Book Company, copyright © 1964 by Louis A. Allen), p. 274, lines 3-38; p. 275, lines 1-9.

requires. He asks those on his own level for information and suggestions on matters of common interest.

Listening: If we wish to communicate fully, that is, to understand what others are trying to convey to us, we need to *listen*. This is a most difficult skill to learn and one that we do not always associate with the communication process. It requires self-discipline and rigorous control of our own urge to talk. When mastered, however, the skill of listening is the best guarantee that we will receive and understand the messages that are being transmitted in our direction.

Understanding: The most important aspect of communications—and the one most often overlooked—is understanding. Most communications have both an emotional and a logical meaning. Often they must be heard by both the head and the heart. To understand in this sense, the manager must have a keen insight into human motivation and must be able to hear or read not only words, but the meaning behind the words.

We hear a great deal but we *understand* only what we want—this is known as *selective listening*. Even though people are in the proper listening posture, their eyes alert and their faces interested, often they understand only part of what we say to them. Psychologically, it is entirely possible for a person to hear two sentences, one spoken after the other, of equal weight and intensity, and to understand one and apparently not even to hear the other.

The president of a small company in Georgia, for example, hired a secretary, a competent, well-experienced girl. In his interview he mentioned that the pay range for the job was $400 to $525 per month. "Newcomers and people with minimum experience start at $400," he stated explicitly. After she had received her first paycheck, the young lady approached the president indignantly. "You told me experienced people get $525 for this job. I'm experienced and you are only paying me $400," she said. The president's explanation did not placate her and she quit in a huff.

Where these failures in communication occur, the most significant result is lack of understanding. We fail to understand the thoughts and feelings of others; they do not understand—friction and frustrations are likely to be the twin handmaidens of error. Personal relationships then often deteriorate and the prevalent tone becomes one of apathy and disinterest.

12

Establishing
Performance Objectives
for Line and Staff Personnel

Most companies today have some form of regularized employee evaluation programs. Companies differ in their approaches but this exercise usually includes a face-to-face meeting, held at least once a year, preferably on the anniversary date of their employment with the company. This occasion offers both employee and his supervisor the opportunity to exchange views—the boss discusses the employee's performance, both good and bad; and the employee has the option to ask questions and submit any of his own grievances. Special company forms are made available, and evaluations recorded, which later become part of the employee's personnel department record. These forms are signed by the interviewer and by his superior. Generally, different type forms are provided for executives, line staff, production and office employees. The key individual in these exercises is the interviewer. His actions in conducting these interviews is of the greatest importance.

PURPOSE OF PERFORMANCE APPRAISALS[1]

Managers generally are often in doubt about:

(1) *What* they are supposed to do.
(2) How *far* they are expected to go in doing it—that is, the degree of authority they possess in each area for which they are responsible.
(3) How *well* they should perform their jobs.
(4) How well they *are* doing them.

Appraisals are, of course, valuable in deciding on promotions and raises, and even on occasions for deciding who will be kept on the payroll and who will be dismissed. But they are not conducted primarily for any of these reasons. The primary purpose is to help each man handle his current job better.

---

[1] Virgil K. Rowland, *Evaluating and Improving Managerial Performance,* (copyright © 1970, by McGraw-Hill, Inc. New York), p. 205, lines 1-8; p. 210, lines 16-35; p. 206, lines 1-4; p. 207, lines 1-13; p. 211, lines 1-9.

155

This is a point that should be emphasized in any announcement of an appraisal plan and in the talks each boss holds with each of his subordinates on either the plan itself or on the results of an appraisal. If the promotion aspect is prominently featured, false hopes may be aroused, for higher jobs may not be available or likely to be available in the near future. Continuing improvement as shown by successive appraisals will in many cases mean that a man should have a raise, but it is not always possible to grant one at any specific time; therefore, it should be understood that the boss is not making any promises of more money even if any given appraisal shows that the man is doing an excellent job. And, of course, the boss should endeavor to avoid any tinge of a threatening attitude in the conduct of the appraisal interview. If he does not, his group will become nervous as appraisal time approaches and the work will suffer.

PEOPLE DO WHAT THE BOSS INSPECTS

It might be stated as an axiom (or a principle of management) that "people do what their boss *inspects*." Lawrence A. Appley, of the American Management Association, was perhaps the first to point out—or rather to sharpen—the common management saying, "people do what the boss *expects*," in this way.

The two sentences really mean the same thing, for people identify what the boss expects by what he inspects, by what he comments on, by what he seems pleased about, and by what makes him angry or, perhaps, merely by his casting a cold and fishy eye on a subordinate when he finds him doing it. If what the boss talks about in the appraisal interview differs from what he talks about on the job, or communicates by facial expression or tone of voice, subordinates are not going to pay much attention to what he says in that interview, especially when they know that conducting it is something imposed on by the boss from without and that he doesn't really believe in the program himself.

WHY MANY EVALUATION PLANS FAIL

Many Evaluation Plans fail because line or staff management regards making the appraisals as something extraneous to the real work—an extra chore that interferes with work toward their real objectives and a simple waste of time. In many cases, the line managers are quite right in thinking so because of the nature of some of the forms they are compelled to fill in. These forms often call for information that has no pertinence to the jobs and for judgments that are different or impossible to make, and even more difficult to discuss with the subordinates once they have been made.

Other reasons such plans fail include:

(a) Poorly chosen plan—perhaps too involved.
(b) Plan not properly explained to both parties—managers and workers.
(c) Some supervisors not properly trained in how best to conduct a Merit Review
(d) Top management's lack of *active* support.
(e) Judgment factor still too predominant in many programs—goals, budgets, standards, well-stated objectives, and factual factors are best.
(f) Absolute privacy not maintained during employee's Merit Review.
(g) Impartiality by management, at all levels, not followed.

(h) Low ratings in review not always backed by factual data. (If employee is rated low for his attendance record figures should be provided to substantiate claim. Example: "During six-month period, Mary Smith was absent without cause 24 days and was late 15 times.")

(i) Weak and ineffective administrator of program.

EXAMPLES OF IMPROPERLY MAINTAINED MERIT REVIEW PLAN

The following represents an actual instance where a *Job Evaluation* and *Merit Review* program in an office of fifty employees was not properly maintained.

The president of a company had a consultant make a study of this department, composed mostly of women. A personal and private interview was conducted with each of these fifty employees in an effort to determine the causes of the unrest. Most of these people were very honest and frank during these meetings and "pulled no punches." They were first informed that notes of their comments would be recorded but names would not be indicated. A sampling of these remarks follow:

(1) Unhappy about job salary, has now reached her maximum (an employee with many years of service with company).

(2) Cannot understand taking less money when moving to new job in same Salary Grade.

(3) Hard to get decisions regarding pay increases or questions relating to same.

(4) Employee does not think system is being used properly.

(5) A question of *Cost of Living* adjustments was made by several employees.

(6) One employee suggested that where employees have reached top of their salary range, every three years they be given a five (5) per cent increase. These individuals would then be carried the same as in the red-circle group (those employees, who for one reason or another, receive salaries out of the prescribed limits of their grades).

(7) Employee expects fairness—department isn't handled that way.

(8) Employee does not think Job Evaluation System is now working effectively—due to abuse by supervisor.

(9) Employee stated that in one department of company the employees never have received a Merit Review.

(10) Employee stated that those individuals reaching top of their range in salary should still receive a Merit Review even though they no longer are eligible for a change in rate because *everyone likes to know how he is doing.*

(11) Employee believes her boss uses the system as a "crutch" when he does not want to give an increase but when he wants to favor someone, he skips the established procedure.

(12) Supervisor spends little time with employee and does not point out areas on Merit Review Form (see Exhibit 12-1 and 12-2) where she is deficient or is in need of improvement, nor does he show her the results of each item—only the total. She also stated little time was given, if any, to tell her story to her boss.

(13) Employee thinks the Merit Review interview by supervisor should be conducted in complete privacy, instead of out in public—is usually conducted in front of the entire office force. In addition, hers is conducted when the Auditors are in the

MERIT REVIEW

Name of Employee.. Department ....

Position Title .... Date ....

Position Grade .... Reviewed by ....

Instructions for Department Supervisors

This rating sheet provides a practical method through which the ability of the individual can be judged with a reasonable degree of accuracy and uniformity. Indicate your opinion of this employee by placing a check mark on the phrase in the block which seems best to fit the employee. This appraisal will be reviewed personally with the employee at a later date — be sure your facts are correct. Please follow these instructions carefully —

1. Use your own independent judgment.

2. Disregard your general impression of the employee and concentrate on one factor at a time.

3. When rating an employee recall instances that are typical of his work and way of acting.

4. Make your rating with the utmost care and thought; be sure that it represents a fair and square opinion.

5. Be sure you do not permit your personal feelings to influence and govern your rating.

GENERAL COMMENTS AND RESULTS

(1) Is the employee performing the task best suited to his ability? ....

(2) Is the employee promotable? .... If yes, to what position? ....

(3) What specifically, is he doing to improve himself? ....

....

(4) Along what lines do you feel that he needs to improve himself? ....

....

(5) Total points .... Recommended rate change from $................ week to $............... week.

Approved by (Reviewers' supervisor): ....   Date ....
                                                                 (Over for rating chart.)

EXHIBIT 12-1

EMPLOYEE RATING REPORT

Check appropriate square with red pencil.
To be rated by Supervisor only.

FACTOR	Distribution of points.					Points
	(2)	(4)	(6)	(8)	(10)	
Knowledge of Work	Practically None. Is Unsatisfactory.	Below Average. Needs Help Frequently.	Average. Possesses Enough to Do a Fair Job.	Somewhat Above Average.	Extremely Well Informed.	——
Quantity of Work	Unsatisfactory. Output Very Light.	Just Turns Out the Required Amount.	Output a Little More Than Required.	Fast Worker. Rarely Behind in Work.	Exceptionally Fast. Output Very High.	——
Quality of Work	Very Careless, Not Complete. Many Omissions—Unsatisfactory.	Just Gets By. Could Be Improved considerably.	Work is Generally Acceptable. Average Performance.	Usually Does A Good Job. Rarely Needs Special Attention.	Consistently Does Excellent Work.	——
Accuracy	Very Inaccurate, Unsatisfactory.	Occasionally Makes Error. Work Below Average.	Seldom Makes Errors. Usually Does a Good Job.	Somewhat Above Average.	Exceptionally Accurate. Mistakes Most Unusual.	——
Initiative	Must Always Be Told What to Do.	Needs Considerable Supervision.	Needs Help in Most Cases.	Needs Little Supervision.	Self-Starter. Has Very High Initiative.	——
Responsibility	Careless and Negligent.	Generally Follows Instructions Little Follow-Up Req'd.	Accepts When Asked. Fairly Dependable.	Assumes Without Being Told.	Exceptionally Reliable—Conscientious.	——
Relations with Others	Often Breeds Trouble.	Sometimes Causes Dissension.	Normal—Causes No Trouble With Others.	Promotes Cooperation and Good Will.	Outstanding For Cooperation.	——
Promptness	Always Tardy.	Often Late. Requires Occasional Reminding.	Usually Prompt—Rarely Late.	Never Late Without Cause.	Almost Never Late.	——
Attendance	Very Bad Record Causing Work to Suffer.	Poor Record—Often Absent Without Cause	Fair Record. Could Improve It.	Satisfactory. Rarely Absent Except For Cause.	Nearly Perfect Record.	——
Adaptability	Very Slow to Learn—Requires Repeated Instructions.	Has Some Difficulty in Adapting Himself to New Work.	He is a Routine Worker. Requires Detailed Instructions on New Work.	Adjusts Himself to New Conditions Easily.	Very Open-Minded. Has High Degree of Adaptability.	——
Attitude Towards Company	Unsatisfactory. Only Cooperates when He Has To.	Usually Cooperates—But With Some Reluctance.	Satisfactory. Passive Attitude. Not Too Enthusiastic.	Meets Others Half Way on New Ideas. Generally Cooperative.	Displays High Loyalty. Good Team Worker.	——
Suggestions or New Ideas	Never Has Any.	Rarely Contributes Anything New.	Occasionally Presents a New Idea. Seems to Try to Improve Job.	Comes Up With Good Ideas Frequently.	Presents Outstandingly Constructive Ideas Often.	——

TOTAL POINTS [ ]

EXHIBIT 12-2

boss' office and she is provided little opportunity to speak about her own problems which should be done privately.

(14) Supervisor said some employees "scoff" at Merit Review Plan (could this be because the supervisor also had indicated a lack of interest or had made disparaging remarks about it?).

Note: The above has been reviewed because we can always learn from the mistakes of others.

An appraisal of the supervisor of the indicated department follows:

"During studies covering this assignment Mr. X has been very cooperative and helpful. He also has displayed interest in seeking answers to the current personnel problems, and reflects intelligence, technical competence and of being a very hard worker......On the *liability* side he is considered to be very 'wishy-washy,' lacks courage, is evidently a poor manager and definitely is weak in the art of handling people."

METHODS OF COMPUTING PERFORMANCE OBJECTIVES[2]

(1) Example of Computing the Personnel Manager's Index

Top management is always interested in raising the organization to new levels of performance. The top executive likes to see new records set forth for output, quality, cost reduction, and in general plant efficiency. Thus every plant has certain standards, or "score cards," that are used to compare departments within the organization. One method covering a monthly industrial relations appraisal measuring employment, turnover, absenteeism, overtime, and related items is shown in Exhibit 12-3. The major officials of the company use this report to check against goals and past performances. Ten indices were selected by the before-mentioned company and are listed in Exhibit 12-3.

If these indices are rising, it is assumed that the personnel manager is not doing as effective a job as he should. The data for these factors are gathered monthly from available company records. The indices for the ten factors are then computed and combined. It is quite difficult to combine figures derived from various ratios, trends and percentages. However, it is possible to use *standard deviations* in order to make a combination of like items. Each one of the ten factors is first measured to see how far it deviates from an accepted *norm*.

It is then possible to add together figures from each of the ten indices. There is no problem of trying to add together unlike items, for each index is computed in standard deviations from an accepted norm for each index. The standard deviation for any given month can now be added together to give a composite index covering all ten factors relating to the subject department. For example, the figures for the month of January could be computed for each index and added together in a manner as illustrated in Exhibit 12-3.

Each of the ten factors has been weighed in accordance with its importance in determining the value of this department to the company as well as a good indication of

---

[2] Thomas J. Luck, *Personnel Audit and Appraisal* (New York: McGraw-Hill Book Co., copyright c 1955), p. 27, lines 6-16; p. 28, lines 11-19, 22-42, and Table 4-3 on p. 30.

Computing the Personnel Department's Performance Index

January

Factors	Deviation S. D.	Weight	Weighted Factor
Labor index	0.00	2	0.00
Absenteeism	0.25	2	0.50
Participation in company programs	0.25	− 1	− 0.25
Accident rate	− 0.20	1	− 0.20
Grievance rate	0.05	2	0.10
Wage rate	0.05	1	0.05
Rework-time cost	− 0.10	1	− 0.10
Material consumption	0.05	1	0.05
Personnel load ratio	0.25	2	0.50
Overtime hours trend	− 0.10	1	− 0.10
Total			0.55
Weighted average			0.055

EXHIBIT 12-3

how well the supervisor is doing. The weights used in Exhibit 12-3 are not meant to be absolute, but are merely examples of how weights might be used in a given company. Each company should determine its own list of factors and also decide independently upon the weights, if any, to be used. The final index figure, in this case 0.055, is posted on a graph each month. By following the trend of the graph, a quick picture of the performance of the personnel department supervisor and his department can be obtained. If there is a sudden upswing in the index, it is advisable for management to make a thorough investigation of the causes.

(*Note:* For further information regarding the method used to compute the indices, see L.R. Zeyher's *Production Manager's Handbook of Formulas and Tables,* Prentice-Hall, Inc., Englewood Cliffs, N.J., pp. 128-129.)

(2) Key Employee Bonus Plan

This is a four-step performance plan, based on company profits and the measured performance of the participants in plan:
  (a) Company performance
  (b) Plant performance
  (c) Department's performance
  (d) Individual's performance

(a) **Company Performance:** based on the annual profit results. Usually a lump percentage of the profits, after taxes, is set aside for distribution to employees. This arrangement generally is different for each company, depending on their particular policies. In this particular plan 10% is the maximum for the company performance bonus. Let us assume for this example, that the foreman whose base pay is $9,000 per year is alloted 3% or $270.00 bonus. (See Exhibit 12-4.)

(b) Plant Performance: based either on budgetary performance of plant or annual results against standard costs or similar yardsticks. For the sake of this example we will assume that for the year the bonus for the supervisor is 2% of $9,000 or $180.00, with 5% being the maximum he could receive. (See Exhibit 12-4.)

(c) Department Performance: also either based on departmental budgetary performance, standard costs or similar yardstick. In this example we will assume that for the year the bonus for this same supervisor is 3% of $9,000 or $270.00, with a maximum of 5%. (See Exhibit 12-4.)

(d) Individual Performance: based on performance of all the items listed in Exhibit 12-4 with a 10% maximum. According to the results depicted in this exhibit the foreman would receive 6.6% of $9,000 or $594.00 (See Exhibits 12-4 and 12-5.)

Total Annual Bonus on This Plan

(a) Company performance	$ 270.00
(b) Plant performance	180.00
(c) Department performance	270.00
(d) Individual performance	594.00
Total	$1,314.00

or $\frac{\$1,314}{9000} = 14.6\%$ of base pay.   (maximum allowed 30.0%)

(See Exhibit 12-6 for list of performance elements considered measurable.)

There are many possible variations to this type of plan. Each company can tailor the basic parts of this program to its own specific situation. The plan should be made understandable to all participants—this plan presented here also can be simplified.

FACTORS TO CONSIDER WHEN CONDUCTING AN EMPLOYEE PERFORMANCE REVIEW[3]

The following factors should be given every consideration when interviewing a subordinate for his performance:

(a) Ratings should be conducted every six months.

(b) A good performance rating includes more than just a supervisor's opinion. It should be based on facts—such items as his scrap record, productivity, attendance record, attitude, cooperation with others and related factors.

(c) Make sure you point out employees' strengths and weaknesses—later, on occasion of next review, check on improvements.

(d) Employees like to know where they stand—give each one a clear understanding of how well his boss thinks he is doing his job. Be specific—it cannot be

---

3 From *What Every Supervisor Should Know*, 2nd. Ed., Lester R. Bittle, Copyright © 1968 by McGraw-Hill, Inc. Used by permission of McGraw-Hill Book Co., pp. 135-142 partial.

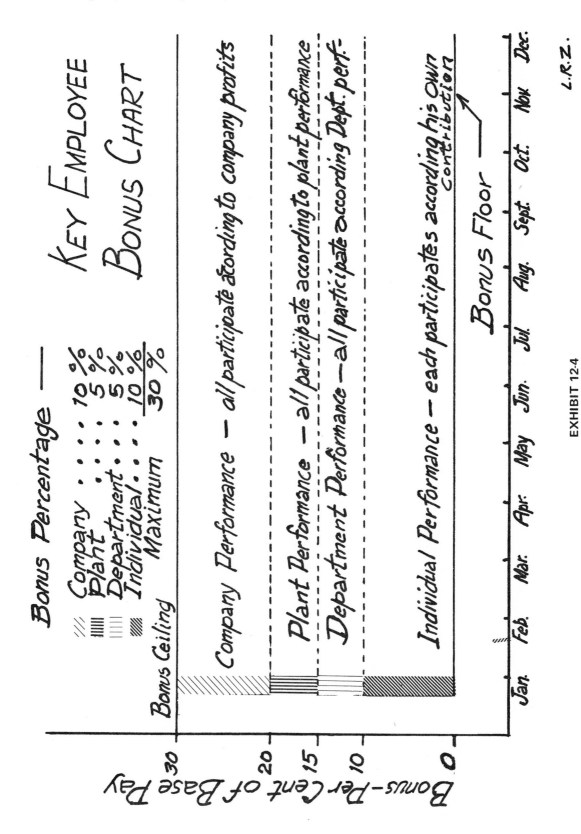

EXHIBIT 12-4

INDIVIDUAL PERFORMANCE
Example: Foreman at $9,000 base

Performance Element	1	2	3	4	5	Credit 6	Points 7	8	9	10	REMARKS
Productivity						X					
Attendance										X	
Cost Reduction		X									
Waste					X						
Housekeeping										X	
Safety										X	
Years Service				X							
Self-training						X					
		2		4	5	12				30	53

Maximum Points Allowed 80

$$\frac{53}{80} \times .10 \times \$9,000 = \$594.00$$

or 0.660 X .10 X $9,000 = 594.00

Year's Bonus $594.00
(for his individual bonus only—
other bonus elements to be added)

EXHIBIT 12-5

overemphasized that *he should be told about the bad things,* so improvement can be expected.

(e) Avoid favoritism or any slight indication of it.

(f) Appraisal interviews *must* be conducted in privacy.

(g) Before an employee interview is scheduled plan your approach. You should be the best judge of how he will take what you have to say to him. Also, be prepared to hear his story.

(h) Use the sandwich technique—this means you should sandwich unfavorable comments between favorable comments. This "softens the blow" when you get to the bad news.

(i) Avoid the halo effect—nearly everybody has a tendency to let one *favorable* or *unfavorable* trait influence his judgment of an individual as a whole.

(j) Don't be too *lenient* or too *tough* in your ratings. Few employees are good at everything. Be fair.

(k) After a performance review, follow up—provide ways for his development, and continue to show interest in his work.

FOUR-STEP PERFORMANCE PLAN
ITEMS MEASURABLE

ITEM	PERFORMANCE ELEMENTS MEASURABLE	comp.	plant	dept.	indiv.
1	Productivity	X	X	X	X
2	General expense	X	X	X	
3	Attendance and tardiness	X	X	X	X
4	Cost Reduction suggestions used				X
5	Inventory turnover	X			
6	Scheduling		X	X	
7	Yield (waste)		X		X
8	Housekeeping		X	X	X
9	Safety and health (Accident Index)	X	X	X	X
10	Telephone expense		X	X	
11	Customer "returns"			X	
12	Labor turnover		X	X	
13	Self-training				X
14	Budgets	X	X	X	
15	Industrial relations		X	X	
16	Machine down-time		X	X	
17	Formalized meetings	X	X	X	
18	Years of continuous service	X			
19	Indirect labor		X	X	
20	Manpower		X	X	
	other				

EXHIBIT 12-6

13

Programming
for Cost
Reduction

This chapter provides you with some tried and proven methods for reducing plant costs and specifically suggests how to program your plant so you can achieve these objectives. Operations most sensitive to a cost reduction campaign are identified, and suggestions advanced for a continuous attack against high cost.

PREPARE A PLAN

Determine Dimensions of Attack[1]

Before embarking on this type of program, it is well to decide beforehand the functions and operating areas you plan to include in your attack on costs. Are you, for example, going to examine just the more obvious and sensitive areas for cost reduction? Is the program going to be a hit-and-run affair—a skimming-off of the cream of excessive costs? Is the plan to be conducted by a few selected staff men or are you going to make it all-encompassing, with everyone participating—staff people and production employees, supervisors and lead-men, alike? Will the plan be in effect every day or just on certain days, when time is available? Will a strong, aggressive leader be assigned full responsibility for results, coupled with corresponding authorities, or will responsibilities be spread over the members of a committee? Do you expect to get top management support and how do you plan to obtain it? Will the employee responsible for results be given freedom from his regular job to work full time on this program or will he be expected to perform this additional task as an extracurricular activity, in his "spare time"? These represent but a sampling of the questions that must be resolved before you initiate a cost reduction attack on operations.

It is recommended that the program be designed to cover all major functions and reach into all operating areas. It is also suggested that a competent staff man, with demonstrated courage, aggressiveness and persuasiveness, be selected to head the

---

[1] Lewis R. Zeyher, *Production Manager's Desk Book,* (Englewood Cliffs, N.J.: Prentice-Hall, Inc., copyright © 1969), p. 95, lines 12-31; p. 96, lines 1-13.

program. He should spend full time on this task, be cloaked with all the authority required and have the full and *active* support of management, at *all* levels. Furthermore, he should be adequately supplied with the necessary assistance and have free access to all departments, their facilities, brainpower and efforts. It should not be a short program. It sometimes takes weeks to build up full steam and produce results.

Establishing Goals and Timetables

These should be determined by the production manager, in consultation with his superior. Plant circumstances may influence these decisions but if possible, make it cover at least a year's time or more, and establish goals by going over the past year's operating statements with the plant controller. The goals should be realistic. Consideration also should be properly given to any reconciliations necessary in the figures due to changes, operating modifications, product mix, and related influences. A brief *sample outline* for a cost reduction program, with goals and timetables, is depicted in Exhibit 13-1. A project report for department foremen or for department results also is shown in Exhibit 13-2.

Example of a Plan Successfully Employed by Major Corporations

Outline of Plan: Briefly, after the management decided to conduct a cost reduction program because of the need of higher earnings and because price increases were out of the question, the following actions were taken.

Each department supervisor was asked to determine the areas within his department where cost could be reduced. Brainstorming sessions were held, a lot of soul-searching took place, ideas were exchanged and made. Each supervisor from Purchasing through Shipping was involved and each one submitted a list of possible cost-saving items. In this particular instance, 350 items were listed. The annual cost of each was then determined—which was a slow, tedious job, and these figures made available.

Simultaneous with the above, eleven meetings were conducted to explain to each salaried supervisor:

(1) The necessity for cost reduction.
(2) The basic concept of the program:
    (a) They would determine their projects.
    (b) They would determine their savings goals.
    (c) They would accept a cost savings project as a personal commitment.
    (d) A progress report would be made monthly to the *Cost Control Coordinator*.
    (e) They would report annually to a top management group.

After these meetings had been completed an overall dinner meeting was held and once again the entire program was reviewed in detail.

A few days later, the supervisors presented the proposed departmental projects (including annual cost of each) to their superiors. The supervisors then were asked to accept one and to commit themselves to an annual cost reduction for the project they had accepted.

A five per cent overall cost reduction for the first year was anticipated.

A newsletter covering important events, including a list of supervisors' cost reduction

DEPARTMENTS	Yearly Savings Expected	First Quarter		Second Quarter		Third Quarter		Fourth Quarter		Yearly Savings Accomplished
Machine Shop	$50,000	$15,000	16,000	$15,000	17,000	$10,000	10,000	$10,000	9,000	$52,000
Assembly	30,000	10,000	12,000	7,500	10,000	7,500	6,000	5,000	6,000	34,000
Toolroom	10,000	3,000	1,000	3,000	1,500	2,000	1,500	2,000	2,000	6,000
Shipping & Receiving	25,000	10,000	12,000	5,000	6,000	5,000	6,000	5,000	7,000	31,000
Plating	5,000	2,000	2,000	1,000	1,000	1,000	1,500	1,000	1,000	5,500
Maintenance	20,000	7,000	8,000	5,000	4,000	4,000	6,000	4,000	7,000	25,000
Production Control	5,000	2,000	1,000	1,000	500	1,000	500	1,000	--	2,000
Quality Control	10,000	4,000	4,000	2,000	2,200	2,000	1,800	2,000	2,000	10,000
Personnel	4,000	1,000	1,000	1,000	1,000	1,000	800	1,000	1,200	4,000
Manufacturing Engineering	11,000	4,000	5,000	3,000	4,000	2,000	1,000	2,000	2,000	12,000
TOTAL	$170,000	$58,000	$62,000	43,500	47,200	35,500	35,100	33,000	37,200	$181,500

EXHIBIT 13-1

Lewis R. Zeyher, *Production Manager's Desk Book* (Englewood Cliffs, N. J.: Prentice-Hall, Inc. Copyright © 1969), p. 97.

COST REDUCTION PROJECT · PROGRESS REPORT

DEPT. _____

Description of project ___ — etc.

	GAIN OR LOSS FOR MONTH	GAIN/LOSS TO DATE	GOAL TO DATE
OCT.	$500	$500	$2,000
NOV.	800	1,300	4,000
DEC.	(1,000)	300	6,000
JAN.	600	900	8,000
FEB.	(1,600)	(700)	10,000
MAR.	(1,000)	(1,700)	12,000
APR.			14,000
MAY			16,000
JUNE			18,000
JULY			20,000
AUG.			22,000
SEPT.			24,000
GOAL FOR YEAR			$24,000

GOAL

PROGRESS

SAVINGS IN DOLLARS

MONTHS OF YEAR

EXHIBIT 13-2

Lewis R. Zeyher, *Production Manager's Desk Book* (Englewood Cliffs, N. J.: Prentice-Hall, Inc. Copyright © 1969), p. 98.

commitments, was distributed to all interested parties. All employees in the plant and office were also made fully aware of the program's aims and cost reduction expectations.

Management had high hopes for this program. The competitive enthusiasm displayed among the supervisors was good and efforts were focused on keeping this spirit alive. Charts were prepared covering each project—these were kept up to date by the Cost Reduction Coordinator and were posted in the respective departments so all employees would know progress (or lack of progress) being made. Departmental comparison charts for plant-wide posting were also developed. Additional dinner meetings were conducted at which recognition was given to those who had made substantial progress and reports were made on the overall plant progress.

This program became effective in the fall of the year with approximately 150 projects aimed towards reducing costs $2,000,000 over a 12-month period. Costs of the previous 6 months were used as a base in practically all cases. Only one project required a capital expenditure.

Throughout the program work simplification principles were used like: Why do we do it? . . . Is it really necessary? . . . Can one job be combined with another one? . . . Can we substitute less costly materials? . . . Do we really need as much material as we have been using? All projects accepted by the supervisors were real challenges. The first month of the program, October, net savings were $60,000, November $200,000 and December $110,000. This was low because of the Christmas season (plant shutdown), and year-end accounting adjustments. To meet their goal an average of $170,000 per month had to be maintained. After the first of the year the program went into high gear and the men began to demonstrate what they could do.

Full running of the plant, of course, was necessary for good results as some unit costs climbed when operations were slack. In addition, the program had complete support and recognition from top management. Many directors visited the plant from time to time and questioned supervisors on results. The company magazine wrote up at least one successful project each month. Wide publicity was provided and all employees were kept informed of projects and performances.

COST REDUCTION HANDBOOK

A cost reduction handbook was developed and distributed to supervisors in the early stages of the program. The purpose of the handbook was to present some of the basic concepts, ideas and rules of cost reduction. It was intended to provide supervision with a reference for training and for use in maintaining an active program.

The handbook did not attempt to provide all the details for an active program as each department had to tailor its own needs. The handbook did present those items which have a bearing in the program.

The index of the *Cost Reduction Handbook* follows:

INDEX

COST REDUCTION HANDBOOK *

Note: These are *not* reproduced in this book because most titles are self-explanatory and because of space limitations. In addition, they must be tailored to fit each plant's particular situation.)

HOW IS AN EFFECTIVE COST REDUCTION PROGRAM ACCOMPLISHED?

A good Cost Reduction Program requires teamwork and is effective when those directing the program pursue a systematic approach along the following lines:

(1) Analysis of factors affecting costs.
(2) Development of methods of reducing costs.
(3) Setting of cost goals and comparison of performance against these goals.
(4) Publicizing performance.
(5) Obtaining the enthusiastic and active participation of every member of the organization.

Cost reduction can result not only through reductions of wasted time, motion, expenditures and other cost-making factors, but also through:

(1) Increased productivity.
(2) Decreased depreciation through prompt write-off of excess and obsolete material and equipment.
(3) Improved techniques and training.
(4) Technical improvements.
(5) Yield improvements.

The group supervisor is the *key man* in the Cost Reduction Program because he is the one who spends the money and controls the operation. He must therefore:

(a) Analyze costs.
(b) Know what the costs are and where they are.
(c) Know what the *variables* are and what *causes* them to vary.
(d) Institute cost reduction action based on this knowledge.
(e) Sell cost reduction to operators and mechanics.

(A) Fix Responsibility

It is the responsibility of each person who initiates an item of cost reduction to forward, through his supervision, all pertinent data to the *Cost Coordinator*. This data should include a description of the item, a description of how it will reduce costs, the date it was or is forecast to be in effect, frequency of use, price data, consumption data, and forecast savings for each quarter for one year from the effective date.

(B) Cost Reduction Goals

Goals in cost reduction, as in other fields, give direction to your efforts and stimulate your activity. Cost reduction goals:

(a) Should be interesting and challenging.
(b) Must be attainable, even though they require much hard work.
(c) Must not be self-limiting. This can happen if goals are easy to meet. Where possible, a cost reduction goal of "dollars per pound" is more realistic than "total dollars reduction."

(C) Securing Budgetary Allowance[2]

The initiation and operation of a program such as this will require the expenditure of additional monies. In consultation with the production manager and the controller, an estimate of this should be compiled by the appointed leader of the program. Costs to consider should include the following:

(1) The Cost Reduction Coordinator's salary.
(2) Clerks' time who compile cost records.
(3) Supervisors' and production employees' time attending meetings.
(4) Awards for outstanding performance.
(5) Plant posters, publicity and displays.
(6) Training time.
(7) Special dinner and final banquet.

---

2 Lewis R. Zeyher, *Production Manager's Desk Book,* (Englewood Cliffs, N.J.: Prentice-Hall, Inc., copyright © 1969), p. 96, lines 14-31.

(8) Outside speakers.

(9) Typing, multigraphing, Xeroxing and miscellaneous services.

After the budget has been approved it should be religiously followed. Programs like this can get out of hand, cost-wise. Misguided enthusiasm can create extravagant ideas that aren't always productive. An accounting clerk should keep a running record of expenditures.

COST REDUCTION CHECKLISTS BY CATEGORIES[3]

(A) Improving Returns from Capital Investments

(1) **Machine utilization:** machines used at less than a reasonable potential—80 to 90 per cent.

(2) **Setup:** machines down for too lengthy setups, too frequent and/or poorly conceived.

(3) **Maintenance:** necessary maintenance work done during scheduled production time and/or poor maintenance servicing, such as neglecting to lubricate or poor repair workmanship.

(4) **Debugging:** excessive labor spent in getting the new machines to run properly, or excessive breaking-in time.

(5) **Installation expense:** excessive costs in moving and installing of the equipment, especially over and above original estimates.

(6) **Production scheduling:** inneffecient scheduling resulting in excessive machine down-time, stand-by equipment and poor judgment exercised in assigning work to proper machine.

(7) **Production standards and/or incentives:** failure to establish a measured work program, implemented with production standards, or incentive pay plans to secure maximum operator production performances.

(8) **Tooling:** modern and effective machine tools designed and made for top quality work, as well as to accommodate high machine feeds and speeds, where practicable.

(9) **Planning:** this could include good planning in floor layout, such as locating machine in close proximity to raw materials, efficient arrangements for the temporary storage and/or material handling of the completed parts.

(B) Product Design and Value Analysis[4]

Note: This is a simple checklist based on the metal working field, which will trigger ideas for the kinds of questions your value analyst should ask even in totally different types of operations.

(1) Locate a cheaper material that will meet your specifications.

(2) Is the cost of a particular feature of the design proportionate to its usefulness?

---

3 Lewis R. Zeyher, *Cost Reduction in the Plant,* (Englewood Cliffs, N.J.: Prentice-Hall, Inc., copyright © 1965), p. 76, lines 23-42; p. 77, lines 1-3.

4 *Ibid.* Pages 48-49.

(3) Emphasize well-balanced design planning, covering new and less expensive materials, processes and equipment.

(4) Does the product need all its features?

(5) Can a usable part be made by a lower cost method?

(6) Can a standard product be found which will be usable?

(7) Is product made with proper tooling—considering quantities used?

(8) Will a dependable supplier provide part or product for less?

(9) Do material, reasonable labor, overhead and profit total its cost? (This is a good insurance against mistakes and poor judgment in estimating from one supplier.)

(10) Have you sought help from your various vendors?

(11) Do you test your products for over-design?

(12) Examine your processes—are the elements in proper sequence, proper machines designated, adequate tools and inspection equipment indicated?

(13) Review capabilities of the foundry processes of the material removal methods, and of the assemble procedure—a most helpful procedure for the design engineer.

(14) Do designers consider using miniature castings instead of light stampings?

(15) Have you thoroughly examined your packaging costs? Can some containers be redesigned, using less material?

(16) Do your design engineers consider using alloys which will enable faster machining—also cut tool wear?

(17) Have you considered combining operations?

(18) Examine your drill jigs—have they been designed according to work simplification principles, MTM, and do they provide maximum production yield per handling?

(19) Caution your designers about too tight tolerances and/or too fine finishes. The tougher these are to meet, the greater the scrap losses.

(20) Design your product for manufacturability?

(21) Assure yourself that castings are *not* over cleaned at the foundry.

(22) Standardize your materials, parts, supplies and equipment as much as is practicable.

(23) When ordering raw material consider such items as its configuration, length, width—seek the shape and size that will mimimize work in your originating operations.

(24) High product rejects may dictate need for design changes in some machines, equipment or tooling.

(25) Can *wire* rather than *bar* stock be used in some of your operations?

(26) When examining tooling costs decide whether product can be machined from a block of metal, forged, cast or molded. Each method has a different tooling cost.

(27) Should you engage in machinery and equipment modernization program? (Some companies fail to keep abreast of improvements in machine tool designs.)

(28) As volume of product improves do you review processes, machinery and tooling used?

(29) Are cross sections adequate to insure design intent?

(30) When increase in volume occurs do you consider changing types of operations' arrangement—fixed position, process flow or product flow?

(C) Preventive Maintenance[5]

By the utilization of the management tools and historical records available, an analysis of many maintenance operations can be initiated. Some of these operating areas where an analysis would be productive are:

(1) High cost work orders.
(2) Repetitive work orders for same problem and on same machine.
(3) Excess hours spent over the estimated hours allowed.
(4) Continued poor work performance by certain employees.
(5) Excessive and careless use of materials.
(6) Too loose or too tight standards or estimates.
(7) Too close frequency of inspections.
(8) Poor maintenance methods.
(9) Prohibitive cost of certain machines culled out from equipment records to determine causes.
(10) Too frequent breakdowns of same equipment.
(11) Machines, equipment, and accessories requiring redesign.
(12) Production operators who may be abusing equipment.
(13) Excessive overtime costs.
(14) Quality of maintenance work.
(15) Line supervisor's complaints.
(16) Control of stores' inventories, spare parts supply, and keeping proper balance of items kept in stock.
(17) Amount and type of emergency orders.
(18) Volume and nature of service orders by departments.
(19) Standardization of parts.
(20) Shoddy paperwork and placing responsibility for same.
(21) Possible procedure improvements.
(22) Improved reports to management.
(23) Review of major overhaul schedules and methods.
(24) Trends in type and frequency of repairs by use of spread sheets combined with work orders.

These checklists are merely samplings of such lists—every plant can easily prepare its own. Other chapters in this book include checklists. By stuying these lists with a specific problem in mind, ideas for improvement are almost certain to occur. The ideas raised by the checklist items must, of course, be thoroughly explored. There is always the danger when glancing over a list of twenty to fifty items that many of the items will be given only superficial consideration. While reading over a checklist, ideas for improvement often generate rapidly. They should be recorded as they occur and given later careful consideration lest some that are really worthwhile become lost and forgotten.

---

[5] Lewis R. Zeyher, *Cost Reduction in the Plant,* (Englewood Cliffs, N.J.: Prentice-Hall, Inc., copyright © 1965), p. 68, lines 31-42; p. 70, lines 1-19.

14

Making
Capital Investment
Decisions[1]

METHODS OF QUANTITATIVE ANALYSIS

Quantitative techniques lead to two general results:

(1) A comparison between two projects to show which is the better. Thus, a new project may be compared with an existing project or two new projects may be compared with each other.
(2) An index for each project which permits comparison or ranking of any number of projects.

Certain implicit assumptions underlie the various methods. Usually these are not stated but are easily recognized once they have been identified. Possible assumptions are that types of equipment being compared on the basis of cost/benefit relationships:

(1) Perform the same function at different cost.
(2) Perform different (improved quality) functions at:
    (a) The same cost.
    (b) Different costs.
(3) Perform improved functions (improved productivity) yielding greater revenue at:
    (a) The same costs.
    (b) Different costs.
(4) Perform new functions (make a different product to yield increased profit by means of a better cost-revenue relationship).
(5) Have different lives and patterns of costs and revenue.

Thus, methods of analysis which compare only costs or cost savings imply that all other factors remain the same.

---

1 From *The Management of Capital Expenditures*, R.G. Murdick and D.D. Deming. Copyright © 1968, McGraw-Hill, Inc. Used by permission of McGraw-Hill Book Company. Pp. 64-72.

SOME BASIC CONCEPTS

The economics of decision making is simple in concept. The management of a company has in its possession a net aggregate of physical and cash (or cash equivalent) assets. The question which management faces is: "How can we best employ these resources so as to yield the greatest on-going return?" It does not matter what the present assets cost, or how long or short a time the company has had them, except as these matters affect future cash benefits. It conceivably might be advisable for a company to liquidate its assets and pay off the owners if the banks offer a higher return on savings than the company can earn for the owners.

The future result of a management decision is represented by a series of cash expenditures and cash revenues which, combined, are the anticipated cash benefits. This stream of cash benefits, discounted to the present time, is the measure of the value of an investment. Management should be seeking those investments which will optimize all company cash benefits in the short run, and particularly in the long run.

A second basic concept is the distinction between accounting data and the cash flows relevant to decision making. The decision maker often must rely on accounting data to compute cash-flow items. One of these accounting or "book" terms which causes considerable confusion is "depreciation" and another is "profit." The relationship between these book terms and the cash-flow items of "investment" and "cash benefits" is indicated below:

Cash benefits (net cash inflow)	Investment (cash outflow)
— depreciation (book entry)	— depreciation (book entry)
Profit (book entry)	Reduces investment (book value)

One important relationship derived from the above table is that cash benefits over the years provide for profits and capital recovery:

$$\text{Cash benefits} = \text{profit} + \text{depreciation}$$

The other more obvious conclusion is that: Investment—book value of investment = depreciation.

A third concept is that while past (sunk) costs and depreciation of equipment are by themselves irrelevant to the decision maker, they do affect the cash flow of taxes in the future. The relationship between depreciation (a book entry depending on past history) and taxes which represent future cash expenditures is shown first in symbolic form (Exhibit 14-1) and then in a numerical example (Exhibit 14-2).

EXHIBIT 14-1: Symbolic Relationship Between Book and Cash Items Taking into Account Taxes

	On Books	Cash Flow
Cash benefits due to savings or increased earnings....	CB	CB
Depreciation on new machine....DN		
Less: depreciation of old machine....DO		
Additional depreciation expense............	$DN - DO = \underline{DA}$	
Additional taxable income.................	$CB - DA$	
Increase in income tax (50%)....	$0.5\ (CB\ -\ DA)$	$0.5\ (CB - DA)$
Net additional income after taxes......	$\overline{0.5\ (CB\ -\ DA)}$	
Net annual cash benefits after taxes..........		$CB\ -\ 0.5\ (CB - DA)$ $= 0.5\ (CB + DA)$

EXHIBIT 14-2: Numerical Example of Relationship Between Book and Cash Items Taking into Account Taxes

	ON BOOKS	CASH FLOW
Cash benefits due to savings or increased earnings	$10,000	$10,000
Depreciation on new machine $2,000		
Less: depreciation on old machine 1,000		
Additional depreciation expense . . $1,000	1,000*	
Additional taxable income	9,000	
Increase in income tax (50%)	4,500	4,500
Net additional income after taxes	$ 4,500*	
Net annual cash benefits after taxes		$ 5,500*

*$1,000 + $4,500 = $5,500

A fourth basic concept is that $1 today is worth more than $1 offered to us at some future time. For this reason, revenues or costs which will occur in the future must be reduced or discounted to make them comparable to today's dollars. Conversely, if we loan out a dollar today to be returned at some future date, we expect a greater amount to be returned for each year it is loaned out.

At the interest rate i, a sum S will be worth A dollars at the end of one year. The relationship is:

$$A = S + iS = S(1 + i)$$

After two years,

$$A = S(1 + i) + iS(1 + i) = S(1 + i)^2$$

After n years,

$$A = S(1 + i)^n$$

If $S = \$100$, $i = 4\%$, and $n = 5$ years, then

$$A = 100(1.04)^5 = (100)\ 1.2166 = \$121.66$$

The present value of the future amount A is found by solving for S:

$$S = \frac{A}{(1 + i)^n}$$

If $A = \$100$, $i = 4\%$, and $n = 5$ years

$$S = 100(1.04)^{-5} = 100(0.8219)$$
$$S = \$82.19$$

Thus $82.19 today is as good as $100 payable five years hence. Some of the cruder methods of investment analysis do not take into consideration this "time value" of money.

The fifth basic concept is also related to the time value of money. When an investment is made in equipment, the company ties up its own funds or borrows money. In either case, there is an expense associated with the use of money. If the company borrows money, it pays interest to whoever loans it. This is an expense easily identified by the accountant and his books. If the company uses its own money, it foregoes the opportunity of loaning out this money or putting it to work in some other way. The opportunity of earning this money represents a cost to the company just as real as the interest rate for borrowing. This cost does not appear in the accountant's books but must be taken into consideration in decision making. It is *implicit* cost called an "opportunity" cost.

Payback Method

The payback method is the simplest and perhaps most commonly used quantitative method for evaluating an investment. It answers the question: "How many years will it take for the cash benefits to pay for the cost of the investment?"

$$\text{(1) Payback time} = \frac{\text{investment}}{\text{cash benefits per year}}$$

For example, suppose we wish to purchase a group of machines to produce a new product. The machines cost $240,000 and the cash benefits are anticipated to be $40,000 per year. Cash benefits are, of course, the excess of revenues over cash expenditures. Then,

$$\text{Payback time} = \frac{\$240,000}{\$40,000} = 6 \text{ years}$$

If we are considering replacing a machine whose salvage value is $5,000 with a new machine costing $23,000, which will save us $4,000 per year in operating expenses, the formula may be restated slightly.

$$\text{Payback time} = \frac{\text{net investment}}{\text{net cash benefits}} = \frac{\text{net investment}}{\text{savings}}$$

$$\frac{\$23,000 - 5,000}{\$4,000} = 4.5 \text{ years}$$

$$\text{(2) After payback} = \frac{\text{investment}}{\text{cash benefits}} = \frac{\text{investment}}{\text{profits after taxes} + \text{depreciation}}$$

If we refer to Exhibit 14-1 and remember that *CB* represents cash benefits and *D* represents depreciation, then

$$\text{After payback time} = \frac{\text{investment}}{0.5(CB - D) + D} = \frac{\text{investment}}{0.5(CB + D)}$$

An investment of $85,000 for plant and equipment and $15,000 for working capital is being considered. Profits of $10,000 per year after taxes are expected. Depreciation charges will be $1,700 per year. What will be the after tax payback time?

$$\text{After payback time} = \frac{\text{investment}}{\text{profits after taxes} + \text{depreciation}}$$

$$\text{After payback time} = \frac{\$100,000}{\$10,000 + \$17,000} = 3.7 \text{ years}$$

Or alternately,

$$\text{After payback time} = \frac{\text{investment}}{0.5 \, (CB + D)}$$

$$\frac{\$100,000}{0.5 \, (\$37,000 + \$17,000)} = 3.7 \text{ years}$$

Return on Investment

The common accounting approach to return on investment is equivalent to the reciprocal of the payback formula.

$$\text{(1) Return on investment} = \frac{\text{cash benefits}}{\text{investment}}$$

$$\text{(2) Cash-flow return after taxes} = \frac{\text{cash benefits}}{\text{investment}}$$

$$= \frac{\text{profits after taxes} + \text{depreciation}}{\text{investment}}$$

$$= \frac{0.5\,(\text{CB} + \text{D})}{\text{investment}}$$

The common accounting approach often uses gross investment rather than the correct value, the net investment, for replacement analysis. In addition, the accounting approach may use a variation which does not represent future cash flows but uses an accounting term in the numerator which reduces the apparent return.

$$\text{(3) Return on Investment} = \frac{\text{Profits after taxes}}{\text{investment}}$$

First-Year Performance

In the first-year performance method, costs are calculated for each of the alternatives for the next year only. This avoids discounting and covers the period about which most is known. Consider the case of a service company which either rents cars or uses them for company purposes such as delivery of sales.

Example:

Cost of new car—$3,000, life—5 yrs		Old car value—$1,500, life—3 yrs.	
Depreciation next year ....$	900	Depreciation next year ....$	700
10% interest on capital	300	10% interest on capital	150
Operating cost 8c/mile		Operating cost 11c/mile	
(10,000) miles)	800	(10,000 miles)	1,100
	$2,000		$1,950

In the above example, the quantitative analysis indicates that both alternatives are about the same from an economic viewpoint. The final decision would be based upon judgment of other factors and of the degree of uncertainty of the data employed.

Total-Life Average or Full-Life Performance

The total-life average lumps together all costs involved in owning and operating a unit of equipment over its life. This sum is divided by the estimated life of the machine to give an average annual cost. The comparison between investments is thus on a cost basis, and it is assumed that the alternatives produce the same revenue.

$$\text{Average Cost/Year} = \frac{\text{operating costs} + \text{depreciation} + \text{interest}}{\text{estimated years of life}}$$

Example:

	Old machine	*New machine*

Given: $2,000 market value $11,000 installed cost
No scrap value $1,000 scrap value 8 years of life
2 years life remaining $36,000 annual operating costs
$4,500 annual operating   excluding depreciation
  costs excluding depreciation 10% interest
10% interest

Costs: $ 2,000   Depreciation over remaining
          9,000 (2 years)   life $10,000
            300   Operating cost . .$28,800 (8 yrs)
        ‾‾‾‾‾‾‾   Interest at 10% .   5,300
        $11,300   ‾‾‾‾‾‾‾
                                                   $44,100

$$\frac{\text{Average cost}}{\text{year}} = \frac{\$11,300}{2} = \$5,650$$

$$\frac{\text{Average cost}}{\text{year}} = \frac{\$44,100}{8} = \$5,512$$

$$\text{Interest on old machine} = 0.10 \times \$2,000 + 0.10 \times \$1,000 = \$300$$

If the new machine is depreciated on a straight-line basis from $11,000 to $1,000 over a period of eight years, the depreciation will be $1,250 per year. The interest on the new machine is computed as follows:

0.10	X	$11,000	$1,100	interest for the first year
0.10	X	9,750	975	interest for the second year
0.10	X	8,500	850	interest for the third year
0.10	X	7,250	725	interest for the fourth year
0.10	X	6,000	600	interest for the fifth year
0.10	X	4,750	475	interest for the sixth year
0.10	X	3,500	350	interest for the seventh year
0.10	X	2,250	225	interest for the eighth year

As a shortcut, the interest may be computed by multiplying the average interest payment (composed of the sum of the first and last payments divided by two) by the number of years.

$$\text{Interest} = \frac{0.10\,(\$11,000 + \$2,250)}{2} \times 8 = \$5,300$$

Note that the last payment = salvage value + the annual depreciation X interest rate = ($1,000 + $10,000/8) (0.10) = $225.

Average Rate of Return

The average rate-of-return method is based upon accounting terms rather than cash flow. It does not take into account the time value of money and assumes profits are fairly constant.

$$\text{Average rate of return} = \frac{\text{average annual net income after taxes}}{\text{average investment over the life of the project}}$$

$$= \frac{\text{after tax profit}}{\text{average investment over the life of the project}}$$

Example:

An investment in a plastic molding machine which costs $12,000 requires working capital of $3,000 for inventory and accounts receivable. After-tax profits are expected to average $2,700 per year over the six-year life of the machine. There is no salvage value at the end of life.

$$\text{Average investment} = \$3,000 + 1/2\,(\$12,000) = \$9,000$$
$$\text{Average rate of return} = \frac{\$2,700}{\$9,000} = 0.30 \text{ or } 30\%$$

Present-Worth Method

The present-worth or present value method is one of the better methods of investment analysis because it takes into account the time value of money. The present-worth method discounts future costs and revenues in order to compare the present value of future benefits with the present value of the investment. If the present value of the benefits does not exceed the investment, the investment should not be made.

When a new project is being considered, a profitability index may be computed. The first example below illustrates this. If two projects which have different service lives are being compared, they must be compared over the same period of time. The comparison may thus extend over multiples of the lives of each.

Thus, if the service life of one project is three years and another is four years, the comparison must be over a 12-year period with replacements occurring for each. The second example below illustrates this point in a very simple fashion.

Example:

A company is considering purchasing a No. 2 Centerless Grinder to produce a new product. The basic data on the machine are:

Initial investment $18,000
Service life. . . . . 10 years
Disposal value at end of life $5,000
Straight-line depreciation $1,000/year
Interest rate 10%

Some refinements are neglected in the table shown in Exhibit 14-3 for simplicity of showing the general approach.

End of Year	Operating Costs	Revenue	Cash Benefits	Cash Benefits after Taxes 0.5 (CB—D)	Discount Factor	Today's Value
1	$12,000	$18,000	$ 6,000	$3,500	0.9091	$3,182
2	12,100	21,000	8,900	4,950	0.8264	4,091
3	12,200	22,000	9,800	5,400	0.7513	4,057
4	12,400	22,500	10,100	5,550	0.6830	3,791
5	12,600	21,000	8,400	4,700	0.6209	2,918
6	12,900	19,500	6,600	3,800	0.5645	2,145
7	13,300	18,000	4,700	2,850	0.5132	1,463
8	14,000	17,000	3,000	2,000	0.4665	933
9	15,000	16,000	1,000	1,000	0.4241	424
10	15,000	16,000	1,000	1,000	0.3855	386
					Present value	$23,390

EXHIBIT 14-3

Present value of the capital investment

$$= \$18,000 - \frac{\$5,000}{(1 + 0.10)^{10}}$$

$$= 18,000 - 5,000 \,(0.3855)$$

$$= 16,072$$

Let V = present value of the cash flow

C = present value of the capital investment

(a) Profitability index $= \dfrac{V}{C} = \dfrac{\$23,390}{\$16,072} = 1.45$

(b) Return on investment $\dfrac{V - C}{C} = \dfrac{V}{C} - 1 = 0.45$

or

$\underline{\underline{45\%}}$

15

Controlling Operations at the Product Distribution Center

The warehousing and distribution functions are usually the most widely neglected areas of company operations. In general, there is a significant lag in the implementation of modern technology in these important cost centers. Inefficiencies are more difficult to detect than in plant processing departments, but progressive managements have begun to recognize major savings potentials existing here. While sales department needs and demands sometime conflict with acceptable operating practices, top management should insist on an optimum balance between service and costs. To bring about the desired results managers must first know and be able to apply the basic principles of modern management and then know how to introduce and properly maintain the most effective techniques of control.

INTRODUCING WORK STANDARDS IN WAREHOUSING

Little progress can be made in improving efficiencies without some form of work measurement. Standards provide a point of reference. Scoring in golf is an example. Every course has par for each hole and for the completion of the game. *Par* acts as a reference point—the player can either make par for the hole, or play so many strokes over or under par. With each game he can try to improve his previous performance. Without scientifically developed work standards, controls are based on estimates, which are subjective and therefore unreliable. (See Chapter 5 for more detail on work standards; also Chapter 9 for handling time and space utilization standards.)

Various techniques are available for the proper introduction of standards, including time study, methods-time-measurement, work factor and work sampling. Due to the many variables encountered in warehousing operations, work sampling lends itself well to the measurement of indirect labor. (See Chapter 4.) However, repetitive operations can best be measured by the other methods mentioned. (Also see L.R. Zeyher's *Production Manager's Handbook of Formulas and Tables*, Prentice-Hall, Inc., Englewood Cliffs, N.J. 07632.)

Example of Dray Delivery Standards[1]

(a) <u>General Data:</u>

		Standard Minutes
(1)	Plant and Personal Time—each Day	120
	" " " " —Overnight—Add	75
	(Total for Both Days . . . . . 195 Minutes)	
(2)	Travel Time—Allowable Average Minutes for Miles and Farthest Zone Travelled. (See Appropriate Table.)	– – – –
(3)	Stop Time—Each Stop—Delivery and Non-Delivery	10
	" Dead Stop	5
(4)	Drums (550 + 400 D). Each Drum Picked Up or Delivered	1
(5)	Cartons-Buckets—1200—Allowance Average Minutes from Appropriate Tables for Total Pieces Delivered (120D = 2 pcs.)	
	A. Total Pieces from 1-25 Piece Orders @ .53 min/pc	
	B. " " " 26-100 " " @ .41 " "	**
	C. " " " 101-500 " " @ .35 " "	
(6)	Delay and Repair Time (Actual) from ARPE 253	– – – –
(7)	Each Additional Trip in One Day Add	45
(8)	Refueling—over 200 Miles in One Day Add	10
(9)	Rest Stop—over 200 Miles in One Day Add	10
	Total Standard Minutes	

Compare Total Standard Minutes and Total Actual Minutes (from ARPE 253).
If Standard more than actual = — (Difference) . . . Favorable
If " less " " = + (Difference) . . . Unfavorable

**Include delivery time for orders or part orders not delivered but returned to package warehouse and unloaded.

Also see Exhibits 15-1, 15-2, 15-3 and 15-4.

Warehouse Operations (with Powered Trucks)

Warehouses using powered trucks must maintain a minimum aisle width of 10 feet for truck maneuvering. Yellow lines should be painted on the floor indicating aisles. When receiving palletized truck loads, stack the pallets in rows no greater than three pallets high leaving at least 3 inches between rows. If the stack height exceeds 21 feet, limit stacking to two pallets high.

(a) There are two types of drums which are received at warehouse locations, open top and bung type. Open top drums must be stored upright, three to a pallet and no more than three pallets high. Bung type drums may be laid on their side on specially constructed pallets two to a pallet, stacked a maximum of four pallets high.

(b) A location chart should be prepared for the warehouse indicating a pre-designated location for brands and grades of products. When locating rows for a

---

1 Used with permission of the Atlantic Richfield Company.

(b) Specific Data:

DRAY DELIVERY STANDARDS
CARTONS—BUCKETS—120 LB. DRUMS
(EACH 120 DRUMS = 2 PIECES)
1 TO 25 CASE ORDERS
TOTAL PIECES DELIVERED

pcs.	min.	pcs.	min.	pcs.	min.	pcs.	min.	pcs.	min.	pcs.	min.	pcs.	min.
1	1	16	9	31	17	46	25	61	33	76	41	91	49
2	2	17	9	32	17	47	25	62	33	77	41	92	49
3	2	18	10	33	18	48	26	63	34	78	42	93	50
4	3	19	11	34	19	49	26	64	34	79	42	94	50
5	3	20	11	35	19	50	27	65	35	80	43	95	51
6	4	21	12	36	20	51	28	66	35	81	43	96	51
7	4	22	12	37	20	52	28	67	36	82	44	97	52
8	5	23	13	38	21	53	29	68	37	83	44	98	52
9	5	24	13	39	21	54	29	69	37	84	45	99	53
10	6	25	14	40	22	55	30	70	38	85	46	100	53
11	6	26	14	41	22	56	30	71	38	86	46	200	106
12	7	27	15	42	23	57	31	72	39	87	47	300	159
13	7	28	15	43	23	58	31	73	39	88	47	400	212
14	8	29	16	44	24	59	32	74	40	89	48	500	265
15	8	30	16	45	24	60	32	75	40	90	48		

.53 MINUTES PER PIECE

EXHIBIT 15-1

DRAY DELIVERY STANDARDS
CARTONS—BUCKETS—120 LB. DRUMS
(EACH 120 DRUMS = 2 PIECES)
26 to 100 CASE ORDERS
TOTAL PIECES DELIVERED

pcs.	min.	pcs.	min.	pcs.	min.	pcs.	min.	pcs.	min.	pcs.	min.	pcs.	min.
1	1	16	7	31	13	46	19	61	25	76	32	91	38
2	1	17	7	32	14	47	20	62	26	77	32	92	38
3	2	18	8	33	14	48	20	63	26	78	32	93	39
4	2	19	8	34	14	49	21	64	27	79	33	94	39
5	3	20	9	35	15	50	21	65	27	80	33	95	39
6	3	21	9	36	15	51	21	66	28	81	34	96	40
7	3	22	10	37	16	52	22	67	28	82	34	97	40
8	4	23	10	38	16	53	22	68	28	83	34	98	41
9	4	24	10	39	16	54	23	69	29	84	35	99	41
10	5	25	11	40	17	55	23	70	29	85	35	100	41
11	5	26	11	41	17	56	23	71	30	86	36	200	82
12	5	27	12	42	18	57	24	72	30	87	36	300	123
13	6	28	12	43	18	58	24	73	30	88	37	400	164
14	6	29	12	44	19	59	25	74	31	89	37	500	205
15	7	30	13	45	19	60	25	75	31	90	37		

.41 MINUTES PER PIECE

EXHIBIT 15-2

DRAY DELIVERY STANDARDS
TRAVEL TIME
ZONE 31

miles	min.	miles	min.	miles	min.	miles	min.	miles	min.	miles	min.
1	2	21	35	41	67	61	99	81	132	200	325
2	4	22	36	42	69	62	101	82	133	300	487
3	5	23	38	43	70	63	103	83	135	400	649
4	7	24	39	44	72	64	105	84	137		
5	9	25	41	45	73	65	106	85	138		
6	10	26	43	46	75	66	108	86	140		
7	12	27	44	47	77	67	109	87	142		
8	13	28	46	48	78	68	111	88	143		
9	15	29	47	49	80	69	113	89	145		
10	16	30	49	50	82	70	114	90	147		
11	18	31	51	51	83	71	116	91	148		
12	20	32	52	52	85	72	117	92	150		
13	22	33	54	53	86	73	119	93	151		
14	23	34	56	54	88	74	121	94	153		
15	25	35	57	55	90	75	122	95	155		
16	26	36	59	56	91	76	124	96	156		
17	28	37	60	57	93	77	125	97	158		
18	30	38	62	58	94	78	127	98	160		
19	31	39	64	59	96	79	129	99	161		
20	33	40	65	60	98	80	130	100	163		

EASTERN SHORE

EXHIBIT 15-3

particular brand and size, all fast moving items or special sales items should be located closest to the order assembling area.

(c) When assembling orders for loading, keep the same size package on the same pallet for each order or mix orders the same way. This will make square pallet loads and result in safer packing in the truck.

(d) It is important to continuously rotate warehouse stocks. In all cases the oldest material is to be shipped first.

Warehouse Operations (Manpower Only)

Warehouses where only manpower is used to handle packages will adhere to the following:

(a) All drums are to be stored top side up, only one high except where horizontal drum racks are provided. When it is necessary to handle the drums, use a hand truck. *Never* put a drum on its side and roll it by pushing it with your foot or hand.

(b) Generally where there are no powered trucks the packages are not received palletized. When not palletized, stack packages no greater than 7 boxes high and five gallon buckets no greater than 6 high.

(c) A location chart should be established indicating the designated areas where each brand and package size is to be stored. When locating rows, all fast moving

DRAY DELIVERY STANDARDS
TRAVEL TIME
ZONE 2
3

miles	min.	miles	min.	miles	min.	miles	min.	miles	min.	miles	min.
1	5	21	97	41	189	61	282	81	374	200	923
2	10	22	103	42	194	62	286	82	378	300	
3	14	23	106	43	198	63	291	83	383	400	
4	19	24	111	44	203	64	295	84	388		
5	23	25	116	45	208	65	300	85	392		
6	28	26	120	46	212	66	304	86	396		
7	33	27	125	47	217	67	309	87	401		
8	37	28	130	48	221	68	314	88	406		
9	42	29	134	49	226	69	319	89	410		
10	46	30	139	50	231	70	323	90	415		
11	51	31	143	51	235	71	328	91	420		
12	56	32	148	52	240	72	332	92	424		
13	60	33	152	53	245	73	337	93	429		
14	65	34	157	54	249	74	341	94	433		
15	70	35	162	55	254	75	346	95	438		
16	74	36	166	56	259	76	351	96	443		
17	79	37	171	57	263	77	355	97	447		
18	83	38	175	58	268	78	360	98	452		
19	88	39	180	59	272	79	364	99	456		
20	93	40	185	60	277	80	369	100	461		

W. PHILA.
N. PHILA.

EXHIBIT 15-4

items or special sales items should be located closest to the order assembling area. Line with yellow paint.

(d) Small packages should be piled so that they will not overturn or fall down. Packages should never be stored on top of drums. Cases should be stacked securely. All drums and other package goods in storage should be kept tightly sealed at all times. Drums and packages should be handled in such a manner that breakage or leakage will be minimized. If leakage does occur, the damaged container should be removed, and any fire or slipping hazard should be eliminated.

Warehouse Receipts

Drums and packages are received by truck and may arrive damaged. All damaged material must be segregated as the truck is unloaded. Before unloading the truck, obtain a bill of lading and the package stock manifest from the driver. Count the entire shipment including damaged material, if any. If the received quantity differs from the quantity indicated on the package stock manifest, indicate the actual received quantity on the package stock manifest in ink. All deficiencies must be reported to the Stock Group in Philadelphia, using the post card which accompanies the package stock manifest.

All new material is to be stored behind older stocks of the same brand and package size or in rows side by side so that stock removal can be alternated. It is important to continuously rotate all stocks.

Because loads may shift while in transit, and because packages may fall from the truck when the door is opened, it is advisable to stand to one side and open the door slowly. A dock board should be securely anchored between the loading dock and the truck.

When unloading trailers, be certain the brakes are set and wheel chocks placed under the rear wheels to prevent the trailer from rolling.

The flooring of trailers shall be checked for weaknesses or damage before any powered trucks are driven into them.

Handling of Damaged or Leaking Packages

Damaged or leaking packages result from shipment or mishandling while in storage. Whenever a stored case exhibits damaged contents, remove the case from storage immediately to avoid staining the surrounding boxes. All leaking cartons, either from storage or from receipts, are to be opened and the leaking cans removed. The remaining good cans are to be wiped clean and repacked when enough good cans have been assembled. The defective or damaged cans are to be emptied immediately into a 55 gallon drum. Some leakers are hard to detect. Suspected leakers and good cans must stand several hours in clean paper or cardboard to detect a leak. Check both ends.

Order Disbursement Procedures

Obtain from the package stock clerk the B-30 D's in order of their delivery. Starting with the last delivery, pull the stock for each order and load the truck in the same manner. For orders which are palletized, place the same size package on each pallet for each order or mix orders.

Package trucks should not be loaded beyond their capacity, and packages should be placed so that one person will be able to move or handle them if the driver must unload alone. Drums and cases should be secured to prevent shifting or falling.

Package goods should never be loaded on top of drums, except with dunnage between drums and cases.

> *Caution:* A frequent source of injury is the carrying, placing and removing of dock plates. When manual handling of plates is the rule, it is a common practice to man-handle the plates into position, and then to drop them into place. Dropping them into place is prohibited because the practice is a source of many injuries. Plates should be lowered or slid into place.

Enough men should be assigned to carry a plate to prevent strains and other lifting injuries.

Lifting and placing of plates safely can be enhanced by the use of hooks and holes, lifting rings, forklifts, hand trucks and safe storing and unloading practices.

Loading Trucks

The same general precautions regarding trailers indicated under Receiving shall also be followed when loading trailers. The trailer to be loaded must be kept clean to prevent staining the case goods.

Warehouse Housekeeping

The warehouse, warehouse tools, hand trucks, etc. should be maintained in first class repair at all times. Broken panes in windows should be replaced immediately. Doors should be weathertight and in satisfactory condition, and should be kept free of obstructions. Defective hinges, hangers, or tracks may result in personal injury. Any time that the warehouse is left unattended, even for short periods, all doors should be locked.

Doorways, aisle space, and passageways should be kept clear. A clear space marked by yellow lines should be maintained around fire protection equipment and the location of such equipment should be distinctively marked. Fire doors, if provided, should be maintained so they will operate automatically in the event of fire. Fusible links should not be painted.

Smoking shall be prohibited except in a designated area. No smoking signs shall be posted in prohibited areas.

Floors, loading platforms, and stairways should be kept free of oil spills, projecting nails, splinters, and worn or weak spots. Broken planking and floor members should be repaired immediately. Supporting timbers should be regularly inspected. Holes or breaks in concrete floors should be patched to prevent falls or injuries. Floor areas in which drums are stored and in which hand trucks are used should be as level as possible. As stock is removed, sweep the empty floor spaces clean.

Operation of Forklift Trucks

Only drivers authorized and trained in the safe operation of the forklift truck shall be permitted to operate such vehicles. A written record must be maintained for all training given to an operator.

Before operating, drivers shall check the vehicle; if is is found to be unsafe, the matter shall be reported immediately and the vehicle shall not be put in service until repairs have been made.

Special consideration shall be given to the condition of tires, horn, lights, battery, controller lift system (including forks, chains, cable and limit switches), brakes and steering mechanism.

Forklifts shall be operated at an authorized safe speed, consistent with conditions, always maintaining a safe distance from other vehicles and keeping the truck under positive control at all times. No riders shall be permitted and no one shall ride on the forks.

Stunt driving and horseplay are prohibited.

Whenever operator leaves truck, it shall be shut off and the emergency brake set. Never leave truck with engine running.

General Precautions

(1) Make certain you know the operation procedure and capacities of every piece of equipment you handle. Run through a safety check of the truck before starting.
(2) Operate the truck from the operator's seat or platform only.
(3) If operating conditions prevent the use of overhead guards and backrests (both are provided as standard equipment on all trucks), use extreme care. Under these conditions, never lift a load higher than the load backrest or mast.
(4) Never overload the truck.

(5) Drive carefully and slowly across secured dockboards and never exceed the rated capacity.

(6) In forklift trucks, spread the forks as far apart as the load will permit and seat the load against the backrest.

(7) Do not handle unstable loads.

(8) Use extreme caution when handling wide or high loads, and when it interferes with visibility, face the direction of travel.

(9) Always keep the load as low as possible when moving.

(10) Never turn on a ramp. Always keep the load uphill by backing down a ramp when truck is loaded.

(11) Start, top, change direction, travel and brake smoothly.

(12) Use extreme care when tilting a load, particularly when high-tiering. Never tilt an elevated load forward except when in a deposit position. Use only enough backward tilt to stabilize the load.

(13) Allow no one under or near load or lifting mechanism.

(14) Carry no passengers, and never elevate anyone/anything without a secured safety platform.

(15) When leaving the truck unattended or parking, make sure it is properly shut down, key removed and wheels blocked or parking brake set.

(16) Avoid running over loose objects.

(17) Slow down for wet or slippery surfaces.

(18) Fuel tanks shall not be filled while the engine is running. Do not operate any truck which has a fuel leak.

(19) All forklift trucks must be kept clean, and free of lint, oil and grease.

(Also see Chapter 3.)

16

Managing
Trucking
Operations

Today most commodities are transported by truck, due largely to its many advantages over its main competitor—the railroads. Maneuverability and flexibility are the most important advantages. Transportation performance usually is difficult to measure, causing many companies to neglect this important function of warehousing. The capital investment in truck fleet equipment alone demands close attention to such considerations as: proper selection of equipment, well-trained drivers, proper maintenance, competent scheduling or routing, adequate material handling equipment, well-planned loading and unloading docks, expeditious handling of paperwork by warehouse personnel, safety and accident prevention programs, able dispatchers, constant awareness to delays and obstacles and their prompt elimination, controls and other related actions.

[1]It is recommended that, where practical, the warehousing and shipping functions report directly to the production control Manager. To insure minimal receiving cost, close cooperation between the purchasing and traffic departments is mandatory. An aggressive traffic department, working in concert with the purchasing function, can arrange to use transportation services where optimum operating economies can best be effected. The types of equipment used by suppliers in delivering merchandise should fit your receiving dock's requirements, and the carrier's method of unloading should dovetail with your material handling facilities. Deliveries should also be made at times convenient for the department and when adequate manpower is available, thereby obviating the need to pay overtime premiums. In addition, the goods unloaded should be packaged to permit economical movement. Incoming material should be loaded directly onto conveyors, trucks, pallets and similar handling devices and not placed on the bare floor, resulting in double handling.

---

[1] Lewis R. Zeyher, *Cost Reduction in the Plant*, (Englewood Cliffs, N.J.: Prentice-Hall, Inc., copyright © 1965), p. 51, lines 7-21.

TRAFFIC MANAGERS' DUTIES IN WAREHOUSING[2]

In small warehouse operations the traffic function can be carried out on a part time basis by one of the office staff. Large operations may require a full time traffic manager. In either case, the warehouse manager should not delegate too much of his own responsibility. There are too many ways for wasteful practices to get into the traffic function. It should have a prominent place in the warehouse manager's scope of responsibilities.

The traffic manager's duties in warehousing are to:

(1) Determine which carriers will provide the most reliable and economical delivery service.

(2) Assign proper tariff classifications to freight and obtain the minimum legal rates.

(3) Know freight charges in advance of shipments, and audit freight bills against these predetermined charges. (The warehouse manager should authorize freight bill payments.)

(4) Follow up and expedite shipments as required to meet warehouse schedules.

(5) File carrier claims for loss and damage.

(6) Work with the responsible warehouse personnel to save money on freight through consolidations, stop-offs, etc.

(7) Give the responsible warehouse personnel advice on freight tariffs and other government regulations affecting warehouse freight and the use of warehouse trucks.

COST REDUCTION POSSIBILITIES[3]

Areas where cost reduction possibilities generally exist are listed below:

(1) Select proper freight classifications, which should be reviewed periodically.

(2) Use most economical small package shipment method (air freight, less-than-carload freight, parcel post, express, and first class mail.)

(3) Protect against possible damage in transport by efficient loading of carrier's equipment, and by adequate blocking and bracing of freight car shipments.

(4) Keep less-than-carload and less-than-truckload shipments to a minimum.

(5) Select most economical routing and also periodically review your selections—conditions and rates change.

(6) Use proper packaging and adequate as well as economical packing of products.

(7) When a number of deliveries or stops are to be made, assure yourself that the sequence of the loading of materials in the truck conforms with routing specified.

(8) Arrange to control and minimize demurrage costs. Unload cars promptly and notify railroad freight agent immediately when cars are ready to be moved from company siding.

(9) Look for careless and substandard markings on packages.

---

2 Creed H. Jenkins, copyright © 1968 by McGraw-Hill, Inc. Used with permission of McGraw-Hill Book Company. P. 196, lines 7-29.

3 Lewis R. Zeyher, *Cost Reduction in the Plant,* (Englewood Cliffs, N.J.: Prentice-Hall, Inc., copyright © 1965), p. 54, lines 25-41; p. 55, lines 1-6.

(10) Insist on legibility of your bills of lading. Avoid handwritten copies and make sure your carbons on typewritten copies are legible.
(11) Check quantities and condition of packages received from vendors. Also check same when you make shipments to customers.
(12) When notifying carriers to pick up materials be sure to advise them in advance and arrange to secure the best equipment for your particular shipping needs.

PIGGYBACK SHIPPING[4]

One new method that offers great cost reduction possibilities to many companies is the railroads' piggyback plans. Piggyback combines the flexibility of over-the-road trucks with the low-cost long-haul characteristics of the train. This is done in five different ways:

- Plan I calls for the railroad to carry the trailers of common carriers.
- Plan II puts the railroad in the trucking business, offering door-to-door service to shippers.
- Plan III calls for the railroad to haul piggyback shipper-owned or leased trailers at a flat charge, whether loaded or empty.
- Plan IV calls for the railroad to move shipper-owned trailers on shipper-owned flatcars.
- Plan V puts the railroad and the common carrier in partnership giving joint service to shippers. *

CONTAINER HANDLING

A refinement of piggybacking that has interesting possibilities is containerization. You can load your trailer at your warehouse in Chicago, drive it to the railroad yards, transfer the body (container) from the chassis to a flatcar, move it by train to the docks at San Francisco, load the body into hold of ship, have it taken to Japan, reload the container on a trailer chassis, and deliver the goods to your customer's door in Tokyo. All this without having to rehandle the product, and for a single rate.

Piggybacking is probably still in its infancy, but it shows great promise of cutting costs. Shippers that have used this means of transportation are enthusiastic. Therefore, even though it may not now fit into your distribution plans, keep an eye open for future developments. The chances are some will be worth your consideration.

OPERATING YOUR OWN TRUCKS VS. COMMON CARRIERS

Before a proper analysis can be made it will be necessary to gather up all the costs involved in the operation of your trucks. Exhibit 16-1 suggests a possible breakdown of expenses. Note that there are some "hidden" costs included such as management time and office expense.

---

[4] From *Overhead Cost Control,* by Phil Carroll, copyright © 1964 by Phil Carroll. Used with permission of McGraw-Hill Book Company, p. 234, lines 18-31; p. 235, lines 1-26; p. 237, lines 23-33; p. 239, lines 1-8; p. 238, Figure 74.

*All subject to revision at any time.

FIXED EXPENSES

Interest on borrowed capital ....$_____

Interest on equity in equipment ...._____

Depreciation on trucks and trailer ...._____

Depreciation on garage and maintenance equipment ...._____

License fees ...._____

Property taxes ...._____

Federal highway use taxes ...._____

Insurance ...._____

Paint and lettering ...._____

Truck and trailer accessories.._____

Washing and polishing ...._____

Garage supervision.._____

Garage expense (heat, light, telephone, etc.) ...._____

Fleet supervision.._____

Management time allocated to fleet operation ...._____

Office expense caused by having fleet.._____

Payroll taxes and fringe benefits ...._____

    TOTAL FIXED EXPENSES ...._____

OPERATING EXPENSES

Fuel ...._____

Tires (repair and replacement) ...._____

Lubrication ...._____

Antifreeze, tire chains, etc ...._____

Maintenance parts ...._____

Maintenance labor ...._____

Maintenance costs in outside shops ...._____

Road service charges ...._____

Toll road fees ...._____

Rental charges for substitute equipment ...._____

Drivers' salaries ...._____

Drivers' payroll taxes and fringe benefits........................_____

    TOTAL OPERATING EXPENSES ...._____

TOTAL FIXED AND OPERATING EXPENSES........................_____

    LESS BACKHAUL INCOME ...._____

TOTAL NET EXPENSE FOR FLEET ...._____

COST PER MILE $ _____

COST PER 100 POUNDS_____

EXHIBIT 16-1

Many common carriers argue that companies would become disenchanted with private trucking if they included *all* costs in their analyses of their operation. But, quoted carrier rates don't tell the whole story either. You still have "hidden" costs when you use for-hire truckers. Some are processing freight bills, tracing shipments, slow delivery, filing claims, and auditing bills. To make decisions, therefore, you must compare like things—*all* the costs for private, with *all* costs for common.

While you're at it, compare your expenses with the rates offered by a leasing company. It may be that it can provide better equipment at lower cost. Too, many a financial man would prefer leased equipment even if the cost was slightly higher because he can make productive use of the money by investing it in other phases of the business.

THE TRAINING OF DRIVERS[5]

The following data was excerpted from *Drivers' Handbook,* American Petroleum Institute, API Publication 1609, 1972 Edition, Washington, D.C. 20006.

Vehicle Inspection

Before driving the truck, you should make certain that:

(1) Truck fuel tanks are full.
(2) Motor oil level is adequate. Check before starting your engine and do not overfill.
(3) Radiator is full. Antifreeze or water should be added, if necessary.
(4) Tires are properly inflated, and wheel lugs are tight.
(5) Trailer coupling devices and connecting-hoses and cables are properly engaged and in good condition.
(6) Wheel chocks, fire extinguishers, emergency electric lanterns or reflectors, and flags are on the truck.
(7) Water is drained from air tanks.
(8) Hoses, fittings, and tools are all in place and in good condition.
(9) Evidence of previous damage to the uit is reported.
(10) License plates and signs are clean.
(11) Brakes are working properly, including low-pressure alarm for air brakes.
(12) Windshield wipers operate.
(13) Horn operates.
(14) Lights operate.
(15) Steering mechanism operates properly.
(16) Mirrors and windows are clean.
(17) Dash instruments are in proper working order.
(18) Tire chains are in good condition or sanders work properly, if required.
(19) Leaks in tanks, valves, or piping are reported.

General Instructions

(1) Before attempting to remove a radiator cap, make sure no pressure has built up as a result of overheating. Radiators of pressure systems build up pressure in normal operation; therefore, the cap of such a radiator must be removed in two stages: (a) relieve the pressure; and (b), remove the cap. Be alert for delayed pressure release—keep face in the clear and protect hands with gloves or heavy cloth.
(2) Do not race or overchoke the engine during warmup period.
(3) Avoid unnecessary idling of the motor.
(4) Have pride in the appearance of your truck.
(5) Keep the cab and all cabinets clean and free of oily rags, waste, and other unnecessary items.

---

5 American Petroleum Institute, *Drivers' Handbook,* API Publication 1609, 1972 Edition, Washington, D.C. 20006, p. 8, lines 1-29; p. 9, lines 1-31; p. 10, lines 1-24; p. 16, lines 15-29; p. 17, lines 1-33; p. 18, lines 1-33; p. 19, lines 1-33; p. 20, lines 1-31; p. 21, lines 8-28; p. 22, lines 1-6; p. 31, lines 18-30; p. 32, lines 1-33.

(6)   At the end of your shift, report automotive defects to your supervisor in order that the truck may be ready and safe for the next shift, and to comply with DOT (Department of Transportation) regulations if applicable.

Tires

(1)   The tires on the vehicle you are driving are in your care. Their life depends upon you and your life depends upon them; under-inflation can easily reduce the life of a tire by 50 per cent. Tires must be inflated when cold and maintained at the proper pressure.

(2)   Never bleed air from hot tires.

(3)   When inflating tires, stand to one side in order to avoid serious injury in the event of a tire blowout or of a rim becoming dislodged. Do not place your hands between dual wheels.

(4)   Inspect lugs and rims each time tire pressures are checked. Inspect lugs more frequently on newly mounted tires.

(5)   Keep valve caps on the valves.

(6)   Inform your supervisor of any tires that are incorrectly matched, worn smooth, or have bad cuts or breaks.

(7)   Do not drive a flat or soft tire. To do so will cause it to generate enough heat to start burning and may dislodge parts of the tire assembly, making re-inflation or changing of tire dangerous.

Driving Practices

A defensive driver is always courteous and expects and makes allowances for the mistakes of others. He is constantly alert and thinks far enough ahead to be able to take the necessary preventive action before dangerous situations cause accidents. He adjusts his driving to meet all hazards of weather, roads, traffic, and other conditions. He avoids even momentary distractions and realizes the need for split-second reaction to the road.

Prior to leaving the plant, you should become familiar with the truck you are to operate, and, if necessary, make a short trip around the plant.

You should:

(1) Plan your route so as to avoid congested areas whenever practicable.

(2) Always follow authorized truck routes, or those designated by your employer.

(3) On unfamiliar routes, drive at a reduced speed and out of the heavy traffic flow as much as possible.

(4) Start the truck in the lowest transmission gear, whether the truck is loaded or empty.

(5) While driving, shift the transmission to the gear at which the engine will operate economically and without strain. Maintain the engine speed at the revolutions per minute recommended by the truck manufacturer.

(6) Check air-, hydraulic-, or vacuum-brake pressure before moving the vehicle and frequently while underway.

(7) Let the engine help to act as a brake and depress the clutch only when the truck is almost stopped. Much of the braking power of the truck is lost by disengaging the transmission at the time the brake is applied.

(8) Test brakes when approaching the crest of a hill. Drive the truck downgrade in the same gear that would be required to go up the grade.

(9) Keep a frequent check on the dials of the instrument panel.

(10) When it is necessary to park the vehicle on an incline, cut the front wheel to the curb or bank, shut off the engine, set the parking brake, put the wheels, and take every precaution to prevent movement.

(11) When stopped for any cause, other than traffic, on the traveled position of the highway or shoulder, place flags, electric lanterns, or reflectors.

(12) If necessary to remain in your cab while parked, shut off the engine. (Carbon monoxide poisoning is deadly.)

(13) Drive slowly through school, hospital, or other restricted zones, and not over legal limits.

(14) Reduce speed under adverse conditions, such as snow, sleet, rain, fog, darkness, in crowded or congested areas, and when approaching curves. Approach all intersections cautiously and be prepared to stop or yield the right of way, if necessary to avoid collision with cross traffic or pedestrians.

(15) Always keep at least one vehicle length, for each 10 mph of speed, between you and the vehicle ahead. Allow a greater interval when conditions are unfavorable.

(16) Avoid crowding or crossing the roadway center line unless turning or passing. Cross only when the law permits.

(17) When preparing for a turn, correctly position your vehicle in the proper lane, flash the turn signals well in advance, and glance frequently in the rear view mirrors as you turn slowly. Remember that pedestrians have the right of way. Ordinarily vehicles already in a traffic circle have the right of way, but observe the law of the state in which you are operating.

(18) Never pass fires on or near the road without first making certain that the passing can be accomplished safely.

(19) When overtaking another vehicle, look for ample visible space ahead before passing. Never pass on hills, curves, bridges, or at intersections when passing requires entering the opposite traffic lane.

(20) Use care when passing stopped or slowing streetcars, buses, and other vehicles.

(21) Observe local laws applicable to passing a school bus that is loading or unloading passengers.

(22) Keep constantly alert for any vehicle that may be trying to pass you. Be courteous, reduce speed if necessary, and let it pass. Keep to the right and at proper interval on hills.

(23) When changing traffic lanes, slowing down, or stopping, give proper signals in ample time to warn other drivers. Be on the alert for drivers who may not heed your signals.

(24) Switch on the driving lights when there is not enough light to see 500 ft ahead. Lights are required from one-half hour after sunset to one-half hour before sunrise.

(25) Never overdrive the headlights. Adjust your speed to allow for reaction time so you can stop within the distance of visibility.

(26) Dim the truck lights for approaching traffic and also when following other vehicles.

(27) Never take the chance of driving without lights when they are required. If the lights are defective, move your truck off the highway until they have been repaired.

Special Precautions—Railroad Grade Crossings

When approaching any railroad grade crossing, make a full stop not more than 50 ft. nor less than 15 ft. from the nearest rail.

Display proper regard for traffic following you by slowing down well in advance of the stop, using your stop lights as a warning, and by pulling to the right as far as possible. With the window open, listen and look for signals in each department, along all tracks, for approaching trains.

Do not proceed until caution has been taken to ascertain that the course is clear. Watch out for additional trains from either direction. Proceed only in gear of sufficient power to avoid stalling and shifting gears when crossing tracks.

Breakdown

(1) If your truck is disabled on the highway, drive off the traveled portion of the road, if possible, and place a reflector, electric lantern, or flag 100 ft. to the front, 100 ft. to the rear, and one on the traffic side not less than 10 ft. behind the truck. If your truck is disabled at a curve or crest of a hill, these distances should be increased to suit the condition.

(2) If it is necessary for you to park the truck on a grade, cut the front wheel to the curb or bank, set the handbrake and put the truck in proper gear. Set chocks under the rear wheels of the truck or drive wheels of a trailer-type vehicle.

(3) Try to determine, as accurately as possible, the trouble and send word to your supervision. Give all details and ask for instructions.

(4) If it is necessary to remain in your truck with the engine running while parked, keep the windows open to provide ventilation. (Carbon monoxide poisoning is deadly.)

Traffic Accidents

By observing the rules of the road and driving defensively, you stand a good chance of never becoming involved in an accident, but should you become involved in an accident:

(1) Stop at once and turn off engine.

(2) Take all possible precautions to prevent further accidents or damage. (Place reflectors or flags as prescribed previously.)

(3) Assist injured persons. Unless you have been trained in first aid, do not move an injured person unless it is necessary to move him out of danger. Have someone call a physician or an ambulance, if necessary.

(4) Obtain names and addresses of:
　(a) Other drivers, passengers, or pedestrians involved. Take information from drivers' licenses whenever possible.
　(b) Owner of damaged property.
　(c) All witnesses—regardless of their version of the accident. If a witness in a vehicle refuses to give his name, get the license number of his vehicle.

(5) Call an officer of the law if the accident is of a serious nature or involves other persons or property. Inform your employer.

(6) Do not argue at the scene of an accident. Be courteous and show your license willingly.

(7) Do not leave the scene of an accident unless necessary. Send someone else for help and to make telephone calls.

(8) Do not make any statement to any person unless you have been authorized to do so by your employer.

(9) Report every accident to your employer as soon as practicable, regardless of who was at fault or how minor the damage.

(10) Do not stop for an accident in which your truck is not involved unless help is needed. If it is necessary to stop, place your truck in a safe position. Do not discuss the accident.

(See Exhibits 16-2 and 16-3.)

TRUCK ACCIDENT LOG

Facility: _____   Time Covered: _____

Date	Driver	RESULT						Description of the Accident	What Driver Was Doing?		Type of Accident	Class'n A or U	ARCO Driving Record			Action Taken
		Injury		Fatality		Property Damage			Our Truck	Other Vehicle			No. of Accd	No. of Avoid.	Years	
		Arco	Other	Arco	Other	Arco	Other									

EXHIBIT 16-2

DISTRIBUTION
TRUCK ACCIDENT EXPERIENCE

ORGANIZATION	TOTAL NUMBER VEHICLE ACCIDENTS		FREQUENCY RATE		TARGET—35% REDUCTION	
	LAST YEAR	1ST. QTR. THIS YEAR	LAST YEAR	1ST. QTR. THIS YEAR	TOTAL ACCD. 2.3.4. QT. THIS YEAR	AVG. NUMBER PER QUARTER THIS YEAR
AREA 1 NORTHEAST						
AREA 2 MID ATLANTIC						
AREA 3 EASTERN SHORE						
AREA 4 GREAT LAKES						
AREA 5 MIDWEST						
TOTALS						

EXHIBIT 16-3

17

Reducing Excessive Paperwork

In many plants new paperwork is constantly being devised and introduced, while at the same time the old procedures and reports continue undeminished, even though in a number of instances, the need for them no longer exists. This indicates that the processing of forms, orders, reports and related transactions is out of control. At one time clerical operations were considered as just a necessary evil and little attention was focused on them. Today, with office operations growing at a precipitous rate, the potential for improvement and for cost reduction attack has now become a major area for attention. The purpose of this chapter is to present an engineering approach to the solution of this problem.

EXAMINE FLOOR LAYOUT AND CONDUCT SPACE ANALYSIS[1]

Try your hand at a "puzzler" offered its readers by the *Navy Management Review:*
The technical reference branch whose office layout is shown in Exhibit 17-1 is about to receive a new file, and is trying to decide where to put it. The file will fit in only the three places marked X, Y, and Z, and it appears that no one in the office will be satisfied unless the file is next to his desk. Mr. B., the supervisor who occupies the corner cubicle, "couldn't care less" where it goes, since he will not use it. However, his employees have been raising such a fuss that he has decided to ask the Methods staff to help him. This much is known:

(1) The office layout is optimally suited to work flow and should be left unchanged if at all possible.

(2) All will use the file; it cannot be broken down into smaller units.

(3) Desk 1 is occupied by Mrs. C. who will use the file 40 times a day. She is a pleasant woman, about 50, and has a picture of her husband, Admiral C, on her desk.

---

1 Carl Heyel, *The Supervisor's Basic Management Guide* (New York: McGraw-Hill Book Company, copyright © 1965 by McGraw-Hill, Inc.), p. 244, lines 25-33; p. 245, lines 1-18; p. 246, lines 1-10; p. 247, lines 1-10; and Exhibits 0-1 and 0-2.

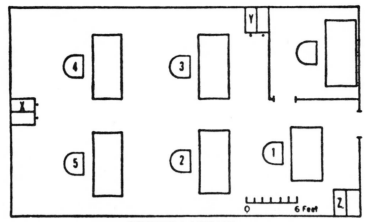

OFFICE LAYOUT:
TECHNICAL REFERENCE BRANCH

EXHIBIT 17-1: Office Layout - Technical Reference Branch

(4) Miss A. sits at desk 2. She is an attractive girl of 23 who will use the file only about 7 times a day while serving as secretary to Mr. B.

(5) Mr. D. sits at desk 3. He is bald, 40, and jolly. He will use the file an average of 11 times a day.

(6) Desks 4 and 5 are occupied by Mr. E. and Miss F. who are engaged. Miss F. at desk 4 is the newest member of the office and will use the file 32 times a day while Mr. E., the next junior member, will use it 12 times a day. Both are 21.

Where would you put the file cabinet?

Answer to Puzzler

The Methods man constructed a "distance-usage index" based on the scale indicated in the floor plan, for each position. The index is shown in Exhibit 17-2.

Position Y is the "mathematical" answer because it will mean less overall office effort. So the solution is *Position Y*. Correct?

Well ... maybe. Unfortunately, the index can only "solve the problem in terms of the quantitative variables given—distance and usage." But how do you account for such variables as power, prestige, and personality? Though they affect most solutions in problems of this kind, they are still quite unmeasurable, and the supervisor must rely on good judgment as well as arithmetic in problems of this kind.

Desk **	Daily Usage	POSITION X		POSITION Y		POSITION Z	
		Round Trip in ft.	Total Distance/ Usage	Round Trip in ft.	Total Distance/ Usage	Round Trip in ft.	Total Distance/ Usage
1	40	62	2480	26	1040	18	720
2	7	40	280	34	238	44	308
3	11	40	440	20	220	50	550
4	32	14	448	44	1408	76	2432
5	12	14	168	58	696	70	840
		"X" Index**	3816	"Y" Index**	3602	"Z" Index**	4850

EXHIBIT 17-2: Distance-Usage Index

This same approach can be applied in placing duplicating equipment, central filing, stenographic pool area, data processing equipment, mailroom, and related facilities.

FORMS DESIGN AND CONTROL[2]

Forms Design

Each piece of paper introduced into the plant and office operations must be paid for—in the expense of creating the form, and in the time spent by the employees in filling it out and physically handling each. It is important for management, then, not only to restrict the growth of such transactions, but also to insure themselves that existing forms serve a definite need. They should also insist that forms be designed so that an absolute minimum of time is consumed in their processing and handling. A condensed list of requirements and further points to consider in the designing of forms follows:

(1) The form should be acceptable to those who are to use it.
(2) It should be well planned, so that information can be quickly and easily inserted.
(3) It should be simple and also complete.
(4) It should be conceived with proper consideration given to the way its ultimate use will affect such paper characteristics as—weight, color, standard sheet sizes, finish, ease of duplication, strength, durability, opacity, price, and comparable physical properties.
(5) It should either be pre-numbered or have a space provided for such an entry as a means of identification.
(6) As many items as is practicable should be preprinted on it.
(7) Spaces should be adequate for the entry of the required information.
(8) It should provide for the efficient entering of required data by the arrangement of printed items in a proper sequence. First, examine the records from which these data are to be transcribed.
(9) Its layout should be planned so that a typewriter can easily accommodate it; printed lines should be properly spaced.

(See questionnaire covering objectives of forms review and analysis—Exhibit 17-3.)

Control of Forms

To control properly the use of forms and to systematize and coordinate this activity, a staff function should be established. In a large organization this may require the full-time efforts of one individual or of an entire department. In the smaller companies, this function might be assigned to an appropriate employee as a part-time responsibility. The duties of this function should consist of the following:

(1) To approve or reject the introduction of new forms by the various departments of the plant.

(2) To exercise a surveillance function over the correctness of the forms design.

(3) To keep a record of form numbers and to assign numbers in proper sequence to newly authorized forms.

(4) To effect the consolidation of previously established forms when practicable.

---

2 Lewis R. Zeyher, *Cost Reduction in the Plant* (Englewood Cliffs, N.J.: Prentice-Hall, Inc., copyright © 1965), p. 207, lines 16-40; p. 209, lines 1-12; p. 211, lines 37-44; p. 212, lines 1-12; p. 213, lines 1-45; p. 214, lines 1-39.

QUESTIONNAIRE COVERING OBJECTIVES OF FORMS REVIEW AND ANALYSIS

(1) What forms are in use?_____

(2) Are all the forms in use necessary?_____

(3) Are copies of forms and reports filed permanently in too many places?_____

(4) Is all the "logging" done necessary? _____

(5) Can more of the paperwork be centralized?_____

(6) Can any forms be redesigned to improve them?_____

(7) Can any two or more forms be combined into one single form?_____

(8) Can number of copies of forms be reduced?_____

(9) Can forms be used less frequently?_____

(10) Should any forms be consecutively numbered?_____

(11) Is it possible to use any special time-saving forms?_____

(12) Is punching, perforating, scoring and padding of current forms correct?_____

(13) What forms are used in the greatest volume? _____

(14) Is the present office floor layout the most efficient?_____

(15) Can use be made of a faster communication device such as an intercom system?_____

(16) Should a flow chart of each form that is used by positions covered by a job description be inserted in back of such employee's description folder?_____

(17) Are there enough "check" points on completeness, accuracy and legibility of forms submitted?_____

(18) Are filing systems used adequate and physically properly located?_____

(19) Should a centralized filing system be considered due to compactness of floor layout?_____

(20) Can more copies of forms be destroyed after their usefulness has been served?_____

(21) Has proper use been made of "spread sheets" for analysis purposes?_____

(22) Has work place layout and special design of desks, tables, cabinets, etc. been considered?_____

(23) Can back of forms be used for any purpose? _____

(24) Are present mailing practices acceptable? _____

(25) Is routing (flow path) of forms the best obtainable?_____

(26) Can anything be done at one work station that will make the succeeding operation at the next work station easier?_____

(27) Can the department cycle time on handling any form, from its origination to finalizing, be shortened?_____

(28) Was a check made to determine whether all supervisory approval signatures are necessary? _____

(29) Do all approval signatures have proper significance (does supervisor actually review, question, check, add, delete or contribute anything to form before affixing signature)?_____

(30) Can anything be done to minimize or eliminate peak work-load periods, either monthly, weekly and/or daily?_____

(31) Has a system been suggested that will provide a "policing" function to insure proper compliance with established methods and procedures?_____

(32) Are there any instances where the proper execution of a form is necessary before a certain function can be performed, but the function is actually completed without the necessary paperwork?_____

(33) Have checklists been recommended for those work stations where they can be used to advantage?_____

(34) Are all forms that are distributed clear and legible?_____

(35) Are any important instructions given verbally (without written confirmation), particularly those involving engineering data, procedures, methods and related information? _____

(36) Are there are instances where there are "pockets" of idle time (due to poor distribution of work load and/or poor planning at certain work stations)?_____

(37) Are there any instances where data and information provided by engineers, clerks, factory supervision, often require a decision regarding a choice of alternatives (multiple choices) covering engineering data when there should actually be only one choice and that one *clearly indicated?*_____

EXHIBIT 17-3

(5) To review continuously and examine forms currently in use for the purpose of effecting economies through their elimination, improvement, and extension of their usefulness; to keep minimum but adequate supplies on hand; to insure economical reordering quantities; and to maintain proper quality standards.

These responsibilities should, of course, be expanded or reduced as the size and type of the company might dictate.

PREPARE AND ANALYZE PAPERWORK HANDLING CHARTS

Review and Examine All Your Paper Flow Charts

After all forms flow charts have been prepared depicting their movement among the various departments (see Exhibit 17-4) and the necessary written procedures covering the proper handling of each completed, a thorough analysis can be initiated.

Problem areas and distinctive patterns are then detected, remedial actions are formulated and become the basis for your final recommendations. A few examples of the kinds of situation to look for are:

- Executives and supervisors handling and processing too many clerical papers. Could these be delegated to others or eliminated? (Review Exhibit 17-5.)
- Too many departments involved in the transactions of paper work routine. Could their travel paths be shortened and some steps eliminated?
- Work checked too frequently; some never checked.

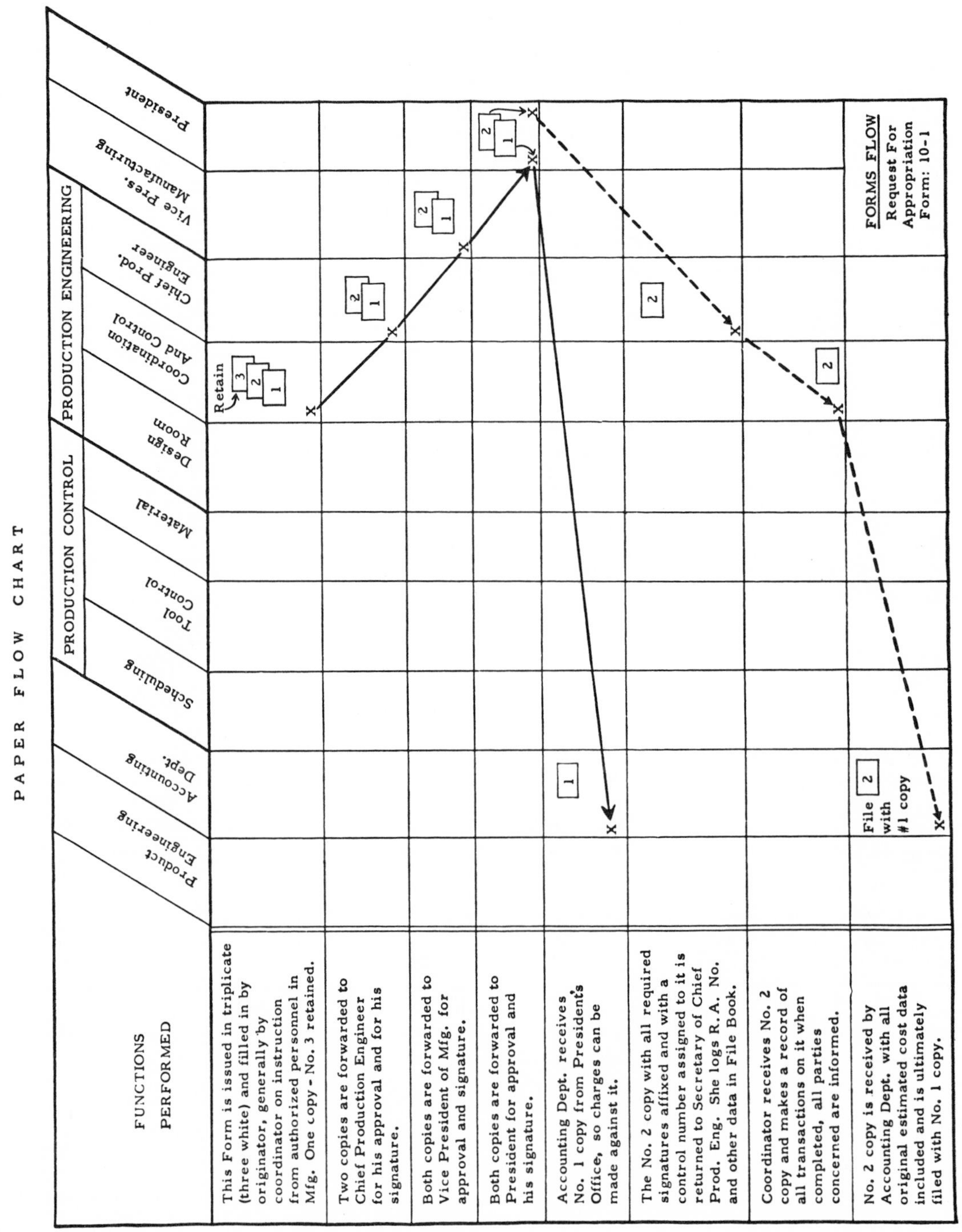

PAPER FLOW CHART

PRODUCTION CONTROL | **PRODUCTION ENGINEERING**

Columns (left to right):
Product Engineering | Accounting Dept. | Scheduling | Tool Control | Material | Design Room | Coordination And Control | Chief Prod. Engineer | Vice Pres. Manufacturing | President

FORMS FLOW
Request For
Appropriation
Form: 10-1

FUNCTIONS PERFORMED
This Form is issued in triplicate (three white) and filled in by originator, generally by coordinator on instruction from authorized personnel in Mfg. One copy - No. 3 retained.
Two copies are forwarded to Chief Production Engineer for his approval and for his signature.
Both copies are forwarded to Vice President of Mfg. for approval and signature.
Both copies are forwarded to President for approval and his signature.
Accounting Dept. receives No. 1 copy from President's Office, so charges can be made against it.
The No. 2 copy with all required signatures affixed and with a control number assigned to it is returned to Secretary of Chief Prod. Eng. She logs R.A. No. and other data in File Book.
Coordinator receives No. 2 copy and makes a record of all transactions on it when completed, all parties concerned are informed.
No. 2 copy is received by Accounting Dept. with all original estimated cost data included and is ultimately filed with No. 1 copy.

EXHIBIT 17-4

Each form column carries the subheading "Form No." The label at the right margin reads "Activity Schedule / Positions / Handling Forms."

Departments and/or Positions	Mfg. Order	T.E.D.	E.C.O.	Work Order	Work Order	C.E.R.	Eng. Release	RRSC	R.A.	P.O.F.	E.D.R.	EMPL. SUG.	T.R.N.	N.O.R.	P.R.	R.S.O.	N.G.R.R.	D.A.P.	Proc. Dgw.	ROUTE SH.
Chief Production Engineer		X	X					X	X	X	X	X		X	X			X		
Ass't. Chief Prod. Engineer		X	X					X	X		X	X		X				X		
Secretary Chief Prod. Eng.		X		X	X				X		X	X			X			X		
Group Leader—Print Control		X	X	X	X	X	X	X	X		X	X	X	X	X				X	X
Ass't. to Gp.Ldr. Print Control		X				X					X		X		X	X	X		X	X
Technical Clerk Print Control																				
Group Leader Routing	X	X				X	X	X		X	X			X	X	X			X	X
Technical Clerk Routing		X				X		X			X			X					X	X
Chief Design Engineer		X				X								X						X
Group Leader Project Engineers		X	X		X			X	X		X	X		X						
Project Engineers			X		X			X	X		X	X		X						
Group Leader Time Study								X			X	X								
Prototype Expeditors		X								X				X	X	X			X	
Technical Clerk Tool Room			X	X	X															
Blue Print Room			X	X	X	X	X						X	X					X	X
Production Control		X	X	X	X	X	X	X					X	X	X					

EXHIBIT 17-5

- Too many forms being used—are they all necessary?
- Several forms serving the same purpose or overlapping in functions. Could a composite, single form be designed, or one or more eliminated?
- Evidence of poor communications. Do all interested departments receive the necessary copies of forms? Are more copies required?
- Unnecessary filing being performed, and evidence of excessive distribution of copies to individuals who do not need them.
- Final disposition of all copies of clerical papers not always indicated.
- Unnecessary logging of paperwork usually done for the protection of department actively involved in the processing of them.
- Sequence of flow of paper through various departments inefficiently planned. Operations performed on forms not always done in the most logical order.

NOTE: To see how measured work can be applied to office operations refer to Lewis R. Zeyher's *Production Manager's Handbook of Formulas and Tables,* Prentice-Hall, Inc., Englewood Cliffs, N.J., 07632, Chapter 3; also Chapter 5 here.

A CHECKLIST FOR PAPERWORK IMPROVEMENT

(1) Initiate a plant-wide study to determine if you have a serious problem with paperwork.

(2) You should seriously listen to your supervisory staffs' complaint about their excessive paperwork responsibilities and take remedial actions.

(3) In large companies you should have a forms control coordinator.

(4) You should have a Form and Procedure Committee that continually reviews the need for forms, procedures and other clerical transactions.

(5) You should have a central and master filing system in order to eliminate or minimize the need for individual and departmental filing.

(6) Make sure all the forms in use are necessary.

(7) Make certain all the "logging" performed is necessary.

(8) Check on whether any forms can be redesigned and improved.

(9) Determine if any two or more forms be combined into a single form.

(10) Determine if some forms can be used less frequently.

(11) Where possible use standard or special time-saving forms.

(12) Investigate any forms in use that you have printed to order to determine if they can be replaced by a less expensive standard form that can be purchased in the open market.

(13) Make sure there is correct punching, perforating, scoring and padding of the current forms in use.

(14) Determine if the present office floor layout is the most efficient.

(15) Check for more effective use of better communication devices, such as intercom systems, pneumatic tubes, and autotelegraph equipment.

(16) Design flow charts depicting the proper movement of all paperwork.

(17) Prepare written procedures describing the manner in which forms should be processed.

(18) All interested personnel should be immediately informed when required changes or modifications are made in existing paperwork.

(19) All interested personnel should be instructed and well briefed about the handling of new forms or procedures.

(20) Make sure there are enough checkpoints strategically located along the path of all paperwork so that the completeness, accuracy, and legibility of forms can be easily detected.

(21) Determine whether more copies of forms can be destroyed after their usefulness has been served.

(22) Make certain that special and efficient design of desks, tables, and cabinets has been considered, particularly from the standpoint of reducing physical effort and time required for the tasks involved.

(23) Determine if the reverse sides of some forms can be used for any purpose.

(24) Make sure present mailing practices are efficient and acceptable.

(25) Determine if the routing (flow path) of forms is the best obtainable.

(26) Determine if anything can be done at one clerical work station that will make the succeeding operation at the next work station easier.

(27) Shorten department cycle time in the handling of any form, from its origination to finalizing.

(28) Determine if all approval signatures have the significance that management intended. Supervisors should actually review, question, check, add, delete, or contribute something to forms before finally affixing their required signatures.

(29) See if anything can be done to minimize or eliminate peak work-load periods during the day, week, or month.

(30) Make certain a system has been provided that introduces a "policing" function into the handling of paperwork to insure proper compliance with established methods and procedures.

(31) When the proper execution of a form is necessary before a certain function can legally be performed, make sure your system prevents such transactions from being carried out without the necessary authorization.

(32) Checklists should be established for those work stations where important details and operating information must not be omitted by personnel when processing certain forms.

(33) All forms should be clear, legible, and understandable.

(34) Check to determine if there are any instances where "pockets" of idle time (due to poor distribution of work loads, poor planning, inadequate supervision, and inefficient scheduling) can be corrected.

(35) Have your system ensure that data and information supplied by technical personnel are sufficiently clear and explicit for non-technical personnel to make correct decisions.

(36) Arrange your print control system so it will direct you to the location of a required print, when it cannot be found in its proper drawer or file. Have good control of prints.

(37) Determine if too much time is wasted by personnel searching for information because of inefficient paperwork handling by others, and have these conditions corrected.

(38) The disposition of all copies of paperwork should be clearly indicated.

(39) Your system should indicate the final disposition of all forms to either destroy, permanently file, or temporarily file for a limited time.

(40) You should have up-to-date organization charts.

(41) You should have properly maintained job descriptions for all personnel.

(42) You should make use of standard procedure instructions.

(43) Each employee involved in a clerical transaction of a form should have a paper flow chart in his possession that depicts its path and the steps described for its processing.

(44) All forms should be designed so that a minimum of typing time will be consumed in the transcription of information from one form to another.

(45) All office machines insofar as is practical should be segregated in an area where the noise from them will not disturb other office workers.

(46) You should have office standards covering specifications for materials, supplies, and office equipment.

ACTIVITY SCHEDULE—POSITIONS HANDLING FORMS
Analysis of Exhibit 17-5
Covering (20) Major Forms

Position Title	Number of Forms Handled	Per cent of Major Forms Handled
Chief Production Engineer	10	50
Assistant Chief Production Engineer	8	40
Secretary—Chief Production Engineer	8	40
Group Leader—Print Control	18	90
Ass't. to Group Leader—Print Control	7	35
Technical Clerk—Routing	2	10
Group Leader—Routing	12	60
Chief Design Engineer	6	30
Chief Design Engineer	6	30
Group Leader—Project Engineers	8	40
Project Engineers	7	35
Group Leader—Time Study	2	10
Prototype Expediters	6	30
Technical Clerk—Tool Room	3	15
Blue Print Room	2	10
Production Control	11	55

Total Handling Possibilities 116

Total Potential Handlings. 320
  (16 Positions x 20 Forms)

Per Cent Handling to Potential 35

COMMENTS AND ANALYSIS

(a) The above statistics depict the following:

(1) That all key personnel handle at least a third or more of the forms.

(2) That the Group Leader—Print Control has some contact with most of the forms (as this position calls for).

(3) That the Time Study Group Leader sees or has contact with very few forms.

(4) That the Chief Production Engineer, his assistant and his secretary may collectively handle or have contact with too many forms. (Which responsibility might be split up between them and/or assigned to other appropriate group leaders.)

(5) That the Production Control Department is involved in or with more than half

of the forms used in the Production Engineering Department. This emphasizes the need for reducing the cycle time currently required to process them and the importance of keeping them informed promptly of changes, delays, errors and related matters.

(b)An examination of Exhibit 17-5 provides a "panoramic view" of the entire forms activity in the subject department—names and numbers of forms in use, the departments concerned, the activity or non-activity of forms as well as highlighting those of greatest importance.

(c)On the basis of this analysis, a combined form was designed covering the use of the T.E.D., E.C.O. and E.C.R. forms.

(d)The Time Study Group Leader should either receive copies of the T.E.D. and/or E.C.O. forms, or have the opportunity to review the pertinent information and data culled from them, which is of interest to his position. This would be any information that may affect his time study incentive rates in the factory.

(e)The Form No., Tool Revision Notification, has little activity, but an investigation of it disclosed the fact that it is a form used between Print Control and Tool Control. While such a Speediset form would not normally be designed for such limited use, the forms are now available and it does serve a useful purpose.

(f) This analysis also disclosed the fact that a number of positions covered by a job description do not always indicate all of the forms used by each position, nor a description of its handling by such position, which should be corrected when job descriptions are later finalized.

(g)It would appear that most positions that get copies of forms have a need and a use for the information contained therein.

(h)There is some indication that Form No. P.E., Request for Route Sheet Change, is not used as widely and as often as it should be. Changes are being made without the proper issuance of this form and without proper approval.

(i) A Central Filing system is recommended—this will eliminate approximately 50% of unnecessary filing.

(j) Set up a new position to be known as Coordination & Control supervisor, or for brevity, Coordinator. In connection with this construct a Dispatch Cabinet, like the drawings that are attached to this report. (See Exhibits 17-6 and 17-7.)

DISPATCHING CABINET
Coordinator's View

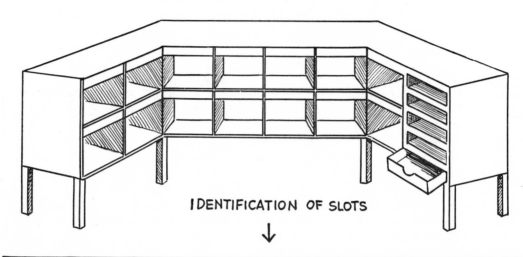

IDENTIFICATION OF SLOTS
↓

CHIEF PRODUCTION ENGINEER	ASS'T. CHIEF PRODUCTION ENGINEER	ROUTING	TIME STUDY	PRINT CONTROL	PROJECT ENGINEER	TOOL DESIGN	T.E.D.'s
							E.C.O.
							E.C.R.
BLUE PRINT	PRODUCT ENGINEER	PRODUCTION CONTROL MANAGER	TOOL CONTROL	MATERIAL CONTROL	SCHEDULING	SPARE (MISC.)	OTHER
							FILE

(ALL DIMENSIONS APPROXIMATE)

SLOTS: 9" WIDE X 6" HIGH X 12" DEEP
IDENTIFICATION SPACES: 1½" HIGH
LEG HEIGHT: 8"
OVERALL HEIGHT: 23"   (6" X 2 + 1½" X 2 + 8")
NO. OF SLOTS: 14 (OUTGOING)
    "   "   "   5 (INCOMING)

(OVER)

EXHIBIT 17-6

DISPATCHING CABINET
Aisle View

INCOMING DEPT. MAIL ↓	TOOL DESIGN	PROJECT ENGINEER	PRINT CONTROL	TIME STUDY	ROUTING	ASS'T. CHIEF PRODUCTION ENGINEER	CHIEF PRODUCTION ENGINEER
T.E.D.							
E.C.O.							
E.C.R.							
OTHER	ETC.	ETC.	ETC.	ETC.	ETC.	ETC.	ETC.
FILE							

ELEVATION (TOP VIEW)

LEWIS R. ZEYHER   (OVER)

EXHIBIT 17-7

18

Computerization of Operating Control Reports

A common complaint of operating managers is the lack of prompt and accurate information regarding events and actions occurring in the areas of their responsibilities. The executive is confronted with many obstacles to a reliable flow of information covering operating intelligence. He should not be compelled to make major decisions on the basis of speculative information. The executive must have a reliable feedback apparatus to keep him advised of the unsuccessful results of his directions. It is the poor results that he must learn about quickly so that he can immediately take remedial actions.

Computerization of operating control reports provides a solution to this problem by reporting quickly timely and accurate data for management decision-making.

This exposition will not cover the techniques and procedures of this comparatively new discipline but will emphasize the many advantages that it offers as an effective tool the plant executive can use for reducing expenses and improving profits.

IMPORTANCE OF INVOLVING OPERATING PERSONNEL IN DEVELOPING THE SYSTEM FROM THE BEGINNING

Too frequently operating personnel are ignored when introducing new systems or methods into plants. People can make or break innovations of all kinds—systems do not run by themselves. It is important that those involved fully understand the processes they are responsible for, and that they participate in their development.

Examples of Poor Personnel Involvement

A case in point involved a consulting firm partner who sold a project for a production control system to the president of a manufacturing company—the decision having been made without prior consideration and consultation with the plant manager. When the installation was initiated, the consultant, on his weekly visits to the plant to check with his field engineers, devoted most of his time to the company president. The plant manager, who would ultimately be responsible for the successful maintenance of this new program, was almost totally ignored. The results, of course, were disastrous.

In another case a multi-plant metal working company developed a new preventive maintenance and repairs system. This company with headquarters in New York City had three geographical divisions—Eastern, Central and Pacific. The engineering and management group of the Eastern Division plants fully participated in the origination and development of this plan. Mutual plant problems were discussed and solutions found; bugs occurred and were eliminated. After many meetings and consultations an excellent system finally evolved. It was then installed in all the plants of the Eastern Division. After three or four months of operating under the plan, top management was pleased with the results. Maintenance and repairs costs were now under control and substantial savings were indicated.

Now the "Standard Procedure Instruction Manuals" were written up and copies sent to the Central and Pacific Divisions with instructions to immediately install the plan.

After six months of operations, the Central Division showed alarming losses in their repair and maintenance expenses—the very items the new system was designed to control. A staff engineer from the corporation's office was sent to the Central Division in Chicago to determine the causes for these poor results. The answer was that the Chief Engineers of the division plants were angry because they had a new program forced upon them without being consulted. A study of their operations indicated that all the necessary paperwork was being performed but nothing was being done to take the required remedial actions. Passive resistance to the program was definitely indicated.

The staff engineer submitted the results of his study, supplemented with recommendations, to the corporate vice president of manufacturing. With the implementation of a number of these suggestions and the cooperation of the chief engineers the program became equally successful in the other divisions.

MANAGEMENT INFORMATION FOR DECISION MAKING[1]

A total information system is a planned program for communicating throughout an organization the same single individual bits of data in a variety of ways so that the requirements for information are met with a single entry into the system. Based on these individual entries a bank, or *data base,* is developed and is constantly updated. Such a data bank can be built in a modular manner using the block concept. All demands for information, the total requirements, are extracted from this bank of data.

This is not really a new approach. The mom and pop corner grocery store operates on a total information system. It is made possible by the proprietor knowing all, seeing all, and being capable of making timely decisions because of the totality of the information he has available to him instantaneously. This totality begins to break down as specialization takes over, as more people become involved, and as the operation physically spreads out. The corrective mechanism is paperwork to communicate data until this becomes so cumbersome, costly and inaccurate that another solution is needed. The other solution is an effective information system, operated economically.

The capability to have such a system is provided by the *third generation* computer.

---

1 Arthur E. Wolf, *Computerized Plant Information Systems* (Englewood Cliffs, N.J.: Prentice-Hall, Inc. copyright © 1974), p. 17, lines 1-26; p. 18, lines 1-21; p. 20, lines 27-33; p. 22, lines 30-41; p. 23, lines 1-26.

Used effectively by management, this tool changes the ability of managers to make more profitable decisions. That's what this chapter is all about: building the system in a block manner the same as constructing a building, based on practical experience and accomplished proficiency. It is not an idea for using computers or solving business problems, but it is a presentation of a working system which is dynamic enough to react and respond to changing operations and other conditions affecting the business. The construction of the data bank is presented as a step-by-step building process, which has tangible results from the initial step and continues to grow and improve as additional blocks of data are added to the base.

This, and subsequent blocks, present a workable, effective, and efficient total information system for operating a manufacturing facility. Plant management conceived the original idea and then presented the opportunity for operating managers to design and implement the information system, aided by systems and data processing technicians. It is important to recognize the sequence of responsibility for developing the system, for unlike many systems installations, *the operating managers were primarily responsible for the system* and were aided by the data processing and systems technicians instead of the reverse being true. The *managers of the operation decided what they wanted* and needed for more timely and thus more profitable decisions and the hardware technicians reacted to these requirements. The broad outlines of the system took place during the earlier stages of the data processing capability using second generation equipment, but didn't become a reality until the third generation hardware and software technology was developed and available. To repeat, it is significant to realize that operating managers were directly involved and primarily concerned with the system from its inception.

An information system to be effective must be accurate, and to be accurate the input data must be correct and timely; this can only be accomplished with the enthusiastic support of operations managers. Since it is they who are being served by the system, from a purely selfish viewpoint they are interested and concerned about the accuracy and timeliness of the input to the system and ultimately a concern for the whole process develops.

Accounting reports are more meaningful and now become management oriented, because they *are skillfully prepared to meet specific management requirements.* This allows the accounting staff to function in the role of an advisor to the managers of plant operations, from foreman to plant manager. Without being a part of the plant operations complement, the accounting effort remains independent and thus continues the primary role as controller of data reports, valuation of assets, and statement of liabilities.

MANAGEMENT'S NEW AWARENESS

Improves Inventory Turnover

Frequently economic indicators point to the skyrocketing increase in investment in inventories when the economy slows down. This results not so much from the lack of interest of managers in the inventory investment, but as a slow reaction to the problem because of a lack of proper information. A dramatic improvement in inventory turnover is realized by giving management the information needed to do the job the managers have been capable of doing before but were unable to accomplish because of inadequate, inaccurate, or untimely data. Built into the computer system are the rote decisions involving inventory replenishments leaving managers with more time to exercise judgment based on improved information.

As a demonstration of the fruits of a total plant information system, inventory turnover rates have been cut in half with commensurate reductions in committed capital. Not only is the investment reduced, but as the level of inventory goes down, operating efficiency goes up. More space is available to store and handle material and less time is spent searching for stocks relocated because of long-term storage and overcrowded storage conditions. Obsolescence of stocks and the need to reexamine and repair old stocks is minimized as turnover improves and stocks are rotated in a normal and efficient way according to an inventory plan. The most enthusiastic supporters of such an improved information system have been the inventory managers because they can manage the warehousing of the physical inventory better and can achieve improved customer satisfaction.

Scheduling Improved

Likewise, production costs drop as more beneficial production runs are scheduled. Timely recording of shipping demands provides more accurate production scheduling, which in turn provides for more economical production runs. Production labor and equipment efficiences improve as better initial scheduling of production is done, schedule changes are held to a minimum, and a neat circle is completed with scheduling aiding production which aids scheduling. The computerized plant information system has the reduction of production costs as its main benefactor, since all plant costs are reflected either directly or indirectly in cost of production.

Lowering in Costs of Maintenance and Repairs

The improved scheduling of production operations also has a direct effect on improving the costliness of maintenance and repairs. Knowing when to schedule preventive maintenance and being able to stick to it have the same cost savings as improved production scheduling. The information system has built into it the data required by maintenance management to do a more effective preventive maintenance job. Once again, the effectiveness of timely information regarding maintenance and repair activities reemphasizes the point of reporting bits of data promptly and accurately. Preventive maintenance is a constant process, and is only helpful and desirable when it is timely enough to avoid more costly breakdown repairs.

SOLVING BUSINESS PROBLEMS BY QUANTITATIVE ANALYSIS[2]

The first category of business problems is terms *quantitative*. Problems expressed in numbers or in symbols that will ultimately have numerical values are quantitative. There is hardly a business problem that is not partly quantitative.

Exploring the quantitative problem briefly, we note its fundamental characteristics. The first of these is *precision*. Aided by tools of statistics, the system analyst is able to

---

2 Stanford L. Optner, *Systems Analysis for Business and Industrial Problem Solving* (Englewood Cliffs, N.J.: Prentice-Hall, Inc., copyright © 1965), p. 15, lines 32-39; p. 16, lines 1-43; p. 17, lines 1-29.

state, for a given relationship, a value or range of values. With a computer, the analyst may structure a problem and solve it twenty times. He may then offer management the three best solutions with the most favorable mix of profit and risk for a given project. The analyst may estimate the reliability of a solution by establishing its confidence limits, or its probability of occurrence. Closely linked with reliability is its mirror reflection, *accuracy*. Using mathematics, the analyst can establish the critical state of a value with a fineness unequalled in any art.

Another characteristic may be called *manageability*. This is characterized by ease of manipulation. The use of numbers and the system for managing them (statistical method, calculus, algebra) make it possible to carry analysis to an arbitrary level of interest. Some problems are answered by simple arithmetic, and the use of advanced mathematical techniques would serve no purpose. However, as problems requiring solution become more complex, the tools for expressing relationships tend to become more complex. Complex tools of mathematics (multiple regression, matrix algebra, linear programming) use the same arithmetic processes as the non-complex problem. However, at some point on the scale of complexity, matehmatical tools may be better machine-managed than manually performed.

Another characteristic of the quantitative state comes forward: the ability to reduce numerical expressions to an objective form that is *machine readable*. Any idea may be given a symbol or a value, irrespective of its state. However, quantitative problems are most easily introduced to a wide range of data processing machines to provide computational assistance. The majority of these can be managed by the trained analyst. Note that the participation of the human is altered when computational devices are introduced. Instead of randomly exploring or trying a mathematical expression, the analyst is called upon for an integrating and planning function as well. In the case of the electric adding machine, the operator's biggest problem may be to find the plug, or to do his sums twice to be certain that error has not been introduced. At the other end of the spectrum, however, are the electronic data-processing devices. Computers require minute, *a prioi* planning of each step in a completely defined machine instruction program, which might consist of thousands of steps. Each step may have a mathematical state, or may provide the linkage to make possible automatic machine operations.

An additional characteristic of quantitative problems is their *unambiguity*. An equation for a curve, or a construction provable by geometric axioms and trigonometric rules, has a unique quality. Ambiguity and generality go hand-in-hand. Numbers are specific; words, loosely used, become confusing generalities.

Versatility may also be called a characteristic of the quantitative state. By manipulating numbers, the analyst may create novel, interesting, or new relationships among complex variables. He may easily alter his procedure and obtain new results without changing (or requiring change from) any part of the world reflected by his equation. He can produce bizarre maxima and minima to demonstrate the facility and generally elastic characteristic of numbers. Some philosophers of science point to the need for expressing accepted relationships in new ways. To the extent that this alone produces increased insight, the versatility and manageability of numbers serve the systems analyst or the mathematician.

Another characteristic of numbers may be termed *consistency*. Consistency describes a number of attributes: congruity, coherence, uniformity, and lack of contradiction.

Consistency implies congruity; for example, the same system may be operated twice in exactly the same fashion. If the experiment is consistent, the operations are superimposable, as are the results of the operations. Consistency is obtained through the uniformity of content, procedure, and program. The essence of uniformity is its non-varying state and its internally homogeneous condition. Consistency relies upon the lack of contradiction. Contradiction arises through an observed or unobserved logical incompatibility, bringing a procedure into conflict with reality.

It is not true that the analyst won't make mistakes if he uses numbers. Nor is it true that the use of mathematics is in itself an assurance that all of the foregoing conditions will prevail. Certainly one of the two overriding goals of experiment is to demonstrate untruth, or to bring about an understanding of an impermissible course of action. The other overriding goal is to represent adequately the phenomena of the real world and to explain its behavior in unambiguous terms. In this latter goal, the fundamental intent underlying the use of numbers emerges: *It is the capacity for representing conditions, events, relationships, or systems objectively and in easily manipulable form.*

ADVANTAGES OF COMPUTERS FOR PLANT MANAGEMENT[3]

- It aids in making better and faster decisions.
- Improves communications throughout the plant.
- You need only the equipment needed to accomplish the task—no more.
- Provides more and better control for operating managers.
- Eliminates the costly practice of repeating data merely for the sake of the accounting record.
- Stresses accuracy and reliability of information fed into the system.
- Provides the answer to controlling the paperwork avalanche.
- Minimizes storage and filing problems.
- The total management information system keeps management up to date, day-by-day, hour-by-hour, minute-by-minute, second-by-second.
- Dramatic improvement of inventory reductions of 50% or more.
- Production costs drop as more beneficial production runs are scheduled.
- Features exception type reporting—the key to the system; managers can "red-flag" variances or exceptions to the norm and evaluate flash reports.
- A single input is shared commonly from the data base; the need for reconciling various reports is eliminated, thus saving additional clerical effort.
- Allows the accounting department to make full contribution to the plant profit effort.
- Flexibility is built into the system so as to enable it to respond to management's needs through continual retrieval from the data bank.
- Operating people are involved in the computer system from the very beginning—thus creating an air of confidence with the machine and full knowledge of its potential.

---

[3] Arthur E. Wolf, *Computerized Plant Information Systems* (Englewood Cliffs, N.J.: Prentice-Hall, Inc. copyright © 1974), p. 5, lines 19-35; p. 6, lines 1-22; p. 17, lines 1-26; p. 18, lines 1-21; p. 20, lines 27-33; p. 22, lines 31-42; p. 23, lines 1-26; p. 171, lines 7-20; p. 172, lines 17-38; p. 173, lines 16-30; pp. 171-176, partial.

- Flow of customer orders is streamlined through daily report of orders not shipped as scheduled and a brief explanation made by the responsible department.
- The system has a built-in corrective action mechanism, flagging the manager as to when to take corrective action before the damage is done.
- In effect, the system produces a "master" monthly report—tying together all reports, such as labor reporting, control laboratory time reporting, maintenance costs, product costs, budgeting and cost standards for speedier, more accurate decision making.
- The system presents the facts *as they are, not what someone thinks they should be*—the best kind of motivation for cost reduction.
- Control remains in the hands of plant and financial managers—the key decision makers—who themselves design and manage the system.
- The system allows plant management to alert top management to changing market situations in time to take corrective action.

EXAMPLES OF COST SAVINGS REALIZED THROUGH USE OF THIS SYSTEM
[A Sampling Only]

(1) Reduced Labor Complement—10%

The most simple, the easiest to install, and the example first described, is the communications improvement in reporting time of workers in the plant and on the job. With this collection and recording of work effort, managers become more knowledgeable of the labor hours involved in performing work; with this information it is the role of the manager to improve productivity by better utilization of the labor force. It is unnecessary and undesirable for a foreman to chase after his men and to observe them on the job. It is just as distasteful to have a "big brother" approach where every action is observed through instrument observation. The correct approach is to record the work effort and improve productivity; when the results do not match the production goals, there is a recorded basis for reviewing the effort and taking corrective action. The cost of labor is probably the significant element of cost, other than purchased materials in your product cost. What would a 10 per cent reduction in your labor costs do for the statement of income?

(2) Reduce Inventory Investment—$ 6,000,000; Improve Annual Cash Flow—$ 600,000

With improved information on finished and intermediate materials it was possible in one plant to reduce the investment by one-fourth—which amounts to five million dollars. Fantastic, impossible, grossly exaggerated, you say? You are right; the inventory information system did not reduce the investment by five million dollars. Good managers working with better information did this. The point is, the managers were good before they had the information system, but by being even more knowledgeable concerning present inventory conditions, they were able to make better decisions. Similarly, the raw material investment was reduced almost one million dollars and these reduced levels have been maintained without sacrificing customer service. Supplies and container inventories were not reduced but held level, which prevented increased costs. With investment reductions of this magnitude, the profit effect is compounded, for other profitable uses can be made of the funds now available as a result of the improved cash flow. Figured conservatively at the present rate of borrowing money and maintaining required compensating balance accounts at lender banks, the six-million-dollar inventory reduction reduces the cost of borrowing money by 10 per cent, or six hundred thousand dollars each year. This is a conservative figure, for reinvestment of funds in other projects that are vying for company financial resources certainly have a return on investment greater than 10 per cent. If they do not, then why borrow money?

(3) Maximize Production Scheduling—$ 500,000

Production scheduling is a difficult job even when good forecasts of demand are available, but it becomes even more difficult when unexpected customer demands or raw material stock-outs occur. Improved raw material inventory conditions have a distinct beneficial effect on production scheduling. As the information system responds to the customer order volume and correlates this with the inventory status as was described concerning the daily operations report, production is optimized by scheduling economic order quantities. A proper sequencing of grades or blends or products can be scheduled, which not only permits runs of a size to obtain the most production at least cost, but also aids in having an adequate inventory condition to prevent customer order stock-outs. This also is difficult to quantify, but when productivity was increased five per cent in one plant, it was calculated that net after tax income increased one-half million dollars. Did the information system save one-half million dollars? Maybe not, but without the improved information the production managers were making less profitable decisions.

(4) Other Cost Savings

(a) Reduced absenteeism—$1,675 Per Man Year.
(b) Optimize purchase of materials—$250,000.
(c) Improved customer service level—$500,000.
(d) Reduced warehouse expenses—$$$$$.
(e) Reduce accounting expenses and better budget controls—$$$$.
(f) Better quality control testing, maintenance costs, etc.—$$$$.
(g) Practical application of situational theory of management simulation.
(h) Picking the right manager for the system.
(i) Picking the right equipment for the system.

The success of the Computerized Plant Information System depends on the plant manager. Under his enthusiastic leadership, a meaningful and profit-making information system can be developed.

> *NOTE:* For more detailed information regarding this subject, Arthur E. Wolf's book *Computerized Plant Information Systems,* © 1974 is recommended. Write Prentice-Hall, Inc., Englewood Cliffs, New Jersey 07632.

Index